WANDERING ON HEATHEN WAYS

Writings on

Heathen Holy Ones, Wights,

and Spiritual Practice

WINIFRED HODGE ROSE

WORDFRUMA PRESS
2023

Text copyright ©2023 by Winifred Hodge Rose. All rights reserved. Brief quotations with full citation are permitted, for the purposes of criticism, teaching, or scholarship.

My thanks to John T. Mainer for permission to quote his copyrighted poem and email about Viðar.

Many thanks to Laurie Inn and Creel Lancaster for permission to use their artworks, which are copyrighted by them.

Wordfruma Press
Urbana Illinois USA

WordfrumaPress.net
WordfrumaPress@gmail.com

ISBN
979-8-9855536-7-3 (Paperback)
979-8-9855536-8-0 (Hardback)
979-8-9855536-9-7 (EPUB)

Library of Congress Control Number: 2023922629

Cover and book design by Winifred Hodge Rose.

Dedication

To the Gesithas, the companions who travel together, exploring the Worlds. Though we may never meet one another in person, we share the pathways of the spirit.

As we walk these Heathen ways today, may we be mindful of those who walked them in the past.

Let us also be mindful of those who will walk these paths in times to come, realizing that the enrichment of their paths depends in part on sharing our Heathen explorations today and passing them on to future generations.

> *Thus are the threads of companionship*
> *woven through Time and Space.*
> *We are the Heathen Gesithas*
> *who walk the Worlds in frith,*
> *seeking and sharing*
> *the gifts of the Holy Ones.*

This icon shows 'X', the Gebo rune, which means 'Gift, Giving.' It marks each chapter in this book.

Oden som Vandringsman.
(Georg von Rosen, artist. 1886)

Odin the Wanderer,
Seeker and Bringer of Wisdom

Table of Contents

As We Set Off... 1
Part I: Heathen Holy Ones 5
  1: The Kindly Gods Go Wandering: 7
    The Gods Ride Over the Bridge 9
    Encountering the Holy Ones 11
    Goddesses and Gods Together 15
    Gand-Shot 20
    Norns and Others Bind the Fylgja 21
    Traces of Heathen Names or References 26
  2: Of Frigg and Odin 31
    All In a Day's Work: Frigg and her Ladies 31
    Call to Frigg: A Prayer 40
    Of Being and Knowledge: Frigg, Nerthus, and Odin 41
    The Winds of Odin's Will: A Song 50
  3. Mimir, Odin, and World-Mind 53
    'Friend of Odin' and his Uncle (?) 53
    Mimir's Relatives 57
    Mimir as a Cosmogonic Sacrifice 58
    World-Mind 61
    The I in Mimir's Well 63
  4: Vør: Goddess of Awareness 67
    Awareness 68
    Meeting Vør 70
    Rune-faring: Year / Jera 71
    Mythic Awareness 74

    Asynja's Flight: A Tale 75

    A Strand for the Weaving: The Tale Continues 80

5: To Honor Viðar 83

    Silent One's Service *by John T. Mainer* 84

    Landvidi 88

    The Testing of Young Viðar: A Tale 89

6. Thor and his Family 99

    The Farmer's God 99

    Sif: Kinship and Hospitality 101

    The Thorlings 104

    Magnetic Power 107

    Thor's Act of Compassion 109

    Love Songs of Sif and Thor 111

7: Walburga and the Rites of May 115

    Witches and Walpurgisnacht 115

    The Roots of Walpurgisnacht 118

    Saint Walburga 118

    Walburga's Dog 120

    Walburga Chased by the Wild Hunt 121

    Walburga's Symbols and Domains of Action 124

    King and Queen of the May 126

    A Sampling of Walpurgistide Customs 127

    What Does This All Mean? 129

    Returning Life 131

    A Between-Time of Magic 132

    A Springtime Goddess 133

The Name of the Goddess	134
8: Eostre / Ostara	137
Ostara's Dance: A Song	139
In Honor of Eostre	141
9: A Tale of Nanna and her Kin	143
Mani	143
Sol	145
Young Nanna	145
Nanna, Warrior-Maid	147
Balder	150
Hatafjord	152
Wedding	153
Forseti	154
Balder's Dreams	155
Odainsakr	156
Hoðr's Blindness	157
Mistletoe	159
Balefire	162
The Hidden Halls of Peace	164
A Commentary on Sources	166
10: Syn: The 'Just Say No' Goddess	171
A Prayer to Syn	174
11: Heimdall	175
Heimdall: Warder of the Atmosphere	175
The Gifting of Heimdall: A Tale	179
Heimdall's Call: A Song	189

12: Earth-Mother, Nerthus 191
    Earth Blessing: A Prayer 191
    Erce, Eorðan Modor 194
    Nerthus: A Poem 197

13: Matrons and Disir: The Heathen Tribal Mothers 199
    Matron Worship in Germanic Lands 199
    General Conclusions about Matron Worship 205
    Moving North 207
    The Disir of Scandinavia 209
    Heathen Disir Today 214

14: Hallow-Streaming: A Meditation on the Mothers 217

15: Werthende: Song of Becoming 221
    More on Werthende's / Verðandi's Domain 223

16: Perkwus: The Tree of Life and Soul 225
    Gods, Soul, and Trees 226
    Table 1: Gods, Earth, Sky Powers 228
    Trees and Souls 230
    Table 2: Trees and Life-Soul Words 230
    A New Tale of Ask and Embla 233
    Trees and the Community of Life 234
    In Closing 238

Part II. Wights: Heathen Otherworldly Beings 241
  17: Landwights and Human Ecology 243
    Systems Ecology and Eco-dynamics 245
    Sourcing and Cycling Resources 248
    Impacts on the Landwights 250

Communication with Landwights 253
Blessing-water 255
Our Homestead Landwight 256
Thundering Across the Prairie 257
Children of the Earth 258
Ing-Frey's Blessing 259

18: Renewable Energy Installations as Jotun-Shrines 261
A Human-Jotnar Switch 261
Another Look at Jotnar 264
Jotun-Shrines 268
Example: Wind Turbines 270
Your own Virtual Jotun-Shrine 272
The Thorn, or Thurs, on the Rose 274
Grotte-song 275

19: The Vision of the Seeress: A Giantess's Tale 279

20: An Anglo-Saxon Charm against a Dwarf: 289
The Charm Against a Dwarf 290
Line 1: *Here came striding in* 292
Line 2: *He had his hama in hand,* 293
Lines 2-3: *Said that you were his steed,* 295
Lines 3-4: *They began to set off from the land* 299
Line 5: *Then came striding in   The Dwarf's sister;* 301
Lines 6ff: *Then she ended it* 303
The Final Instructions 305
Conclusion 307
Old English Text 310

21: Dwarves and their Powers 311
    Origin of the Dwarves 311
    It All Hinges on 'Mod' 314
    Móðsognir and Durinn 316
    Implications for Personal Practice 319

Part III. Heathen Spiritual Practices 323

22: The Living Jewels of Brisingamen 325
    What is Brisingamen? 326
    Forging Brisingamen 328
    Echoes of Brisingamen 333
    Vitality, Life-Energy 334
    Beauty 335
    Joy, Delight 336
    Self-Possession 338
    Working with your Brisingamen 340

23: Wigi Thonar: The Powers of Thor's Hammer 343
    Wigi Thonar 343
    Thor Véurr 346
    Hallowing your Inner Vé 347

24: The Great Gift: A Perspective on Heathen Prayer ... 351
    Problem, Prayer, and First Response 352
    A Cost-Benefit Analysis 353
    Weighing the Benefits and Costs 354
    The Great Gift 355

25: Experience and Practice of Compassion 357
    The Nature of Compassion-Energy 357

Managing Compassion-Energy 359
Keeping Compassion Flowing 360
The Mystery of Compassion 363
Compassion in Heathenry 363
How the Deities Shape Compassion 364
Thor's Compassion 365
Freya's Compassion 366
Tyr's Compassion 366
Frigg's Compassion 367
Odin's Compassion 368
Sigyn's Compassion 370
Frau Holle's Compassion. 371
Frey's Compassion 372
Frith and Generosity 372

26: Earth, Water, Wind, Fire: Relating to the Deities 375
The Mode of Earth 376
The Modes of Flowing and Still Water 381
The Modes of Air and Wind 391
The Modes of Fire and Wode 398

27: Trance and Power Chants 411
Nied-Runa Song 413
Nied-Runa Ceremony 416
The Dancer of Dreams 418
Call-back 421

28: Contemplation: The Resonance of the Heart 423
Contemplation versus Meditation 424

The Planes of Being	427
Resonance	429
The Resonating Heart	435
How to Approach Contemplation	437
Using a Seed-Image for Contemplation	438
'Seedless' Contemplation	443
In Thanks to Frigg	445
In Closing	448
29: Vafrloge: Hidden Fire and its Runic Channels	451
Vafrloge	452
Attuning to the Hidden Fire	457
The Eihwaz Rune	458
The Kenaz Rune	459
Runic Channels of the Hidden Fire	461
Word-Hoard / Glossary	463
Book-Hoard / Bibliography	477
Photo Credits	483
Index	495
About the Author	507
A Word about Wordfruma Press	509

As We Set Off...

The publication of this anthology marks thirty years of my Heathen writing and celebrates many years of 'wandering on Heathen ways!' Though it is divided into three parts, "Heathen Holy Ones," "Wights," and "Heathen Spiritual Practices," in truth everything I've written is either *about* spiritual practice, or the *result of* spiritual practice; spiritual practice is embedded throughout the book. Modern Heathens generally have quite lively spiritual lives—one of the blessings of our troth, for sure! And we often like to share in a give-and-take with others. I'm walking in honored footsteps here.

I believe that my perceptions are rooted in traditional Heathen lore, but they do move beyond those roots into personal experience and insights. The Heathen Holy Ones are still here, active in our lives and in today's world, and our experience of them varies based on who we are. Scholarly

As We Set Off....

research and analysis are important to our troth; so is personal experience and exploration. Both approaches are represented here. Every kind of approach: intellectual, spiritual, experiential, intuitive, sharing and learning from each other, can contribute to the growth of Heathen understanding and practice today.

This isn't a book that systematically describes all the Heathen Gods, Goddesses, and other spiritual beings or wights; there are other good books that do that. My book is an anthology of my wanderings through inner space and time, as I encounter Heathen Deities and other spirit-beings, begin getting to know some of them, and learn new ways to interact with them.

Among our most meaningful challenges as Heathens and polytheists is to get to know all of our Gods and Goddesses to some degree, even if we are most devoted to just one or a few of them. This includes the various Deities from different Heathen pantheons, such as Frau Holle or Holda from the German pantheon, and other German, Saxon, Anglo-Saxon as well as Norse Gods and Goddesses. I've spent thirty years on this and feel I still have far to go on this project! Even the ones I feel I know pretty well are constantly surprising me with new insights and new dimensions of their being. I actively explore as many different ways as I can think of, to approach more knowledge and more interaction with more of them.

Often, becoming more familiar with Gods and Goddesses we don't know well requires learning new ways of interacting with the Deities. In this book, for example, I have chapters presenting my understanding of less-known Deities such as Thor's three children, Viðar, Mimir, the Goddesses Syn, Vør, Sif, Walburga, Nanna, the Matronae, and others. I've taken various approaches for each one, such as research articles,

As We Set Off....

tales, poems, personal experience, illustrations, and creative spiritual practices. My chapters on personal practice with Freya's necklace or girdle, Brisingamen, and with the powers of Thor's Hammer are examples.

This isn't a Heathenism / Asatru 101 textbook; this is for people who have gone past that level and want to dig deeper into Heathen spirituality. It is an exploration of Heathen mysteries, of which there are an endless number. In particular, the chapters on Heathen spiritual practice are designed for those who already have some knowledge and experience of Heathen ways, and some familiarity with basic spiritual practices as well, such as meditation, prayer, and interactions with our Gods and Goddesses.

I offer my own perspectives on these mysteries; you may see things differently and that's fine. I often find that thoughtfully *disagreeing* with someone else's perspectives can stimulate and clarify our own thoughts more effectively than agreement does. So whether you find my ideas here compatible with yours, or disagree with them, you may still find some useful stimulus for thought in this book!

To those who have read my Heathen Soul Lore books or articles: this book does not go into my perspectives on Heathen soul lore in any depth, though there are occasional brief references which are explained in the text. I wanted to offer a book that would be of interest even if you have not studied my perspective on soul lore and don't wish to. Here I offer approaches to Heathen spirituality that do not depend on the soul lore that I teach. But of course, the approaches here are very compatible with soul lore and can be used with it to excellent effect if you wish to do so.

Because I cover so many subjects here, I've provided several ways for you to hunt down specific topics if you wish.

As We Set Off....

First, a detailed table of contents. Second, an extensive Word-Hoard or glossary. And third, I've included an index.

Enough chatting; let's set off on our wanderings! Come explore the terrain that lies before us, opening a vista for our minds and souls to expand toward new horizons. See where these paths might take you: past the horizons of my sight, heading toward your own shining peaks of knowledge, whispering groves of experience, and hidden trails that only you can follow.

Gods speed you on your faring through the Worlds!

Section I: Heathen Holy Ones

Part I: Heathen Holy Ones

An image of Odin from the Epcot Norway Pavilion.

Section I: Heathen Holy Ones

An image of Freya from the Epcot Norway Pavilion.

1: The Kindly Gods Go Wandering:
Norse Spells as Clues to Heathen Deities

Many years ago in the bowels of our university library, I came across a wonderful book of old Norwegian spells. This extensive (1,576 spells!) and detailed scholarly collection was published in 1901-2, entitled *Norske Hexeformularer og Magiske Opskrifte* (Norwegian Witch-Formulas and Magical Recipes), by Dr. Anton C. Bang. It provides an amazing collection of folklore ranging back through the Middle Ages. The author includes, among many others, 34 charms that are variants of the German *Second Merseberg Charm* about Odin's healing of Balder's horse after it sprained its leg, and 27 charms calling on Disir / Norn / Valkyrie / Freya-figures.

The Kindly Gods Go Wandering

The primary figures in these spells overall are Jesus, the Virgin Mary, and Saint Peter, yet it is clear that in many cases these were originally substitutes for Odin, Frigg / Freya, and Thor. Indeed, in several spells from Ullinsaker (Ullr's Field) dating from as late as the 1880's, the final lines read "in the names of Thor, Odin and Frigg" in place of the customary Christian power-names "Father, Son and Holy Ghost."

The connection between Odin and Jesus as 'chief / self-sacrificing Gods,' and between Frigg and the Virgin Mary as 'mother / helping Goddesses' is easily apparent. In Christian lore, Saint Peter is portrayed as a large, strong man with a hot temper: the similarity with Thor cannot be doubted! In the following discussion of the charms I make these substitutions: Odin in place of Jesus, Thor in place of Saint Peter, and Frigg in place of the Virgin Mary, except as otherwise noted.

Most individuals who used these charms probably did so with Christian holy beings (Jesus, angels, saints) in mind; certainly I would not presume to say what each person thought. But as I describe some of these spells and the overall picture that they portray, you will see how deeply Heathen are the beliefs and world-view on which they rest.

In this essay I reinstate our own Deities in a selection of the most Heathen-oriented spells. One of many things this collection offers is a much bigger picture of the activities of the Goddesses, Disir and other womanly wights than we are given in the ancient poetic lore, which deals for the most part with the struggles of warring kings and heroes and with mythological themes. These spells deal, instead, with the concerns of everyday life where the Goddesses as well as the Gods play a great role.

I view these spells as inspirational vignettes, keeping me mindful of our Gods' and Goddesses' interest in our daily affairs, and reinforcing a Heathen understanding of life and the world. As is told in folklore throughout the Germanic lands, when the Gods and Goddesses fare about the land they bring blessings and fertility, gather up wandering souls, chastise those who deserve it, and sometimes challenge our courage and faith by the roaring of the Wild Hunt. These spells give a picture of their everyday kindnesses, their gifts of help, healing and warding, as they walk the hills and vales of Midgard.

I have translated these spells to the best of my ability, and where I am unable to translate certain words I have left them in their original form.

The Gods Ride Over the Bridge

Almost every time the Gods and Goddesses appear in the charms, they are portrayed as riding, walking, or going 'on their way,' 'on the road,' often mentioning a specific, local location where they are met by a person in need. Sometimes Frigg or Odin are found, not wandering, but seated in a place of power: on an earth-fast stone, or inside / outside a God-house. Spell #95 (dated 1800) conjures in the name of "the heavy stone below which Frigg (Virgin Mary) speaks judgement *('dom sag')*" – obviously another place of power. Just as obviously, this image is not consistent with Christian belief, where Mary, a human, does not have the right to judge.

These are not Gods to whom prayers are sent to a distant, heavenly address, far beyond the bounds of Midgard. These are Gods and Goddesses whom we can meet over the next hill, across the river there, or in person in the God-house of our own village. They spend, according to the assumptions of these charms, a great deal of their time wandering around in

Midgard, with the simple aim of being available to their folk in need.

Most interestingly, the Holy Ones are very often described as 'riding / coming over the bridge,' sometimes even the 'shining bridge' and the 'broad bridge'. For example, Spell #3 begins: "Jesus and St. Peter (Odin and Thor) rode over the shining bridge *(bilne bro)*". The parallel with the Bifröst Bridge is clear, and so is the implication that these are indeed our own Heathen Gods, riding over the Bridge between their World and ours to join us here in Midgard.

Bridges play no particular role in Christian mythology, but in our lore any being who comes toward us over a bridge is known to be an Otherworldly being of one kindred or another. Here is an example of one of the many 'coming over the bridge' charms, one of my favorites. The spell is against an *Aakast*, some kind of evil wight. Mentioned here is a 'church-aakast'; this may be similar to the northern English 'church-grim,' a dangerous wight that lurks around churches.

Against Aakast
I make (this magic) for myself and you,
Against all nine Aakast, whether flying or faring,
Dwelling in Himmel and Jord (Heaven and Earth),
Dwelling in Maane and Sol (Moon and Sun):
Against Church-Aakast,
Against Mountain-Aakast
And against Vas-Aakast (probably poltergeist).
Fare away, whether Aakast or Aakast's father,
Aakast or Aakast's mother,
Aakast or Aakast's brother,
And all their relations and friends.
Some fared up

And some fared down,
Some fared north
And some fared south.
Then came Odin riding over the bridge.
Odin said: "Where are you going, Aakast?"
"I will rake flesh and blood from bones."
"No," said Odin,
"I shall turn you back
To the one who sent you
And to the blue mountain.
There shall you stay
In stock and stone
And not bring harm to anyone.
(#79, dated 1750)

Some of the charms featuring Frigg show her being encountered on the road or coming across the bridge by herself, or with Odin, or occasionally with both Odin and Thor. But often, rather than wandering around, a person will go to the 'church,' the God-house, knowing she or he will find Frigg sitting there in person. This is reminiscent of the public and private temples and *Disirsalar* (worship-halls of the Disir) in the older lore, where the statues of the Gods, Goddesses, Disir and others were considered to be living representatives of their divine models. Further below, I will show several examples of Frigg spells.

Encountering the Holy Ones

There are three 'encounter' patterns with the Gods and Goddesses. In one pattern, a person meets a Deity and a conversation is held: the Deity asks what is the matter, the petitioner tells this, and the God or Goddess speaks words of power which fix the problem. This kind of spell builds on the assumption that what happened 'some other time' between the Gods and 'somebody with the same problem I / you have,' will happen again now as we work this charm. Most of the spells seek help from the Gods against evil wights, sorcery and curses. The following spell is a little different, giving a delightful example of trust that the Deities will help us with any of our needs.

Hunter's Prayer
Odin fared forth and went to a Grinn-Le (?),
There stood a hunter and held himself beside it,
And wept bitter tears.
"Why are you grieving so sorely?"
"Well may I grieve,
I can fetter no birds,
Eider ducks, roe-deer, hare,
Nor other kinds of wildlife."
Odin came toward him and said,
"Come and sit you down;
I shall teach you so you can remedy this
And work magic so you can fetter eider ducks, roe-deer, hare, and all sorts of wildlife."
(#132, dated 1815)

A second type of encounter is - quite charmingly! - between a Deity and a domestic animal directly, unmediated by the animal's owner. The pattern is the same as for humans: a distressed animal meets a Deity, tells its problem, and receives a remedy.

Here is an example featuring the affliction called 'envy' *(avunds-hed)*, caused by an ill-wishing person against another person's cow. In Dag Strömback's wonderful essay, "The Concept of the Soul in Nordic Tradition," he shows that a powerful person's *avund* / envy / evil eye is able to act physically upon another being or object by the power of the envious person's Hugr-soul. This is a spell featuring an envy-struck (Hugr-struck) cow:

Against Avundshed
Odin fared over a bridge,
There he met a cow.
It cried out, lowing; it cried out, mooing.
Odin said:
"Why are you lowing?
Why are you mooing?"
"Well may I low, well may I moo,
Since it is sucking blood from my body,
Flesh from my bones,
Marrow from my limbs,
Milk from my udder."
"That isn't right, my blessed cow," said Odin.
"I shall work (magic) for you against envy,
And weaken it with my ten fingers and my twelve angels
(think Valkyrja)
So that you shall get
Blood in your body,
Flesh on your bones,
And marrow in your limbs,
And milk in your udder.
Your milk shall remain fat,
And your cream remain frothy."
(#152, dated 1750)

The Kindly Gods Go Wandering

The third type of encounter is not between the Gods and an ordinary human, but between them and various kinds of evil wights, as I showed in the spell above about the Aakast. This also includes evil human witches, warlocks, etc. Very often these beings are illness-wights: the spells show a great variety of personified spirits of sickness. There are also many other kinds of wights, Dwarves, ghosts, and *'aande'* or spirits in general.

Note that *aand* is the same as Old Norse *önd*, the gift of Odin to humankind. *Önd / aand* does not only mean 'breath of life' but also 'spirit.' This comes across clearly in the use of *'aand'* in these spells to mean 'evil spirits' as well as the name of the Christian Holy Spirit in the Scandinavian languages: *Hellig Aand* and variants thereof.

In this pattern, the Gods are 'going on their way' and encounter evil beings. They ask the evil beings where they are going and what they are up to. The evil ones, apparently constrained to tell the truth, answer that they are going to a specific village or person's house (the charms list "NN" meaning "insert the relevant name here") to cause harm, or they simply describe the harm they intend to do in general. The Gods reply that they will do no such thing, and bind or curse them in some way so that they are powerless. Here is an example of this type of charm:

<u>Against Blod-Ægten</u> *(spirit of the plague)*
Odin and Thor went forth on their way,
met the Blod-Ægten, the plague.
"Where are you going?" said Odin.
It said:
"I shall go to NN and tear out and munch on his cartilage, bones, veins, flesh and sinews."

The Kindly Gods Go Wandering

"No," said Odin,
"You shall go backwards into an earth-fast stone,
and nevermore harm mankind!"
(#136, dated 1780)

Goddesses and Gods Together

Both Gods and Goddesses are shown to help both men and women in the charms: there is no strict bureaucracy of who is supposed to help whom! While it may be logical, in principle, to call on a Deity who can especially 'relate' to your problem, the more important method is simply to meet a Deity—any Deity—and ask for any kind of help from him or her. For example, we saw in a previous charm and many other similar ones that Odin gives back strength to an afflicted cow so it can produce milk, a supposedly 'feminine' function. And in many spells it is Frigg who ousts vicious wights, rather than Thor or Odin as one might expect; or else she works in concert with them.

Here is an example of Frigg's role:

<u>Against Trolldom</u> *(witchcraft, sorcery)*
Frigg and Thor walked and 'lotted,' and Odin walked and 'laid'. They saw a huge troll in the mountain: "He is no good." "Yes, he is no good for visible or invisible (beings)," said Frigg. "Troll-men and troll-wives we will bind in the blue mountain; there they shall sit until doom comes, from sunup to sundown." (#126, dated 1865)

[Norwegian 'loted' is translated online into English 'lotted,' as in 'allotted.' The three Deities are apparently 'laying' the dangers of trolls in a magical sense, choosing and 'allotting' their fates, as well as I can figure.]

Frigg in her fierce aspect! ('Fricka,' by Arthur Rackham.)

In one of the most peculiar spells—if one looks at it from a Christian viewpoint—Frigg / Virgin Mary heals her son of a troll's attack. In the Christian version, Jesus has taken the place of Balder rather than replacing Odin. As I discuss below, the title 'Herre' (Lord) is applied to Balder in another charm as well as in this one.

The Kindly Gods Go Wandering

<u>To Conjure Against a Troll</u>
Frigg went and sat herself down in the house of her lord (Herre) and his father. "Here you lie, my son," she said to him. "Mother, a troll came and caused swelling in all my bones." "My son, sit you upon an earth-fast stone" - and that he did.
(#201, variants from various places and ranging between 1750 to 1830).

The "earth-fast stone"– a stone which is held fast in the earth, rather than a loose stone—comes up very often in these spells. Clearly it has the power to hold fast something that we want to imprison such as bad luck or an evil wight. Sometimes Frigg works her magic seated on an earth-fast stone, which serves her as a source of earth-power; this is her recommendation to Balder in the spell. In the Christian version of the spell, of course it is Virgin Mary who is the healer.

But the whole situation is a very unchristian one: would Christians really expect Jesus to be injured or sickened by a troll and be unable to heal himself without his mother's help? This would not happen in authentic Christian mythology. Yet our own mythology tells of Balder's afflictions and the efforts of his mother Frigg to help him, and in our tales it is a sorcerous being, a *troll-maðr*, Loki, who attacks Balder. This spell seems more characteristic of Frigg and Balder than it does of Jesus and Mary.

Odin and Frigg very often work together in these spells. I think that in Heathen lore, Odin and Frigg worked together (or in contest with each other!) far more often than the traces we find in the lore. What little is mentioned there hints at more, for example Odin and Frigg fostering the shipwrecked boys on the island in *Grimnismal (Poetic Edda);* and Frigg and Odin giving the Langobardi their name (Paulus Diaconus, section 8). There is also the old German *Second Merseberg Charm*, which shows four Goddesses, in addition to Odin, galdoring over the wrenched leg of Balder's horse (discussed further, below).

In our book, Spell #122 shows Odin and Frigg standing together upon a sod of earth, working magic against all the *Onde* (evil spirits) that fare under the heavens: a truly magnificent image! Another spell against an evil wight begins with a picture of Odin and Frigg together as farmers: "Odin and Frigg drove their livestock *(boskap)* over the broad bridge..." (#191).

Consider this: these spells in their Christian forms speak of Jesus and Mary as though they were together, wandering about on their own, a great deal of the time. This is not the case according to Christian scripture and tradition: Mary mother of Jesus did not generally go wandering around the countryside alone with her son, working wonders together on an equal basis with him, though she may have been among the crowds that followed him.

The whole point of Christian wonder-tales about Jesus was to show that only he could do these things, by the power of his father. By having Jesus and Mary working together as magician-companions so often, these Norse spells are, I believe, following a traditional Heathen model where Gods and Goddesses work together and companion each other. In order for the Heathen spells to be Christianized, Christian mythological accuracy had to be distorted to fit Heathen tradition, showing how strong the Heathen tradition really was.

Here is an example of Odin and Frigg patrolling together as wardens of Midgard:

Against a Giant
Odin and Frigg walked upon the white sand,
There came a giant flying to the land.
"Where are you going, then?" said Odin.
"I'm going to Middel-Heim,
To suck blood and munch bones."
"No," said Odin, "you shall no longer come;
You shall be put
Upon a very high mountain,
In Day's tree,
In Night's tree.
(#146, dated 1862)

An interesting thing about this spell is that clearly it takes place somewhere other than Midgard, since Odin and Frigg meet the giant on his way to Middel-Heim (Middle-World, Midgard) and prevent him from ever getting there. So where is it that they are patrolling? As 'Jesus and Mary,' they would not be in 'Heaven,' because they could not have met a giant there. They would not be in 'Hell' because they don't go there. In a Christian context this is a very difficult question to answer. In a Heathen context there is no problem at all: they are patrolling the borders in another Heim or World: perhaps Jotunheim, perhaps the approach to Bifröst Bridge, perhaps some nameless borderland between one world and another. The fact that they are on the sand, therefore next to a body of water, definitely implies a borderland of some kind between the worlds. The fascinating "Day's Tree" and "Night's Tree" must also be in another World outside of Midgard: I wish I knew more about them!

Gand-Shot

Evil wights often use a form of attack called 'shot' *(skud)* - the same approach used by wights in other Germanic lands, like the Elf-shot and hag-shot of the Anglo-Saxons. In Norse languages it is often called *gand-skot* or *gand-skud.* Gand occurs in Old Norse as well as medieval Scandinavian dialects. In different contexts it seems to mean 'a spirit, usually associated with a magician,' 'a type of magic,' and 'a magic staff or wand'. As I see it, *gand* is a spirit which can work magic and resides in the staff or wand of a *vitki, seiðkona* or other magic-user, or alternatively can reside within them as an extra soul or spirit.

In the charm below, *gand* refers to injury or illness 'shot' by magic at domestic animals. 'Troll' as mentioned below refers to a sorcerer or magic-user, who sometimes may be human, sometimes not. This spell is another example of Frigg's power against evil.

> ### *Against Gand-Skud*
> *Frigg said "What is harming your creatures (domestic animals)?"*
> *"Troll-craft and shot are flaying my creatures."*
> *Frigg shall work well in return (for the evil):*
> *Against Berg (mountain)-shot,*
> *Against Earth-shot,*
> *Against Troll-karl's (sorcerer's) shot,*
> *And against (all) shots*
> *Which fly along wind and way.*
> (#116, dated 1864)

There are many other 'shot' spells featuring Odin or Frigg or both together; sometimes Thor is included as well, and sometimes it is three Norn or Valkyrie-figures who do this. The typical symptoms of 'shot' are sudden pain, 'accidental' injury, or other sort of physical disablement. The following spell offers some kind of pain reliever, a *døvelse,* against typical symptoms of 'shot.' The magical beings invoked in this spell are clearly Valkyrja, reminiscent of the spear-maidens protecting their chosen heroes in battle.

When One Wants to Magically Make a Døvelse
There came three maidens Moier (?)
Down from heaven,
The one bore light,
The other bore a spear,
The third bore 'døvelsen'
To relieve pain and injury.
(#249, from 1800-1880)

Norns and Others Bind the Fylgja

The author of our book, Dr. Bang, put 27 charms into a category which he called "The Three Norns and Freya-Maria;" the preceding spell is one of these. These are among the most fascinating and Heathen-oriented of the spells in this book. A number of them deal with an entity that is in all likelihood the *hama / hamr* or *fylgja* of a child in the womb, or of a domestic animal in the womb.

In the modern and older Scandinavian languages, the afterbirth and the caul (birth-membrane) are sometimes called the *fylgi* ('follower') or the *hama* (skin, membrane, covering), showing the connection between gestation and some of the Heathen souls we possess or are accompanied by: the Fylgja and Hamr. Apparently this entity can sometimes get loose from the fetus and escape the womb, causing two serious problems: (a) probable miscarriage, and (b) haunting and harm done by this entity on the loose.

There are several terms used for this entity in the spellbook: among them are *bølen,* and *barne-mora. Barne-mora* would translate into English as 'bairn-mara;' the Mara or Mare is well-known in English and other lore as a phantom which haunts and afflicts sleeping people. Our word 'nightmare' does not refer to a horse, but rather to a night-mara, a haunter of the night.

Regarding the word bølen, it seems to be derived from *bøl* (related to Old English 'bale') meaning bad luck, harm, and shild or debt due to misdeeds. These meanings are very clearly connected to the idea of the fylgja and other 'soul-followers' like the Disir and the Hamingjur, which carry with them our luck, our wyrd, and our shild for misdeeds we have done. The connection with the Norns and wyrd is also clear. The identity between the bølen-spirit and the afterbirth comes across in the title of this spell:

To Bind an Afterbirth (Efterbyrd)
I bind the bøln with my five fingers,
As Odin and Frigg bound with their five fingers.
It shall stay with might (be mightily bound) in an earth-fast stone,
It shall cause no more harm to anyone.
(#300, dated 1800)

Here the *bølen* is treated as an evil spirit and immobilized; there are other spells that also treat 'afterbirths' as evil spirits which are sometimes collected and sent out by sorcerers. In these cases, the afterbirths are probably those of miscarried or stillborn babies which were not 'laid' by magic after the event.

They could also be Hamr-souls stolen by a witch or sorcerer from living persons: a *hamstolinn* person is considered witless, lacking their Hama soul which enables speech and social interaction. Even when not directed by a sorcerer, these afterbirth apparitions wander around and cause trouble.

In most of the spells involving Norns and Goddesses, a different approach is taken: they seek to bind the *bølen* or *barne-mara* back to the fetus immediately, as soon as it gets loose. This prevents a miscarriage and prevents the permanent creation of an evil phantom unattached to a living person who would control it.

Norns with their binding-cord.

Here is an example of binding the *bølen* in a healing way:

To Bind the Bølen inside a Woman
There come three maidens from East-lands,
The first can spin gold,

The other binds the barne-mora,
The third lays it in its right place within NN (name of mother).
(#240, dated 1780)

These are clearly the Norns acting, reuniting spirit with baby and laying it properly in the womb for a safe birth. This may bear some relation to the mysterious statement about the Norns in the *Völuspà* where they:

> *There lay laws, there choose life*
> *Of mortal children; speak ørlög.*

I suspect that these lines of the *Völuspà* refer in some way to the Norns' role in binding the soul and ørlög to the child in the womb, as Frau Holle, in German tradition, draws the souls of new babies out of her pond.

Another spell features a different group of women:

Against the Mora
There came three maidens wandering,
One was the Sun,
The other was the Moon,
And the third was the Virgin Mary (surely Freya).
They bound the slimy / slippery Mora
With silver bands
And gold bands
As fast (firm) as the Aand (spirit)
In the chains of motherhood.
(#246, 1882)

The Kindly Gods Go Wandering

I assume that the last two lines are talking about fastening the Mora-spirit into the womb, but it's not exactly clear. The grouping together of the Sun, the Moon, and Freya is very reminiscent of our Heathen lore. Several of our myths tell of giants seeking to win, as a prize, "the Sun, the Moon, and Freya" – the most well-known instance is the building of Asgard's walls by the giant and his stallion (Sturlason, p 35-6).

In the charm it is clear that all three entities—Sun, Moon, and Freya—are seen as female beings. The Goddesses Sunna and Freya are clear enough. Though Mani, the Moon, is a male God in Heathen lore, there are also hints of a Moon-Dis in our lore. Verse 39 of *Grimnismal* (Poetic Edda) speaks of Hati, the wolf who is known to be the Moon-Bane, the pursuer of the Moon, chasing the "bright bride of heaven" – obviously a Goddess or Dis. The Swedish scholar Viktor Rydberg identifies Nanna, Balder's wife, as a Moon-Dis – in fact as Sinhtgunt the sister of Sunna who appears in the *Second Merseberg Charm* (see below).

Hati the Moon-Bane chasing the 'bride of heaven' does imply that he is chasing the Moon or a being associated with the Moon. The reference to the 'bride of heaven' could also point toward Balder, Nanna's husband, whose home is called *Himinbjorg* or Heaven-Burg and who is associated with the Sun and the heavens. (See Chapter 9, *"A Tale of Nanna and Her Kin"* for more about Nanna as a Moon-Dis.)

I suspect that the precursor of this charm originally featured three of our Heathen Goddesses, most likely Sunna, Nanna, and Freya. The silver and gold bands in the spell, besides reflecting the colors of Moon and Sun, bring to mind Freya's magical girdle / necklace Brisingamen. Restoring a wandering soul-form to a baby may be one of the powerful magical uses to which Freya puts her girdle or necklace.

Here is another Norn-spell:

For a Hexed Bull
The three wise, wandering women
Went upon their way,
Met my bull weeping bloody tears.
"What is wrong with him?"
Asked the three wise, wandering women.
"My bull is mod-stolen and blood-stolen,
All might and strength is stolen from him."
"You shall go hence,
To the blessed (velsignede) Vendels-Rod*."
"Stand you there, you fair Ven* ('friend'? Or contraction of 'vendels-rod'?)
What are you good for?"
"For mod-sickness and blood-sickness,
For all ill that can happen to the bull....(continues)
(#253, dated 1815)

[*Vendels-Rod translates online to 'vendels-root', but the meaning of 'vendel' isn't clear. Is it a specific plant? 'Vend' means 'to turn' in English, so I wonder whether this is a magical root for 'turning' or transforming something. 'Ven' means 'friend,' but perhaps it is a contraction of vendels-rod?]

Traces of Heathen Names or References

As I explained earlier, in most cases the Deities figuring in the charms are Christianized ones, for which I have substituted our own Deities' names. In a few cases, however, actual Heathen names or references creep in, as I describe below.

Balder

In the following example I retain the original version with "Jesus" to emphasize the strangeness of the other character in this spell:

> *Jesus and "Herren" ride*
> *Over the desolate heath.*
> *Herren's horse slips,*
> *And wrenches its leg.*
> *Jesus alights there*
> *And sets in order*
> *Herr's foal:*
> *Hide to hide,*
> *Bone to bone,*
> *Then it (the leg) held its place,*
> *As it had held before.*
> (#5, dated 1670)

Now, this charm is especially interesting because among Christians Jesus's father "God" is normally called "Herre" = Lord. Alternatively, Jesus is also referred to as Herre / Lord. But here, Jesus is riding with someone else called Lord, implying that Jesus is not "Lord", or at least that there is someone who is more lordly and more deserving of the title than he is. "Lord" is unlikely to be the Christian Father-God in this case, since one never hears tales of him walking on earth in human form (not since the Garden of Eden, anyway). Who this "Lord" is becomes clear when we compare this with an Old High German version of the same charm dating from the tenth century:

The Kindly Gods Go Wandering

Phol and Wodan fared to the wood,
Then was Balder's foal's leg wrenched.
Then galdored Sinhtgunt and Sunna her sister,
Then galdored Friia and Volla her sister,
Then galdored Wodan, as well he could,
Be it bone-wrench, be it blood-wrench, be it limb-wrench:
Bone to bone, blood to blood,
Limb to limb, as if they were glued.
(Second Merseberg Charm, Barber p. 65)

Here, Phol is probably a variant German name of Balder. Comparing the two charms, it is clear that in the Norwegian charm, Jesus plays Odin's role and Herre / Lord is Balder. The Norwegian version, ostensibly Christian, not only implies the presence of a Heathen God, but places him higher than Jesus by calling him Lord.

Wodan heals Balder's horse, by Emil Doepler.

In another of the 34 Norwegian variants of this charm (#17), it is the Virgin Mary who heals Jesus's / Balder's horse, which parallels the healing role of the Goddesses Sinhtgunt, Sunna, Friia (Frigg) and Volla (Fulla) in the German charm.

These examples show very clearly that Christian Deities replaced Heathen ones in traditional spells, and that there was a good deal of creative flexibility about the replacements. For example, sometimes Jesus replaced Odin, other times he replaced Balder. In another 'wrenched horse's leg' variant (#1), Jesus plays Balder's role and Saint Michael (archangel) plays Odin's role.

Odin

In another of the 'wrenched leg' charm variants we see "Eg" riding over a bridge, which probably refers to Odin's name "Ygg." (#28, dated 1811.) Another charm works against "Eddin's daughters." "Eddin" is surely Odin, and his daughters may perhaps be Valkyries. The charm orders first one, then two, then three "Eddin's Daughters" to go out of the person, into earth and sea and air. (#99, dated 1847.)

Thor, Odin and Frigg

There are a couple of spells which I mentioned earlier, that actually name three Heathen Deities outright: Thor, Odin and Frigg. Here is one:

> ### To Bind Bad Luck into a Sending-Stone
> *Put the black upon the blue,*
> *Put the blue upon the white,*
> *Put the white upon an earth-fast stone.*
> *In the names of Thor, Odin and Frigg.*

The Kindly Gods Go Wandering

Lock (it) in a stone, walk three turns around and strike in the bad luck (strike the luck into the stone).
(#40, dated 1880)

Your guess is as good as mine, concerning the "black, blue and white"! Another similar charm mentions "black upon the blue, blue upon the grey, grey upon the white, white upon the red...", and also speaks in the name of Thor, Odin and Frigg (#96, examples found from 1780 through 1885). Perhaps there are clues in folklore that would help one figure out the details of this approach.

So many of the charms in this book, when viewed with a Heathen understanding, can serve to open our awareness of how near the Holy Ones always are. We might not see them face to face, walking on the streets, though perhaps this could happen. But there are many other ways they approach us: through the timely words and example of others, in person or through books or media. Through the phenomena of nature, whether powerful like storms or gentle like bird-calls or sunrises. Through feelings in our hearts and insights in our minds. Through synchronicities and luck acting in our lives.

Everything can speak with Gods' voices and powers when we open our awareness. By immersing ourselves in experiences and insights consistent with a Heathen world-view, as we find in these spells, we train our awareness to be sensitive to the voices of the Holy Ones. I hope that you will feel as moved as I do, perceiving in this world-view the closeness, goodness, and power of the kindly Gods and Goddesses as they walk among us: then, now, and always.

2: Of Frigg and Odin

All In a Day's Work: Frigg and her Ladies

"Frigg, Oden's hustru," by Jenny Nystrom.

Of Frigg and Odin

One of Frigg's greatest powers is the ability (and the determination!) to create and maintain a healthy and fruitful condition of orderliness in both the material and the non-material domains. This ability is expressed in her patronage of householding and housekeeping, where she teaches and supports all functions having to do with the well-being of the family. This includes not only housekeeping *per se,* but the management of money and property, hospitality, child-raising and teaching, health, and family relationships.

Frigg's ability to order these matters is not confined to the small scale of the individual household, though that is one essential aspect of it. The same kinds of wisdom, authority, and knowledge required to properly run a household are also needed to run a business, an organization, a city, state, or nation. This is especially true when one remembers how much was done in the household during Heathen times, and how much skill and authority it took. In addition to the functions householding still implies today, it also included the production of food, fiber, pharmaceuticals, and most other materials needed for daily living, and performed the functions of farm, school, hospital, pharmacy, bank, nursing home, clothing and tool factories, and many other operations that are now more often in the commercial sector rather than the household.

The differences between householding and today's commercial and public undertakings are primarily one of scale, and do not relate to the basic nature of what one needs to know and do. Whether in the home or the organization, one must know how to organize materials and work functions, plan work according to daily, monthly, and yearly requirements, manage one's finances, manage supply and production, train and supervise people, ensure good relations among workers, plan for the future, and many other activities.

Our word 'economy' *(oikonomia)* simply means 'the law/ordering *(nomia)* of the household *(oikos)*' in Greek, while 'ecology' means 'the science of the household.' The roots of these words reflect the overall unity between the work, functions and interactions occurring within the household, and those occurring outside it at the larger scales of national economies and natural ecosystems. Differences of scale, while they may mean a lot to us, are not as significant to the Deities since they are not bound by the limitations we are. Thus, for Frigg, one might say that either running a household, or running a nation, is simply 'all in a day's work!'

I'll share here a brief vision of Frigg that came to me years ago in meditation: one of the reasons I can so easily see Frigg as 'chairman of the board!' Her appearance in some high-powered company boardroom was overlaid simultaneously with her appearance at the 'doom-stead' or judgement-stead and meeting place of the Æsir Gods. Here is the scene:

Frigg is dressed in a power-suit, standing at the head of the conference table in a Boardroom / Doomstead. She lays her briefcase on the table, and I see that its combination lock shows runes instead of numbers. I realize that the runes on the lock change, depending on the situation that the Board of Directors / Reginn / Gods are dealing with. Whichever runes appear on the lock guide them in 'unlocking' wise rede and strategies for decisions and actions. As Frigg opens her briefcase I notice her wristwatch. It has no numbers or other figures on it. Instead, it is a silvery, misty hologram of the Well of Wyrd. Through it she can discern the Well and consult with the Norns, bringing knowledge of ørlög, wyrd

Of Frigg and Odin

and shild to the Boardroom / Doomstead and the directions and actions that are decided upon there.

Frigg's ordering function extends to all kinds of relationships: personal relations between individuals, kindred and kinship relationships, larger groups, and society at large. Frigg is the frithweaver, bringing about not only peace, but 'right relationships' that can maintain themselves peacefully over time, without constant struggle, strife, and grief.

In the prose *Edda*, Frigg is listed first among a large group of other Goddesses, who are considered by some to be her companions and co-workers, or possibly aspects of herself (Sturlason pp. 29-31). The majority of these Goddesses are concerned with this right ordering of relationships.

"Frigg and her Maidens"

Var ensures the sanctity of oaths and promises; without this sanctity, relationships become weak and chaotic, and often break down into vengefulness and resentment. Though the Edda apparently limits Var's domain of oaths and promises to those between men and women in romantic relationships, I believe her power extends much further: to business contracts, diplomatic treaties, the 'social contracts' that underlie trust in our public officials at all levels, and good-faith agreements of all kinds.

Sjöfn and **Ljöfn** support the smooth path of love and affection; I see their work supporting not only romantic and sexually expressed love, but all the different kinds of love, affection, friendship, and caring.

Snotra *(Snow-tra)* teaches us about courtesy, manners, protocol, diplomacy—and not just the superficial forms of them, but the wisdom and the social ethics that underlie them. The whole purpose of these ways of ordering social interactions is to maintain good relationships with each other: to reduce opportunities for strife and misunderstanding, and to smooth the path of friendliness and trust.

When these things break down, vengefulness, social chaos, strife and war ensue, bringing danger to all. **Hlin**, the protector, provides a safe refuge from the breakdown of social order and the dangers of embittered relationships, until they can be healed or left behind.

Syn, whom I call the "Just Say No!" Goddess, wards the door and the gate, and also helps us ward our personal boundaries from intrusion; she has a chapter to herself in this book, as does Vør.

Vør is Goddess of awareness; without awareness and understanding of other people, their environments and circumstances, it is difficult to maintain good relations with them. Just as important is awareness of ourselves, our biases, our motives, our habits, the effects our actions and words have on others. True awareness and understanding form the necessary basis for any efforts at ordering anything, at any level, if we don't want to end up making situations worse than they were when we started. This includes anything from teaching self-discipline to children, to deciding to go to war against another nation.

Gna, Frigg's messenger Goddess, can be seen as the process of communication between one person and another. Without this ongoing communication, relationships collapse into complete disorder.

The relationships Frigg is concerned with—and has the power to help with—range from the intimate relations within a family and among close Heathen kindreds, through the everyday social relations within our workplaces and neighborhoods, and all the way up to the diplomatic relations between different countries and cultures. And if we ever end up meeting with extraterrestrial beings, we could most certainly use the assistance of Frigg and her ladies then, as well!

Frigg extends her ordering abilities even beyond the household, work-sphere, and relationships at all levels. Working with **Eir**, another of her companion-Goddesses, Eir and Frigg order the interweaving strands of body, mind and soul to promote health and healing.

She also orders knowledge and wisdom. Frigg is said to "know all, though she does not speak it." (Lokasenna vs.29, *Poetic Edda*). The 'all' referred to in this quotation applies mainly to the knowledge of the Norns, the knowledge of Wyrd. As anyone who has tried to perceive Wyrd directly knows, this kind of information can seem to us like an impossibly confused and chaotic tangle of bits and pieces. To be able to translate 'chaotic tangle of bits and pieces' into 'true knowledge and wisdom' requires a very high degree of ordering power—an ability symbolized by Frigg's spinning and weaving skills.

Saga is seen as another of Frigg's companions or aspects, and her skill is the ordering of disconnected bits and pieces of knowledge into the meaningful whole represented by historical accounts or by a tale, poem or song.

Fulla is Frigg's sister, and though Snorri in the *Edda* describes Fulla as rather subordinate to Frigg, the fact that they are sisters, and other literary clues, shows that Fulla has greater power than Snorri describes. Fulla's primary power is the gift of abundance, of *Fullness:* no small matter, and an attribute of the Great Goddess in every religion. In Snorri's description, Fulla looks after Frigg's possessions, and keeps her secrets. 'Looking after Frigg's possessions' must surely involve putting and keeping them in order. And what are Frigg's possessions? Her power, her knowledge, her wisdom.

It is as though Fulla, with her task of ordering Frigg's possessions, is the secret core of Frigg's ordering powers. Here we have the uniting of Frigg, whose name means 'Beloved' (the essence of relationship) with Fulla, whose name means 'Abundance,' both of them converging in the power of right ordering. This seems to hint that we should see these things as a unity: right ordering and right relationships lead to abundance and fullness—not only material fullness, but even more, they lead to emotional and spiritual fullness, as well.

It is important to understand that the power of right ordering underlies many of Frigg's aspects, abilities and strengths, and is a key part of who she is, in terms of her character and personality. This common thread serves to tie together apparently unrelated aspects of her powers, some of which are represented by her companions. Understanding how and why she seeks to bring about order in all these different ways helps one see the underlying unity of her manifold works and purposes in Midgard.

"Frigg and Fulla," by Ludwig Pietsch.

More about Fulla

There is a reference to Fulla in the myth of Balder. When Hermod visits Balder and Nanna in Hel, Nanna gives him a gift of 'finger gold' to take back to Fulla, and gives fine linens for Frigg. These are the only two Deities to whom Nanna sends gifts from Hel to Asgard, and her choice indicates a certain degree of equality between these two Goddesses, at least in Nanna's affections (*Gylfaginning* in the prose *Edda*, p. 50).

'Volla' is mentioned as Frigg's / Friia's sister in the Old High German *Second Merseberg Charm* (Simek p. 278). '*Voll*' means 'full' in German and is pronounced *foll*. There are a number of references to 'Dame Abundia' in Jacob Grimm's

Teutonic Mythology and other writings about folklore in Germanic lands. I think 'Dame Abundia' must be the same as Fulla and Volla: all of their names mean 'fullness, abundance.' All of these clues lead me to the conclusion that Fulla / Volla was in elder times a mightier and more highly-regarded Goddess than we now realize. Her relationship as sister to Frigg reinforces that impression. Volla is recognized as a Goddess in the *Urglaawe* branch of modern Heathenry.

A chest for Frigg's and Fulla's treasures.

Of Frigg and Odin

Call to Frigg: A Prayer

"Frigga"

Lady Frigg, most magnificent,
Asgard's Queen in your cloak of stars:
We call to you, be with us now!
Send your mighty maidens to us:
Swift Gna, bringing grace and good fortune;
Golden Fulla with her overflowing gifts;
Eir with her healing wisdom;
Gentle Hlin, giving comfort and strong warding
Against all grief, despair and evil
That assail the heart.
Teach us your wisdom, Mother,
To order our lives, homes, and folkways rightly,
For the good of all,
And to reflect your grace and brightness.
Hail Frigg!

Of Being and Knowledge: Frigg, Nerthus, and Odin

This essay summarizes a few of my thoughts, personal perceptions and experiences that help to shape my understanding of Frigg, of her relationship to Nerthus and her relations with Odin. I do not make any claims as to the universal validity of these perceptions. If they make sense to you, fine; if they do not, then toss them out!

Frigg and Nerthus

Here, I am exploring the relationship between Frigg and the Goddess Earth, whether she is named Nerthus, Fjörgyn, Jord, or other names. Frigg's father is named as Fjörgynn in the lore, and I believe that he and Fjörgyn were a pair of sibling-spouses, Earth and Sky / Storm Deities. This would make Frigg the daughter of the Earth-Goddess. In this way, Frigg inherits much of Earth's nature, her Godly standing, and her powers—the family resemblance is certainly there.

But Frigg is a more modern expression of the ancient earth Goddess. Frigg is closer to humanity and to the concerns of civilized human beings—just as one would expect a daughter to be more modern than her mother. She shares in some of her mother's nature and powers, but also embodies much of her own new and unique character, much that is new to humanity since ancient Earth herself came into being. This does not mean that Earth herself is or should be superseded by Frigg—not at all, of course! Nerthus / Earth is and will be what she always has been. But the needs of non-human beings and of primitive human beings are in some (not all) respects different from those of humans and human societies that have moved beyond the Stone Age, and we need Deities with whom to work, to meet these needs.

My view of Frigg goes well beyond that of the mother of a nuclear family, and by extension the mother-Goddess of human families—powerful and significant as that role indeed is. Frigg is also the Goddess of social order, social structuring and social relations. Though Odin is not referred to as a 'king' specifically—he is not really a God of rulership and statecraft—Frigg is referred to as 'queen' of Asgard, and for good reason: she subtly weaves the web of frith that forms the fabric of society, for Godkind and humankind. This is where much of her power lies—a power that can indeed be compared to Earth's power in terms of its significance for the world, but which is really very different from Earth's power, though rooted in it. What would our world be, without social relationships and all that goes into creating and maintaining them, at all levels from individuals on up to cultures and nations?

Mother and daughter share the same power, at the root of it: the power of life itself. But Frigg wields the power of life expressed through different channels—less through the channels of nature, and more through the channels of Godly and human society, which is to say, a great deal of what gives human life meaning, and makes it possible. Nor does Frigg detract from Earth's powers in any way: we will always need Earth, need to love and care for her, and accept her care in return. That cannot change. But Earth cannot give us what Frigg can, and we need both of their gifts in very truth—we could not live, nor would life be worth living, if we were missing either of their powers.

Here I will share with you a brief but very meaningful vision that I had of Frigg many years ago—making no claims for it, other than it being my own personal experience and insight. But I think it has a bearing on this discussion, casting a light on it from a different perspective.

I saw Frigg seated next to Ginnungagap, surrounded by the blackness of the void. Inside the Gap itself, I saw a seething mass of runes, coruscating with intense gold rims and the blackest of shades in their interiors. I had the sense that the runes were so star-hot they were cold, so outer-space-cold they were hot—that they passed beyond the physical boundaries where energies can be sensed and measured. Frigg, enveloped in her mantle of stars, was serenely reaching into the mass of runes, coiling handfuls of them onto her distaff, and spinning from this the thread with which to weave the worlds.

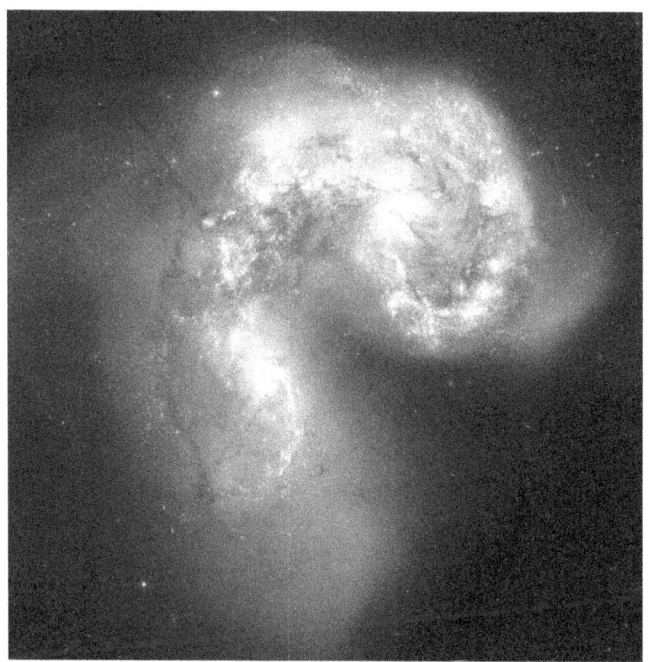

"Antennae galaxies" from NASA...but this looks like Frigg's distaff to me!

In trying to interpret this vision, I think it is not so much the physical world/earth that she is weaving, as it is the nonmaterial worlds of spirit, of culture, knowledge and wisdom. She is weaving some of the underlying patterns, such as the moral codes, the drives toward human interactions, and their links with Wyrd, that shape the physical and social worlds, and the worlds of Spirit. In this respect, she is Earth's equal, or perhaps greater than Earth, but she is of a different essence and wields a different power than that of Earth. They are similar in their powers of bringing forth and shaping, but those things which they bring forth are different, though related or connected with each other.

Seeing Frigg in this form, as I saw her in this vision, makes me wonder whether her spirit in some form does not also precede Earth, being greater than Earth in the sense of being more universal or cosmogonic. It is as though Frigg, in a relatively undifferentiated, cosmogonic form, existed before Earth, but also was born of Earth into her more personified form as the Goddess Frigg. As though her 'birth' from Earth consisted of a reshaping of who she is, into a being with whom it is easier for us to relate than it is to relate to Earth and to Auðhumla or some other form of the cosmic Ur-Mother. Her birth through Earth perhaps helped to bring her more 'down to earth' in a way that we can relate to! But still in the core of herself she retains the powers of the cosmogonic Mother.

Frigg, Odin, and Power
If we hold this view of Frigg, how might this affect our understanding of Odin's nature and powers, and of the relationship between Frigg and Odin?

Another vision that I had, some years ago, is germane to this question. This was before I grew close to Odin. I knew I needed to do that, and part of me wanted to, but I kept shying away from closeness with him, feeling at that point somewhat wary and distrustful. I was working mainly with Frigg at the time, so finally I got the idea of asking her to help. I knew that she loves Odin and thinks highly of him, and he of her. So I asked her to help me understand more of her relationship with him, as a way of getting closer to him through her.

"Wodan and Friia (Frigg) in Heaven's window," by Emil Doepler.

Well, the Gods sometimes give us a little more than we bargain for, and that was certainly the case, this time! Frigg snatched me up one night, unprepared, just as I was falling asleep, and drew me into a place like outer space. I was a tiny mote, and Frigg and Odin were the size and power of supernova suns, with me the tiny mote floating right between them. The two of them were just at that moment turning toward each other, with the thought of love in their minds. The power that flowed from their love and passion was literally awesome—power that generates worlds, even universes—Big Bang power. I was there only a split second,

Of Frigg and Odin

and realized this was no place for a mortal to be. But it's not something I will ever forget!

Here is a thought of mine that follows on from that experience. It involves a rather unusual 'take' on Odin's history, but there are possible examples of the event I describe here in other Pagan pantheons, including the Celtic idea of the king or ruling God 'wedding the sovereignty of the land.' Based on some interpretations of the development and history of our faith, Odin can perhaps be seen as an 'upstart God,' one who in very ancient times was a less-important God of wind and wode, and a psychopomp, in comparison to the overarching Sky Father God represented by Tyr in our pantheon. The fact that the Romans equated Odin with the less-powerful God Mercury rather than with Jupiter (who was equated with Thor) supports this idea.

The scholar Georges Dumezil and others have noted the resemblance between the Tyr / Odin pair of leader-Deities, and similar pairs in other pantheons, such as the paired Hindu Mitra-Varuna, Celtic Nuada / Lugh, and others. The balance of power between these pairs of Gods who represent the light / dark aspects of sovereignty may have swayed back and forth numerous times in the various pantheons.

Here's a speculation on my part as to how Odin gained greater power and somewhat eclipsed Tyr's Sky Father position in our pantheon. If the vision I saw of the power of love between Odin and Frigg is true, then perhaps Odin gained his greater degree of power when he wedded Frigg. He and Tyr could have been roughly equal before then, but after Odin and Frigg wed, Odin's power increased over that of Tyr. Together Odin and Frigg wove this power out of their love and their respective natures.

"Odin and Frigga," by Harry George Theaker.

Making a hard-headed 'marriage of state' to gain power from it, and making a success of his personal marriage relationship nevertheless, are actions that would fit very consistently with Odin's usual way of going about things! Equally so on the part of Frigg, as a Goddess who is supremely at home in her queenly position. It's an interesting idea to consider!

(See a summary here of the Tyr / Odin and similar Deity pairs: https://en.wikipedia.org/wiki/Mitra-Varuna_(Indo-European)).

Frigg, Odin, and Knowledge
In my perception, Frigg and the Norns weave the secret patterns of the multiverse. Odin seeks to unravel the strands of truth that are hidden within these secrets. Weaving and unraveling: between the two processes, the multiverse is in a constant state of Becoming, of re-creation and renewal. It is endlessly woven and mysteries are endlessly generated, which Odin seeks endlessly to learn and understand: because by being understood and known by him, the mysteries attain a higher degree of reality and power.

Of Frigg and Odin

I see 'truth' as generally multi-layered and complex, not simple and absolute. The layers of truth can often conflict with each other, or seem to do so. This is how it seems to me when I am in the Well of Wyrd, peering through layer upon layer of interwoven truths. Simply learning a single truth about a matter does not equate to full wisdom, in my view. Rather, we begin to gain wisdom when we are able to perceive a cross-cutting sample of these layers of truths (I think we generally cannot perceive all of them) and integrate across them, spinning a multi-stranded, multi-colored cord of knowledge by the power of seeing and understanding the layers. This cord is then strong enough to hold the weight of the deeper truths. Sort of like spinning a fishing-line for deep-sea fishing! In this imagery, the 'sea' is the one Well—the conjoined Wells of Wyrd, Mimir, and Hvergelmir; while the 'fish' are the truths worked into its layers.

Frigg knows automatically how to spin this cord of wisdom, knot it into a net and fish with it, as part of her being, part of who she is. For Odin, constant seeking is required of him: exploration, action, learning. He gains something by this requirement, by having the process be difficult for him, rather than having it be a part of his being as with Frigg.

Frigg 'knows all but speaks it not', as Freya said of her in *Lokasenna* (Poetic Edda). I believe this is because there is no way to put into words the arcane knowledge that she has, in the form in which she holds this knowledge. It does not lend itself to verbal expression. But Odin, because of his striving, learns not only the knowledge itself, but also learns the *process of learning about the knowledge*. Because of this, he is more able to communicate it to us directly, to teach us knowledge and teach us how to gain knowledge for ourselves. Frigg is the weaver of mysteries. Odin is the distiller of knowledge out of mystery, drop by inspired drop. He is Óðrœrir's Master!

Frigg is not unable to teach us about the mysteries, of course, but her ways are somewhat different. (Keeping in mind that she teaches *many* other practical things about life and living, in all the usual ways. I am speaking here specifically about knowledge of deep mysteries.) Frigg teaches us her mysteries most often by experience and intuition. Odin teaches his mysteries by runes and inspired words, by language, intellect, and wode. The minds of each of them are subtle and great, and hold far more than we can ever encompass. The power each of them has, alone, is enormously enhanced when their powers are conjoined. I think that the entertaining wrangles which are told in the myths and tales—the contests of wit between Frigg and Odin—are but pale reflections of that primal, creative explosion that happens when they truly come together.

Of Frigg and Odin

The Winds of Odin's Will: A Song

Let fly two Ravens forth from thee,
Singing Thought and Memory!
Naught in any world from them can flee.
Fare ye forth!
Hear one of them call to his mate,
Seeking out the strands of fate,
Crying, "Come! Fare we now on winds of Odin's will!"

Upon yon distant stone-girt peak
Singing Thought and Memory!
There stands an ancient mossy seat.
Fare ye forth!
There, rooted in eldest might,
Thou sendest forth thy wingéd sight.
Crying, "Come! Fare we now on winds of Odin's will!"

Through worlds of darkness, worlds of light,
Singing Thought and Memory!
Two night-hued Ravens, swift in flight:
Fare ye forth!
Gather ye news of each wight,
See what goes ill, see deeds of right,
Crying, "Come! Fare we now on winds of Odin's will!"

Now sinks the Sun in misty vale,
Singing Thought and Memory!
Thou biddest them hence to tell their tale:
Fare ye hence!
From Hliðskalf thy call echoes forth,
Spanning the Worlds from south to north,

Of Frigg and Odin

Crying, "Come! Fare ye now on winds of Odin's will!"

As Night's soft arms embrace bright Day,
Singing Thought and Memory!
Two shining Ravens wend their way,
Faring hence!
Winds bear them to mountain crown,
Upon thy great shoulders gliding down,
Crying, "Hark! Wisdom borne on wings of Odin's will!"

Heed we well the wisdom borne on wings of Odin's will!

Sung to the tune of the medieval English ballad, "Three Ravens."

"Heed we well the wisdom borne on wings of Odin's will!

*For the background to this song
see Chapter 26, section on "The Modes of Air and Wind."*

Mimir, Odin, and World-Mind

"Odin at the Fountain of Wisdom."

Wisdom:
If it's good enough for Odin, it's good enough for us!

3. Mimir, Odin, and World-Mind

Mimir's Head: this is a stone carving by my husband Rosten Dean Rose. It is placed above a small pond on our homestead, overshadowed by a tall Yew, reflected in the dark water here. Together, the head, the pond, and the yew form our Mimir-shrine.

Mimir is a mighty figure in Old Norse lore: a deeply wise being, the warder of a mysterious Well of wisdom and inspiration, a 'friend' of Odin's, a hostage to the Vanir to help end a war, a sacrifice, and one who lives on after his sacrifice as a decapitated head that is nevertheless a source of rede and wisdom to Odin. Mimir's name is probably related to words for thinking and memory (Simek p. 216), and the Well that he wards, *Mímisbrunnr,* lies under one of the three great roots of the World-Tree Yggdrasil, a source of cosmic power. Odin treasured the wisdom of this Well so highly that he gave his eye as a pledge for a drink from it *(Völuspá vs. 28).*

'Friend of Odin' and his Uncle (?)

Odin is several times referred to as 'Mim's friend' in Old Norse lore. Keep in mind that a 'friend' in old Germanic culture did not simply mean someone that a person hangs out with a lot. It implied patronage, as well as what we understand as friendship: a friend was someone that you could rely on to help you out, support you, and promote your success in life. A worthy friend had the power, ability, and willingness to help you. When Heathens took names like *Thorsvin* ('friend of Thor,' Old Norse) or *Oswin* ('friend of the Os / Esa-God himself, Woden,' in Anglo-Saxon), this implied not 'being buddies' but rather claiming a patronage relationship with that Deity. So the phrase 'Mim's friend' implies that Mimir is the patron of Odin—the one who is in a position to grant benefits of some kind to Odin. This includes their ongoing relationship of Mimir being the wise advisor to Odin, even after he has been beheaded by the Vanir.

It's clear from these details that Odin and Mimir have a close relationship, and the suspicion is that they are related as maternal uncle and nephew, a very meaningful relationship in Indo-European society. This suspicion is strengthened by *Havamál* verse 140 (Poetic Edda), which says that Odin learned nine songs of power from the brother of his mother Bestla:

"Nine mighty spells I learned from the famous son of Bolthor, Bestla's father, and I got a drink of the precious mead, I, soaked from Óðrœrir." (Larrington's translation)

We know from elsewhere *(Völuspá vs. 28)* that Odin pledged his eye to Mimir's Well to gain one drink therefrom. Here, just after he comes down from the Tree, Odin says he got a drink of the precious mead. The parallelism is pretty clear, and it's reasonable to assume that Odin's ordeal on the Tree was followed by the sacrifice of his eye to Mimir's Well in

Mimir, Odin, and World-Mind

order to gain the precious drink. All of these events were, in my view, part of Odin's great ordeal: hanging on the Tree, gaining the runes, sacrificing his eye for the draught of wisdom from the Well, and then being taught the 'fimbul-songs,' the nine songs of power, by his unnamed uncle, Bestla's famous brother. 'Famous' is certainly a term that can be applied to Mimir!

The last line of the verse quoted above, 'soaked from Óðrœrir,' reads *ausinn Óðreri* in Old Norse. Let's examine that for a minute. Odin, as he speaks this verse, has just undergone a great ordeal, hanging from Yggdrasil for nine nights and days without food or drink, stabbed with a spear, in order to gain the runes *(Havamál verses 138-139, Poetic Edda)*. He has just taken up the runes, screaming or roaring, and fallen from the Tree. This is definitely some kind of initiation ceremony, and the person who normally oversees such a ceremony is the patron and teacher of the initiate.

After going through everything described here, Odin is *ausinn Óðreri*, soaked, bathed, or sprinkled with Óðrœrir. This phrase tells us a lot, because the Old Norse custom called *ausa vatni*, meaning sprinkled or bathed in water, is the ceremony when the father or clan-head officially accepts a newborn baby into the family and gives it a name. (See the text-box, below.)

In my understanding, when the poem says that Odin was *ausinn Óðreri*, it means that Mimir was enacting a rebirthing / initiation ceremony for Odin as his patron and maternal uncle, the living head of Odin's clan. Instead of being sprinkled or soaked in water, here it is mead: the mead of inspiration. 'Óðrœrir' means 'wode-stirrer, stirrer of inspiration,' an appellation very suitable to Odin's powers. Odin becomes an embodiment of eloquence, wisdom, poetry, prophecy, galdor-songs, and runelore. Based on all this reasoning, I assume that Mimir is Bestla's brother, Odin's maternal uncle and his teacher and patron.

<u>Ausa vatni, from Wikipedia entry on Old Norse religion</u> https://en.wikipedia.org/wiki/Old_Norse_religion: *"A child was accepted into the family via a ritual of sprinkling with water (Old Norse* ausa vatni) *which is mentioned in two Eddic poems, "Rígsþula" and "Hávamál", and was afterwards given a name.[212] The child was frequently named after a dead relative, since there was a traditional belief in rebirth, particularly in the family.[213]"* References: [212] De Vries, Volume 1, pp. 178–80. *Before the water rite, a child could be rejected; infanticide was still permitted under the earliest Christian laws of Norway, p. 179.* [213] De Vries 1970, Volume 1, pp. 181–83.

We're going to leave the topic of Óðrœrir here, because it becomes quite confused with other events and their timing: the coming-into-being, death, and blood of Kvasir; the Æsir-Vanir war; the wooing of Gunnlöð and the mead-theft; the access of humans to the mead, and more. This mead has its own saga, for sure! It's not clear how or why this mead Óðrœrir is in Mimir's Well at the time of young Odin's initiation, and scholars have offered various discussions about it. For myself, I resolve the problem by assuming that Mimir's Well does contain a form of mead of inspiration, but not necessarily the mead made from Kvasir's blood. There are some clear parallels between Kvasir and Mimir as beings of great wisdom who were killed, but continue to impart wisdom and inspiration through their remains—Kvasir's blood, and Mimir's decapitated head. I think this has something to do with the nature of Óðrœrir, but I'll leave this intriguing mystery now, and get back to Mimir's tale.

Odin sips from the Wellspring of Wisdom as Mimir looks on, by Robert Engels.

Mimir's Relatives

I am going on the assumption that Mimir and Bestla are siblings. I also accept Rydberg's argument that Bolthorn Bestla's father was another name for Ymir the primordial Giant (also called Aurgelmir, Blain, Brimir, multi-named as are many in our mythology). Rydberg posits that Mimir and Bestla were the 'boy and girl' who grew underneath Ymir's arm. (See Rydberg's chapter 86, Vol. 2. *Vafthrudnir's Sayings* in the *Poetic Edda*, vs. 33, mentions this 'boy and girl,' but does not name them.) That would put Mimir and Bestla in the same generation as Odin/Vili/Ve's father Borr, son of Buri, the first of the Æsir, which would make complete sense.

First were Ymir, Auðhumla the cow, and Buri, whom Auðhumla licked free of the primordial ice. Though there is no indication of this in the lore, I believe that Auðhumla is the Ur-Mother, a shapeshifting being who can appear as a cow or a woman, and that she was the mate of Buri and hence the mother of Borr and grandmother of Odin, Vili and Ve. I list here the generations as I understand them. **Bold** type shows relationships that are attested in the lore; *italics* show relationships that I am assuming.

First generation:
- **Ymir, Auðhumla as a cow, Buri.**

Second generation:
- **Ymir self-generates two beings** *(Mimir and Bestla)* **under his arm, and the first giant offspring, Thrudgelmir, from his legs.** (See *Gylfaginning* in the prose *Edda,* Sturlason p. 11.)
- **Buri** *(and Auðhumla as the Ur-Mother in woman form)* **produce Borr.**

Third generation:
- **Borr and Bestla produce Odin, Vili, and Ve.** *(Mimir is their maternal uncle.)*

Mimir as a Cosmogonic Sacrifice

Ymir was sacrificed by Odin, Vili, and Ve so that they could shape the Earth out of his body: the physical world with its sky and its encircling waters, where humans and other beings live.

Mimir, Odin, and World-Mind

I believe that Mimir's baffling execution, while he was hostage to the Vanir, was also a cosmogonic sacrifice like Ymir's. *(Ynglingasaga p. 3, in Heimskringla.)* Here's the story, in brief: The Æsir and Vanir became tired of their war and agreed to make peace and exchange hostages. Njorð and Frey, and according to some accounts Kvasir, went from the Vanir to Asgard. (In other accounts, Kvasir was created by all the Æsir and Vanir spitting into a vat together, to signify their truce; wise Kvasir was made from this brew.) Hœnir and Mimir went from the Æsir to Vanaheim.

The Vanir admired handsome Hœnir and made him a chieftain, but it turned out he lacked the wisdom for this role. In their anger and disappointment, the Vanir beheaded—not Hœnir—but Mimir. The Vanir returned Mimir's head to Odin, who preserved it using rune-power and continued to consult it for its wisdom. In the lore, Odin apparently sometimes carries Mimir's head around with him, but in my perception, the head spends much of the time near to or within Mimir's Well.

There is no logic to this tale of the Vanir beheading Mimir when they were disappointed in Hœnir. For one thing, according to *Völuspa 18* (Poetic Edda), it was Hœnir who gave Ask and Embla 'oðr' when they were being turned into humans, which is variously interpreted as 'spirit, consciousness, wit, wode'. How could he have given such a gift if he lacked it himself? The illogicality of Mimir's execution leads me to look for a more mythic, symbolic underpinning. I think that, in fact, Mimir is a cosmogonic—a World-generating—sacrifice, just as his purported father Ymir was. As Ymir's body became physical Midgard, I believe that Mimir's head / brain / mind became the metaphysical space where inspired Thought occurs.

Mimir, Odin, and World-Mind

A cloud-face shows in profile on the right. I see this as an image of World-Mind, where thoughts take shapes like clouds and float around within a metaphysical 'atmosphere.'

The skull of Ymir became the sky of Midgard, and his brains became the clouds. I see Mimir's head / World-Mind superimposed over Ymir's skull and brains as the sky of Midgard, with the movements of clouds and winds in the physical world mirroring the movement of inspired thoughts floating through World-Mind.

So as I see it, both Ymir and Mimir were cosmogonic sacrifices, sacrificed by the Æsir and by the Vanir, respectively. They were sacrificed at different times: Ymir at the beginning, the foundation of the physical world, and

Mimir much later, after beings capable of Thought had multiplied in Midgard and the other Worlds.

World-Mind

Mimir's beheading thus led, in my view, to the coming-into-being of World-Mind or the Noösphere, represented by Mimir's Well of Memory and Inspiration. (Noösphere is a word formed from Greek *nóos* ('noh-ohs') meaning 'thought, mind' plus 'sphere', and is used in a modern context to parallel the biosphere, the domain of physical life. It's a good word, but I like World-Mind even better!) World-Mind is the intangible space, the energetic matrix, where inspired thought occurs: an individual person's thoughts, and the multitude of thoughts arising from all inspired, thinking beings which circulate there, influence and build upon each other.

When I call this the 'World-Mind' I don't mean some kind of horrible supercomputer or AI running the world! I use 'mind' in its old Anglo-Saxon meaning of *gemynd:* 'memory, recollection'; and *gemynde* meaning 'mindful' but also 'the mouth of a river.' 'The mouth of a river' and 'mindfulness' fit perfectly with the image of wisdom and inspiration flowing forth from the water of Mimir's Well. ('Mouth of a river' is also one of the meanings of the Os / Ansuz rune, a rune of eloquence and wisdom-words.)

I perceive Mimir's World-Mind as an echoing, shadowy, dimly-lit cavern under a root of the Tree, holding the deep, reflective Well at its center. Here, it accumulates knowledge and experience from all the Worlds within itself and slowly ferments them into wisdom and inspiration. I see this active, vital process of World-Mind's fermentation as a parallel to Kvasir's origins: the spittle of the Æsir and Vanir, which

Mimir, Odin, and World-Mind

formed Kvasir, represents their essences and wisdoms trickling daily into the Well, as ørlög filters daily into the Well of Wyrd, falling like dew from Yggdrasil. In parallel, Odin's eye and Heimdall's hearing / Gjallarhorn both lie within Mimir's Well, where Mimir drinks from them daily: presumably because the eye and the hearing / horn represent the occult powers of Odin and Heimdall, as well as supporting or feeding those powers.

(Mimir drinks from them, according to *Völuspá 29* that was spoken by the Seeress not long before Ragnarök, even though he was beheaded long before that, during the truce after the 'first war in the world' between the Æsir and Vanir! The whole mystery about Mimir, Óðrœrir, Kvasir, severed head, blood, mead, truce, wisdom, inspiration, Wellsprings and other forms of water is very confused but fascinating and forms an ongoing topic for meditation for me! I haven't figured it out yet, but I continue to work on it....the poem I offer, below, is part of this work.)

Mimir's Well is a deep, reflective place, but it has an 'organ' or 'agent' in the outer world: Odin's raven Muninn, and the powers of *muninn / gemynd* within each of us. When Odin consults Mimir's head, depth and height, inner and outer, are united. Mimir's deep Well links with Hliðskalf, Odin's High Seat of perception where he views the worlds and where his ravens come to him. I associate Mimir's Well with Muninn, and Hliðskalf with Huginn, when viewing this phenomenon of deep versus high wisdom blending together. The powers of Mimir's and Odin's minds, deep and high, thus unite to act with wisdom and inspiration in our own beloved Middle World.

I'll close with a poem of mine and some commentary on it, where I tried an experiment to meditatively place myself in the positions of both Odin and Mimir as they related to the Well at crucial points of their lives. The poem is thus my perception of three beings: myself, Odin, and Mimir, blended together while facing the challenge of this Well. As I write in my commentary, this experience turned out to be an important personal initiation for me, which took the form of 'fermentation.' Though I do not refer to Kvasir in the poem, the experience that underlies the poem led me to him as well. For me Kvasir is the 'master of thought-fermentation' which leads eventually to wisdom, and I honor him along with Mimir and Odin as teachers and initiators on the path of wisdom-striving.

The I in Mimir's Well

Secrets on the wind.
A leaf flutters, floating, drawn
To its own reflection in the Well.
Leaf and image kiss:
Souls & body,
Myth & memory,
Then & now & will-be
Meet at the membrane of water:
The holy kiss of wisdom
In Mimir's Well.

And is it worth an eye?
Worth a self, a soul,
To sip this water,
Cool and silky on the tongue,
Trickling down my throat
Into unseen depths...

Mimir, Odin, and World-Mind

What will happen when this yeasty sip
Reaches the great vat of unknown liquids
Pooled in the depths of myself?
Will a heady brew arise,
Lifting and mixing all parts of myself,
Suffusing me
With Mod and Wode and Wisdom
Till I myself am a poem
Brewed by a Master?

Or will this yeasty sip
Run berserk within me,
Exploding me into fragments
Instead of fermenting me slowly?

What shall I wager on the chance?

Would there be a home for my eye
Within the Well?
For my mind, my memory?
What is it like down there?
What will I Know?

I hear a song I could not sing
Humming from the Well
Like a seashell sings the Sea.
And the water smells like everlastingness:
Rocky and green and echoing through time.
It is full of whispers.

I dip my finger in, take one drop,
Dab it on the eye I do not have.

Mimir, Odin, and World-Mind

Fire and shards and cacophony,
Bursting and breaking,
Shattering, shimmering.
I can't see.
I'm coming apart.
I'm on fire.

I've got to quench this burning eye
Or I'll go mad.
I grope around blindly.....
Water!

With a gasp, I plunge my whole head in.

This wasn't what I expected.

Can I have my head back?

This is just the beginning of my tale,
But all my thoughts & words are bubbles now,
Floating like leaves on the wind,
Fermenting.

Comments:
In this experience-experiment from more than twenty years ago, I tried to blend myself with Odin and with Mimir together and approach the Well while tuned in to the senses and reactions of all three of us. This poem is what happened!

What happened next, after this experience, was a time of wordless inner fermentation that was of great importance to me. A couple of years later this fermentation segued into the beginning and continuation of my Heathen soul lore work. I feel that this and all my work is rooted in Mimir's Well, drawing upon the Memory and Inspiration therein.

Something of mine (maybe my head!) was sacrificed or transformed during this experience of personal initiation in Mimir's Well. I believe, in truth, that it was my Hugr soul, whom I experience as a hunter of hidden knowledge—knowledge that is not apparent to my everyday awareness. Knowledge began to flow for me after this experience and hasn't stopped since. I don't claim 'absolute truth' or 'authority' for this knowledge. It is what it is, to be evaluated as one sees fit. For me, this knowledge is filled with love, delight, and spiritual fullness; it is my life's path, the world of my heart.

4: Vør: Goddess of Awareness

"A woman thinking," by José Luis Fernández.

Snorri Sturlason in his (prose) Edda tells us about the Goddesses of Asgard, explaining that "Tenth is Vør: she is wise and enquiring, so that nothing can be concealed from her. There is a saying that a woman becomes aware (Vør) of something when she finds it out." (Gylfaginning 35, p. 30.) This is the extent of what we are told about the Goddess Vør. The name Vør is used in a very few poetic synonyms or kennings, and other than that, there is no evidence that I know of that indicates any additional status or worship of Vør.

This is very little upon which to build an awareness of the Goddess of Awareness! But that is the case only if we were to look at Vør in isolation. If we envision her as being an aspect of Frigg, and/or as part of a 'team' of Goddesses who work together with Frigg, then Vør can be brought into much clearer focus.

Awareness

Awareness is a great part of Frigg's own powers. Freya tells us that "of ørlög Frigg has full knowledge, I think, though she herself does not speak out." (*Lokasenna* 29, Poetic Edda.) Every appearance Frigg makes in our myths shows that she has her wits about her and has the presence of mind to respond very effectively to challenges that face her. She is aware of people's prayers and needs, both directly and indirectly from her messenger-Goddess Gna, and responds to them. Her skills and powers within the social domains of the family and society at large require as a basis a clear awareness and understanding of people and situations, of societal rules and customs, and of the natures of humans and Holy Ones. Her role as a mother-figure for Gods and folk requires, again, the same kind of deep awareness that all good mothers have about their children's natures, lives, and well-being.

Awareness is also a necessity for the functions of other Asynjur (Æsir Goddesses) described by Snorri in Gylfaginning 35. Eir as physician, Saga as skald and historian, Var as the warder and enforcer of oaths and contracts, Syn as the one who denies entry to those who should be denied: the work of these and the other Goddesses would be meaningless without a foundation of awareness to direct their efforts appropriately. Vør, or the function of awareness, is fundamental to Frigg's nature and to all her 'handmaidens,' companions or aspects of herself.

This being the case, one way of understanding Vør's existence and nature is to postulate that Frigg's power of awareness is so great that it begins to take on its own independent existence in the person of the Goddess Vør. This idea forms the basis of a mythic tale that I will present shortly, after a little more discussion on the nature of 'awareness.'

Awareness encompasses and goes beyond 'information' and even 'knowledge.' Explanation is created to satisfy the need of our rational minds for information and knowledge. To discuss awareness at its deepest level, however, one must delve beneath these phenomena.

Awareness is based upon knowledge, but it must incorporate also experience and intuition, and the ability to interpret knowledge in the light of these gifts. Awareness, Understanding, Wisdom: these go far below the surface, reaching places where logical explanation cannot fully enlighten nor satisfy.

Communicating this kind of understanding requires perception of the trans-rational domains, and appropriate forms of expression in order to explore them: forms such as myth, poetry, and all of the representational and performing arts. These are the reasons why, in discussing my understanding of the Goddess of Awareness, I turn to personal experience, runic meditation and mythic tale-spinning to try to illustrate my perceptions about her, rather than relying entirely on logic and research.

Vør: Goddess of Awareness

Meeting Vør

I have felt strongly called for many years to try to know Vør or the Vør-face of Frigg. For me, she was at first an elusive Goddess–one whom I knew is there, whom I could perceive out of the corner of my eye, whose presence I could sense by an increase of alertness and awareness in myself when she was near, but who was difficult to meet face-to-face. As I began my quest to know her, I had the feeling that the way to align myself more closely with her was to build her a harrow, an altar, in the soul-lands I walk while spaefaring. Thus, every time I go there, regardless of my intended purposes, I bring with me a few 'stones' for her harrow that represent something meaningful to me and relevant to the power of awareness. Before I proceed to the intended purposes of my spaefaring, I first stop by and add my stones to her harrow.

There is a place in the spaelands, a nook or cranny in a large rock formation, where I have set up the harrow and worship site for Vør. Such a place as a nook or cranny is called a *healh* in Anglo-Saxon. We know that the Anglo-Saxon fore-bears used such places for worship, because we have the Angelseax word *healh-halgung*, meaning "hallowing of the healh." Perhaps these places were used especially after the incursion of Christianity, when the 'folk of the heath' had to withdraw to the most secluded locations to conduct their Heathen worship. In any case, such is the place I have for my worship of Vør and my efforts to bring myself and her into closer alignment with each other. Slowly, her harrow is growing as I add my 'stones' to it, and so also is my awareness of Vør, and sense of her nearness.

Long ago, I undertook a spaefaring, a soul-journey, as part of a series I was doing, one on each rune. I drew a rune at random–Jera or Year–and, not knowing what I would find, I set out on my journey. As it turned out, Vør chose to influence this faring with her gentle power, so I share it here as one illustration of this power.

Her power is usually very subtle; in some ways it is quite ordinary and everyday, but it adds dimensions of depth, intensity, and a feeling that one is looking in new and meaningful ways at the everyday and the ordinary. I hope this sense comes through, in the following brief account of this spaefaring under Vør's aegis. Nothing earthshaking was presented to me here, but the dimensions of everyday life were beautifully enriched and deepened.

Rune-faring: Year / Jera

I walk up to the tree outside the spaeland gate and then pass through, the warm scent of fallen leaves about me. A golden, gentle day. I stop by my little harrow that I am building for holy Vør in the *healh,* the hollow of the rock outcrop, and add my stones to the pile. It looks warm, inviting, dear. Standing in front of the harrow I spread my elbows, fists on my hips, into the Year-stadha, and spin around. Year. The leaves fall around me gently, golden, smelling of fall. Now the rangy white longhorn cow is here, Ing-Frey's gift to me, as mysterious as ever, seeming to hold approval in her dark eyes.

Year. I spin and feel the dark earth grow soft and moist beneath me, muddy. A thin film of ice crusts over it, protecting the life buried within. I spin. Now the snow is up past my ankles, fluffy and scratchy against them as I spin. The wind blows hard flecks of snow against me. White cow watches. The bison calf is here, too, and now Ule, the white owl, perches on the rock outcropping that is cleft with the little nook for my harrow.

Year. I spin slower and slower, as life contracts to a hard-shelled seed under the wrapping of winter. Cow and calf watch me, eyes full of wisdom. Ule cocks his head. I am almost stopped now, standing on a balance-point: Yule.

Year. The fore-memory of bird-call echoes in my mind, pulling me onward. Sun gleams on snow and cow and owl. I begin to turn more swiftly and spring breaks forth. Lovely Eostre stands before me, smiling sweetly in her filmy white gown. She wears a crown of flowers, and a garland wreathes the cow's neck. A buttercup dangles from the bison calf's mouth, a dreamy look in her eyes.

Year. The grain grows knee-high, turns to gold: walking through it, I feel the ripeness of life burgeoning in the crops, the soil, in myself. Freya is here, stalks of grain in her hand, in her eyes the same dark, mysterious look as in the cow's. I sit down in the midst of the grain, longing for the presence of the lord of life, for Ing-Frey. He comes, clad in russet and wheat, holding stalks of grain in one hand, two wild apples in the other.

Year. Frith. Peace. Holiness. Things as they should be, holding to the pattern. Blessed gifts. I see lightning and storm, grain tossing in the wind. Now the grain is shaven; the Old One walks through the stubbled fields with his grey horse, gleaning their share. Frigg in her grace presides over the sharing-out of the harvest goods. Deer walk the woods, huge red Hunter's Moon glowing behind their night-shadowed shapes. A little hedgehog trundles across the crackly leaves to where I have spun to a stop in front of Vør's harrow. It curls into a prickly ball between my feet and falls asleep.

Year. Blessing.

Mythic Awareness

Myth allows us to reach levels of awareness that go deeper and broader than the rational mind can encompass. We strive to express and enhance this mythic awareness in tales, songs and poems, in art and drama, dance and music, and in simply, deeply, experiencing the life of the soul for ourselves. Listening to and learning about the myths of our faith deepens our awareness. A way to strengthen the awareness even more is to enter into the myths and live them in some way: through ritual, drama, meditation, and other forms of experience.

One of the ways I am doing this myself is through the process of writing a book–a book of 'fiction' if you will, that I prefer to see as a mythic tale, rooted in the understandings and worldview of our own faith. The book is about Griðr, the Jotunn mother of the God Viðar, and about her world and folk, and the world of the Gods. As I believe often happens when writing fiction, the characters in my tale tend to take on a life of their own and take over the story themselves at every opportunity! This is exactly what happened in the short excerpts of the book that I present below, that involve Vør and her function of awareness.

I had no inkling or plan for this particular twist of the plot, until very suddenly, out of the blue, it evolved itself in this direction. I think this is what happens when one tries, as I am doing with this book, to enter completely and deeply into myth oneself, allowing it to take over one's full awareness. I am striving to make a tale that reaches down into the place where the essence of living myth touches the roots of our minds, and it is no real surprise that this place does contain unexpected insights and awareness.

Implied within these passages of the story is some part of my understanding of Vør and of her relation to Frigg. Another theme that runs through my tale picks up and carries forward the thoroughly-enjoyed contest of wits that is perpetually waged between Frigg and Odin. The two of them have no other match for their minds in all the Worlds and enjoy honing their sharp wits upon each other! The passages from my book, below, begin the weaving of yet another thread into the fabric of this contest. It is no great stretch of the imagination to believe that Vør, Goddess of Awareness, has a role to play in the relations between the subtle and mighty minds of Frigg and Odin.

So, as my final observations here on the nature of Vør and of awareness, here are two relevant passages from my tale. These ideas are not presented necessarily as 'facts.' Rather this is, as with every mythic tale, "how it might have been."

Asynja's Flight: A Tale

The night after Odin left was clear and bright, a full moon shining and the white star-path gleaming like fresh-fallen snow against the velvet background of the night sky. Griðr the giantess sat outside her cave-dwelling, arms clasped around her knees, musing on the strange turn her life had taken. She carried a new child, Odin's child and hers. A God-child with a mighty wyrd, who would avenge his father's death and rid the world of the devouring Wolf when his day came. A child whose life would stretch out into worlds of which she knew nothing. She laid her cheek on her knees and sighed, not knowing how to embrace such strange knowledge, how to weave it into the familiar fabric of her own being.

Vør: Goddess of Awareness

Minutes later, Griðr started and looked up, hearing the whisper of a great bird's wings before she could spot its shape in the darkness. An enormous falcon winged low across the landscape, heading toward her. The rims of its feathers gleamed silver in the moonlight, brighter than the stars. A falcon, she thought, flying at night?

The bird swooped down to land in front of her, cupping the air in powerful wings as it reached with talons outspread to grapple the snow-patched turf below it. Alighted, the bird tucked its wings and fixed Griðr with eyes deep-set under bony brows....eyes that reminded Griðr, strangely, of the dark orbs of Auðhumla the Cow, the great Ur-Mother whom she had seen in her vision. The young giantess and the falcon stared at one another while time passed outside of Griðr's awareness. The falcon's eyes seemed to her to be all there was, everything else around her but a shadow, a memory of a dream.

As Griðr stared bemused, the falcon's form blurred and flickered. Griðr rubbed her eyes to clear them, and as she looked again, she saw a mantle of feathers cast upon the ground. Standing with her feet enwrapped in the feathery cloak was a tall Goddess, clad in silver with silver hair, her eyes as dark blue as the night sky. Overwhelmed, Griðr knew not how to react, but simply stared.

"Griðr." The voice was silvery, firm and shining at once, faintly ringing with the sound that Griðr could sometimes hear, of the stars echoing in the wind of a summer night. "Griðr, I am Frigg of the Æsir."

Griðr felt paralyzed with amazement. No vestige could she feel of her customary challenging fierceness toward the Æsir, traditional enemies to many of the giant-folk. Nor was the familiarity there between her and Frigg, the almost-camaraderie that she had come to feel with Odin as she had stretched her mind to follow his, while they walked a wary path toward peace between them. Neither enmity nor familiarity could Griðr muster, as she tentatively tested different reactions and found that none of them fit the space that lay between herself and the silver-haired Asynja before her, Queen of the Æsir and Odin's wife.

"Lady? How do you know my name?" Griðr whispered. "Why are you here?"

A faint smile crossed the star-dusted face of the Goddess. "I know most things, Griðr, that I want to know," Frigg answered. "And things that I don't wish to know, as well," she whispered, and a cloud passed over the light of her face. "As to why I am here: close your eyes now, and sense within yourself."

Griðr did so, suddenly feeling the deep sense of self-knowledge and completeness that she had earlier been seeking. She sank into this sense of herself as into an ocean of light, filled with quiet delight at her knowing. Within her, she perceived a mote of being that was swimming and frolicking, full of life although it was so tiny. Her heart leapt with joy, greeting the child of her blood and her soul as he awoke into life. Entranced, she watched him play like a fish in the ocean of herself, at home and perfect in every way.

Griðr opened her eyes to look at Frigg, ready to thank her for this gift of knowledge. But her words went unspoken as Frigg caught her mind in a fresh paralysis of surprise. Not one Goddess stood there, but two: one solid and frosted with silver, the younger one shadowy and dim, with feathery dark hair and bright eyes just visible as blue gleams through the shadows of her hair. The young Goddess overlapped the solid outlines of the Æsir's Queen as though she were a soul-shadow of Frigg, a shadow cast by the bright light of Frigg's own wisdom.

Stunned, Griðr watched as the young Goddess slowly drifted apart from Frigg and floated in her direction. As the shadow-Goddess approached her, Griðr was overcome with giddiness. Blackness filled her sight, and the giantess fell helplessly backwards, sprawled on the winter-brown turf. The ocean of herself billowed and churned, sparks of light and chips of darkness flying like wind-tossed spray from the waves, blinding her senses. She was tossed and turned helplessly, losing all sense of time and place.

Slowly, peace and stillness returned to her. Griðr took a deep breath, trembling slightly, and opened her eyes. There was no sign of the shadowy young Goddess. Frigg sat beside her, looking up at the stars. Sensing movement, the stately Asynja turned, and again Griðr was lost in those dark, intensely blue eyes, the eyes of the Ur-Mother.

"Look again now, Griðr. Look into yourself again."

Griðr gazed back at the Goddess, shaken. She was not sure she was ready to face that churning ocean. Hesitantly, she shut her eyes and reached within. Now, as at first, the bright ocean was still and serene, glittering as though kissed by the sun. Griðr felt deeper: there, again, was the tiny son-mote, playing joyfully within his world that was her Self. Griðr caught her breath with astonishment and was struck again by giddiness. A second mote was there, twin to the first! Intently focused, she caught a fleeting glimpse of feathery darkness and a flash of blue as the second mote joined the first, twirling and spinning about each other in an ecstasy of delight.

Griðr floated up out of her ocean-self and let out her breath with a deep sigh. She was overwhelmed yet again by the unfathomable strangeness of everything that was happening to her. She lay staring at the stars, breathing deeply to calm herself, trying to gentle her whirling mind and emotions as she would a frightened animal. Slowly she calmed, lying there on the cold sward, feeling the warmth of the quiet Goddess beside her in the darkness.

"Frigg?" Griðr ventured, and paused for another breath as the tall Asynja turned toward her. Griðr fought to keep from being entranced again as the dark blue eyes gazed into hers. "I have heard a strange tale told: that the God Heimdall was born of nine mothers. No one I know can understand how that could be." Griðr paused, her tongue tangled with questions for which there were no words. Giving up, she asked simply, "Is this the truth?"

"It is the truth, Griðr."

Griðr stared up at the stars, thinking of a shadow-Goddess and of motes playing in the sparkling ocean of herself, and of a Queen who could cast a shadow of being by the bright light of her own wisdom.

"Whose is the child, Lady? The second child, the new one?"

Frigg smiled at her. "Ours, Griðr. She is mine, and yours, and Odin's, although he knows her not. Her name is Vør."

Griðr breathed deeply, turned within herself to sense all the strange new things that resided within her: tiny beings with names of their own, and changed understanding of things she had always taken for granted. Vør, she thought. Aware: my daughter's name is Aware. And she is the child of a Goddess, and a God, and of me.

Griðr lay breathing the chill night air, with questions in her heart that seemed to have no answers. She heard again the faint echo of star-song whispered in the wind, calling her out of herself. As Griðr looked up she saw a great falcon wheeling across the sky, blotting out the stars with the shadow of her silver wings.

A Strand for the Weaving: The Tale Continues

(Several years later Odin visited Griðr to meet his young son Viðar for the first time. He arrived in the dead of night and called Viðar out to him in the moonlight, to take him into the forest for a test of his Mood and courage. This tale is told in Chapter 5, "To Honor Viðar". Afterwards, Odin sent Viðar back to his bed, and then returned to Griðr's dwelling the following morning to make his visit to her in more customary style.)

The two children entered the main chamber of their mother's cave-dwelling hand in hand. They paused in the doorway, looking at their visitor with blue eyes half-hidden under identical falls of dark hair. Odin broke off his speech with Griðr and stared at them in astonishment.

"And who is this other one here with our son?" he asked, looking back at Griðr.

Griðr smiled, hiding her laughter. "She is your daughter."

"My daughter!" Odin was overcome with amazement, staring again at the children. "Indeed, I see that she is my son's twin, his very likeness! How did this come about, then? I had no knowledge of this." Odin held out his hand to the little girl, calling softly. "Come here, my child; let me see you."

Vør came forward and laid her hand in his. He took it gently and bent toward her. "What is your name, little one?"

She answered in a sweet, firm voice, "I am called Vør, Father."

Odin looked at the child for a moment in bemusement, then dropped her hand and began laughing. He threw his head back and laughed until tears fell from his eye and his laughter rolled echoing across the roof of the cave.

"Vør!" he gasped in the midst of his laughter. "Every child of mine since the beginning of time have I foreknown, except for this little maiden. And what is her name, this one who was hidden from her father's knowledge? Aware! Her name is Aware, and I knew her not!" His chuckles shook his frame like an earthquake as he looked toward her again. "But come! I am startling you and I have no wish to do so. I am not laughing at you, dearling, but at myself. I have very seldom been so surprised by anything or anyone!"

He stroked her hair with a strong, gentle hand, but then looked over at Griðr again, a faint frown creasing his brows. "Truly, Griðr, I do not understand how this could have come about, that I would father a child and not know of it. How is this?"

Griðr grinned openly now. "I think, Odin, that you must speak with Frigg about this."

"Frigg?!" Odin looked at her incredulously. "Frigg?" Frowning in thought, Odin dropped his searching gaze to the soft little face looking fearlessly up at him while he held her chin. Then he raised his head and stared into the distance outside the doorway of the cave. A strange, unfathomable expression crept across his face as he whispered again, "Frigg…..?"

…..And so Awareness unfolds, petal by petal, across an endless horizon of knowing which is ever old and ever new.

5: To Honor Viðar

CONSTANTIN HANSEN.

Viðar straps on his boot.

To Honor Viðar

Viðar is considered a God of vengeance, whose cosmic task is to slay the Fenris-Wolf at Ragnarök. Norse myth tells us that all the leather scraps and trimmings leftover from shoe-making end up being made into a great boot that Viðar wears. After the Fenris-Wolf has swallowed Odin during Ragnarök, Viðar takes his oath-sworn vengeance for his father's death by stepping with this boot on Fenris's open jaw and tearing him apart.

Viðar is also called the Silent God, perhaps in reference to an ancient practice among some Heathen tribes of keeping silence until a mighty oath one has sworn is achieved. Odin has not yet been swallowed by the Wolf; Viðar, as yet, has not taken his sworn vengeance. Hence, he is silent.

Here is a powerful, moving poem by Heathen author and poet John T. Mainer, and a brief conversation between him and myself about the God Viðar, whom we both highly honor. My thanks for John's gracious permission to include them here.

Silent One's Service *by John T. Mainer*

For Viðar Odinson, Fenrir bane, who with his boot made of scraps will shatter the All Father's bane, killing Fenrir at Ragnarök. He speaks little, yet weaves of broken things that which will do what the mightiest Godly weapon could not. For those of us whom life has made broken things, his touch is powerful, and his silence holds a purpose, felt if not spoken.

To Honor Viðar

Silent One's Service
He is forever silent
Watchful and dark
His is the second kill
Of broken things he makes
Salvation in the hour
When all is lost
From broken things
He forges
Second chances

Scraps and leavings
Broken and lost
Without a word he takes
Finds purpose in the leavings
Finds strength within the scars
Weaves of the breaking
Wolf-killing strength
Where Victory Father fell
His scraps alone
Prevail

How many of us
From proud might fallen
From beauty broken
From wisdom riven
To scraps are fallen
Yet
In his hands a weaving
In his eyes a purpose
A use yet
For such as us

To Honor Viðar

He never told me
For what purpose gathered
Against what hour he watches
For what need he sees
One use yet
For scraps and leavings
Yet he weaves
And we abide
In silence
      -*John T. Mainer*

From John:
I have always been Odin's man, yet I cannot deny that a part of me has grown in awareness of Viðar for decades. The silent one isn't like Odin, his presence is often very powerful without attempting to grab your attention or influence directly what you are doing. Understanding his purpose for me is far below thought, a dim understanding of purpose, of intent, more of a glimpse of a distant goal and the will to reach it than anything I could put into words.

    Oddly, now that I am less than I have ever been, I hear him better, though understand again only at the instinctive rather than reasoning level. I hope this poem brings you something. It wasn't a choice to write it, but a task I could not rest until I completed it. I don't know if I grasp entirely what I put into it, but I do ACCEPT it. If that makes any sense.

From Winifred:
Your poem, John, has such a grip on me and won't let go. I've spent days exploring why: because this poem speaks to something universal in today's world, as we face the threat of climate-Ragnarök, and so many other dire challenges. In the

face of all this, all of us are scraps and bits. We are not magic swords that can fell our troubles with one mighty blow, but bits and pieces struggling to shape our responses, however small, to the challenges our whole world faces. It is both powerful and comforting to feel that Holy Beings are helping us to shape our bits and pieces into something that is strong enough to matter, whether in the short term, or in the long view that curves over the event-horizon of space-time, into other Worlds.

It's interesting: just as you said you could not rest until you completed this poem, I also could not stop working with it, couldn't put it down, until I understood more deeply why it speaks so strongly to me—it's my favorite of everything I've read of yours. Some of its power, for me, relates to what I just wrote, but some for sure relates to the Viðar connection that you and I both have. I've been close to him for years, and the relationship is much as you describe with regard to yours. Unspeaking, a sharing of sacred space and meaning that has no words.

But for me the relationship is also different. Your connection, as a lifelong warrior, is so strong with its unspoken, dark-night-of-the-soul-and-of-the-world purpose; it speaks to you in the darkness of unknowing, the grimness of Viðar's call to vengeance, and your faith that he has a true use for you.

When I encounter him in shared space, human-oriented space, it is often at night, but a very different night, with shining stars and peaceful woods around. But when I see him on his own, in God-visions of other worlds, he is always the rising morning, the sun coming over the horizon, the power of the Dagaz rune, the sense of fresh, crystalline wind and light sweeping toward us across unguessable horizons. It is so different from his portrayal in the old myths, but I feel it is so true to who he is, or will be, or always has been....I feel that he is not strongly anchored in Time, but moves around to fill his own spaces in different 'spiritual time zones'. And he looks very different, depending on which time zone one encounters him in!

He is calling you to aid him at Ragnarök. He is showing me what lies beyond Ragnarök, whether that 'beyond' is a literal thing in This-World, which I find unlikely, or whether it is a calling to understand and participate in how the Holy Ones themselves experience the time-outside-of-time that represents the deeper meaning of the Gods' return and the renewal of the World's foundations. Viðar's message coming through both of us is that Ragnarök—whatever that truly is— is a bridge that must be crossed, through faith, courage and dedication, in order to reach Viðar's bright land of morning on the other side of the Sun: the realm of the Dagaz rune.

Landvidi

Because of Viðar's reputation as the Silent God, I see him as a patron of hermits and others who treasure silence and solitude. Viðar's broad domain or God-Home, Landvidi, is a vast and quiet land of undisturbed nature.

In meditation, when I am within his domain of Landvidi, he appears to me as a quietly smiling, very large man, young and strong. We do not speak together: he does not teach or guide or direct me; I do not query or request anything, but our silent companionship is deeply precious to me. We sit across from each other at a campfire near a stream on a quiet night, with the stars spread out overhead and the owls calling, and the scent of pines around us. The peace, beauty, and silence are nourishment to the soul.

Other times I walk along Landvidi's rolling hills, woods and brooks, and watch the magnificent sunrises over the roof of Viðar's home where many birds like to perch to greet the morning sun. To me the Dagaz / Day rune, with its toroid shape, represents part of Viðar's mystery: I perceive the roof of his home as being shaped like this rune, though I have never been inside it to figure out the peculiar geometry! I see Viðar shining like the new day spreading over the horizon, overcoming the darkness of night.

The Testing of Young Viðar: A Tale

Here are two passages from a 'fantasy' novel I am writing about the giantess Griðr, Viðar's mother. In the first passage, Odin has obtained a wolf's head from Griðr; the wolf's jaw is wrenched sideways due to the killing blow from her staff. Odin takes it into the forest to perform an enchantment on it. In the second passage, Viðar is a young boy living with his mother and sister in their cave-dwelling; he has not yet met Odin. Odin comes to him during the night and calls him out to the forest for a test of his courage and ability. Does young Viðar have it in him to face the Fenris-wolf one day? Odin and Viðar go to the clearing in the forest where, years ago in the story, Odin had preserved and enchanted the wolf's head and set it on a stump, waiting for this moment in time.

Odin walked toward the forest for a short way, then took a turn down toward the lower stretches of the stream. There, he carefully washed the wolf's head, removing much of the

To Honor Viðar

meat from inside the neck with his knife. He left the head soaking in the stream while he hunted for the herbs he would need. With winter's hold still tight upon the land, it would be hard to find them, but he knew where to look to find roots, bark, shoots and hidden greenstuffs. It took him the better part of the morning to gather them all, and tie them safely into a knotted corner of his cloak. Then, retrieving the dripping head, Odin set off into the forest.

The tall Ase wandered apparently aimlessly until he came to a natural glade, created by the felling of a large tree that left a flat stump in the middle of the clearing. He settled himself on the soft, snow-patched mast under the trees and began his work of preserving the wolf's head.

First he sorted the herbs carefully by kind, each into its own little pile in front of him. Then he gently picked up each pile in turn and sang a soft song over it, holding each bundle of plantstuff up to his mouth so the breath of his song flowed over it. As he sang, he remembered another time he had done such work, long ago: preserving the head of his friend and kinsman Mimir. Mimir had been given hostage to the God-tribe of the Vanir, to settle a war between them and the Æsir. In spite of Mimir's calm wisdom, a blessing to any folk, the Vanir had become angered and beheaded him, sending the head back to his kinsmen in retribution. Odin remembered his grief at the loss of his mother's brother, and his determination that he would not lose the rede of this wise Jotunn, in spite of his death.

Mimir's head lay now within a dim cavern under a root of the World-Tree, warding the Well of Memory that holds the knowledge-treasures of all the ages in its depths. There, Odin had gone to seek the wisdom of this Well, and Mimir had exacted from him wisdom's price: the pledge of Odin's eye to lie in the Well, to see what it could not see if it remained in his head. Shaking his head at the memories, Odin sat quietly for a time, allowing the magic of his songs to blend with the powers of the herbs.

When the herbs were fully empowered, Odin stuffed the wolf's neck-cavity full, and rubbed aromatic leaves carefully over every hair on the surface of the head. He laid large leaves over the wolf's eyes and nostrils, smoothing them down, and breathed over the leaves. Finally, he took two soft, greyish, elongated leaves, snow-dried and withered but still potent, and placed them carefully under the tongue of the wolf, to either side of the center. Odin laid a forefinger along each leaf in place, and sang again: a buzzing, burring song sung deep in his chest, more like a giant bumblebee than anything else. Again, he recalled his similar actions, laying the leaves in Mimir's mouth so that now Odin could sit with his uncle's head in the dim cavern and listen to the low, rumbling voice give forth its words of wisdom.

Odin smiled at the thought and regarded the wolf's head. "Wisdom you may not speak, as others know it," he told the head. "But wisdom will come from what you utter, nevertheless."

Years pass, and then....

In the deepest part of the night as he slept in his giantess-mother's cave-dwelling, Viðar felt a touch on his mind, a call in his dream. He opened his eyes drowsily, and saw a cloaked shape standing in the darkness, outlined by the dim light of embers from the firepit behind his back. Viðar sat up in alarm, brushing his tousled hair from his eyes. The shape bent toward him, whispering.

Wotan, by Arthur Rackham

"Viðar, I am your father, Odin. You must get up now and come with me."

Viðar untangled his skinny little-boy's limbs from the sleeping-hides and rose unsteadily to his feet, still more than half-asleep and wondering whether he was dreaming. Odin led him out into the moon-blanched landscape, where Viðar tripped over ground he was familiar with, groggy with sleep and confusion and the strange light of the moon. He rubbed his eyes and breathed deeply, trying to wake himself up.

"Tell me, boy," Odin began. "Do you play often in that forest out there?"

"Yes, I do." Viðar peered up at the hooded form, trying to get a sense of his unknown father. "Are you really Odin?" he asked hesitantly, knowing that indeed he was.

Odin grinned, giving the question no answer. "Have you ever found anything...unusual out there? Anything unexpected?"

Viðar glanced away from the shadowed face, rapidly awakening now and his mind beginning to work again. "Yes....there's one thing I've seen...."

"Tell me," said his father.

"A head." Viðar took a deep breath and watched Odin, trying to judge his reaction. "A wolf's head."

"A head," repeated Odin, glancing at him. "Just a plain old head? What is it doing out there?"

"Well, I don't know," said Viðar doubtfully. "It's just sitting out there on a stump. It's dried, but most of the fur is still on it. It doesn't even stink, or not much, anyway. It's stuffed with something…with dried plants. I picked it up to look and I saw all the stems poking out. Its jaw is crooked, too, like it was wrenched out of place. It looked like one of our ram's jaws looked, one time when he was fighting with another one and got rammed in the face. It was sticking out sideways, until Mother put it back again."

"What—she put the wolf's jaw back?"

"No! The ram's jaw!" Viðar laughed, and Odin smiled at the sound.

"So what do you think of this not-very-stinky wolf's head out in the woods?"

Viðar looked down at his feet, scuffing through leaf-mold now as they approached the edge of the moonlit woods. "Well…well, it's kind of interesting."

"Is that so? You think it's interesting?"

"Yes. I don't know why, really. I like to go out there and look at it sometimes. I tried to move the jaw one time—see if I could put it back, or open the mouth wider. But I couldn't move it. It was a pretty big wolf, and the jaw is dried in place, I guess. I didn't want to break it off."

"Why not?"

"Why not….? I don't know. I guess I just like it the way it is. It wouldn't be so much fun to play with if it was broken in pieces."

"What do you play with it?"

"Well, I just play like I'm fighting with it, that's all. I have a stick for a sword and I fight with it. But I don't hit it too hard. I only banged a bit of fur off it, once or twice. It's still a pretty good fighter, and it snarls at me sometimes."

To Honor Viðar

"It does, does it? Do you like that?"

"Yes!" The boy grinned fiercely. "I do. I wish it would snarl more often."

They were fully into the forest, picking their way over dimly-lit fallen branches and tangles, moving slowly.

"Why don't you take me to see this wolf's head now? Maybe it will snarl at both of us. Wolves like to howl at the moon, you know, and there's a fine moon up there right now. Worth a try, don't you think?"

Viðar grinned eagerly and took the lead, now moving easily through the darkened woods. "I'll show you, Father. It's not too much farther now. See that great big rock sticking up over there? The stump and the head are over on the other side of that." He trotted along at a brisk pace, moving like an eel through the tangles and blockages on the ancient forest floor.

"Do you come out at night here often, boy?" asked Odin.

"No-oo...Mother doesn't much like me to. She says there's thurses around, and that the old wolf has plenty of friends out here. And she's right, too—I often hear them. Sometimes I do come, though; I like it out here at night." Viðar glanced sidelong at his father, but got no word of criticism or caution from him.

"So your mother knows about the wolf's head, does she?"

"Yes, she knows. But she won't tell me anything about it—who put it there or anything. She just leaves it alone and doesn't want to talk about it. I suppose she's really more interested in her sheep."

"Yes, I suppose live sheep would be more interesting than a dead wolf's head, at that. I think she said something about that to me once. A practical one, your mother."

Viðar lost interest in a conversation that had declined to the mundane level of sheep and mothers, and dashed off at an even faster pace, nearing the clearing where the wolf's head perched on a stump out in the middle of the glade. "Come along, Father! Here it is!"

They approached the stump together, Viðar dancing in excitement. "There! What do you think of that! Pretty fierce, isn't it?"

"Hmmmm..." said Odin, stroking his beard and looking profound. "So tell me, Viðar: how do you get it to snarl?"

Viðar paused, looking thoughtfully at the head. "Ummm...well, it just does, sometimes. It just ups and snarls, and rolls its eyes. There's some of its eyes left here, if you look closely. They're kind of dried up, but they're there." He poked a finger cautiously into a hairy eye-socket. "See? Maybe if I wave a sword at it it'll snarl for us." He dashed off eagerly to arm himself with a long stick, and ran back to flail wildly at the wolf, yelling at the top of his lungs.

Odin watched as the youngster leapt and darted in circles around the wolf's head with a wild light of battle in his eyes. His body was that of a child, unthewed by a man's muscle and bone, but he moved with grace and an instinct so sure that Odin could almost see a ghostly grey opponent whirling and snapping around the boy—an opponent whose every move Viðar anticipated before it was made.

Odin nodded to himself and made a quick gesture with his hand. Two hairy grey shadows glided forward, seemingly from the folds of his cloak, and circled to approach the child from opposite directions. Little could be seen of them save their eyes, gleaming in the moonlight, and the flash of moonlight on a fang. They bore no wolf-scent on them, only the scent of a nightbound forest, earthy and green.

To Honor Viðar

Gliding low on his belly, the wolf Geri tried to seize Viðar's ankle in the darkness, only to be stopped by a sharp crack on the muzzle from the child's stick. The return sweep of the stick caught between Freki's forepaws, tangling them as he raced toward the boy, who levered his stick-sword swiftly between the wolf's own legs to disable his opponent.

Viðar seemed unaware that the two wolves were there. Caught up in his battle-dream, he leapt and swung, shouting at the wolf's head on the stump in challenge. All his attention was focused on the head and on the movements of his imagined opponent, while each move he made countered the grey shadows that slunk around him. Frustrated, their snarls crescendoed in the quiet night. Suddenly, the boy stopped his wild movements, delight in his eyes, and turned toward Odin watching from the shadows.

"Father! Do you hear? It's snarling! It's snarling louder than it ever did before!" Overjoyed, Viðar threw back his head, laughing, and tossed his stick into the air where it fell slowly down, end over end. The wolves circled him, bewildered by this uncharacteristic behavior. This odd little creature neither acted nor smelled like prey at all. They shook their heads, snorting to clear their sensitive noses from the scuffled leaf-mold, and looked back at Odin in confusion.

Odin smiled. "Come, son. It's time you were back in your bed again." He laid his broad hand on his son's small shoulder as Viðar pressed confidingly against him, still filled with delight.

"Didn't I tell you, Father? See what a fine wolf's head it is! And it did snarl, too!"

"That it did, my boy. And it won't be the last time you'll hear a wolf snarling his battle-call at you—not by a long shot."

Viðar sighed in satisfaction and led his father home through the shadowed woods. Behind them, two grey shapes ghosted through the trees, still snarling faintly, still confused.

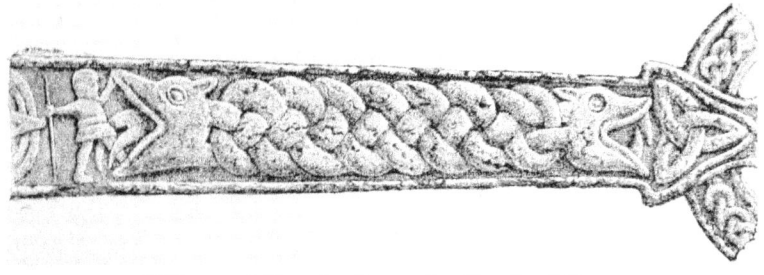

Viðar and Fenris, from the Gosford Cross.

Thor and his Family

"Thor sitting" by Hermann Ernst Freund.

6. Thor and his Family

The Farmer's God

Thor and his Family

I can't agree at all with the portrayal of Thor as a thick-headed oaf or as nothing but a hammer-swinging brute. I have experienced him many times in the form of a down-to-earth yeoman farmer, wise in the ways of the land and the needs of everyday life. Farmers, too, were often looked down on and disrespected by 'aristocrats' of various types. Yet, a successful subsistence farmer must be wise and disciplined in many ways: when and how to plant or slaughter; how much to eat now and how much to save for future planting or breeding. How to make best use of scarce resources. How to adapt to weather and climate. Careful planning and disciplined execution of those plans. Fair management and guidance for all the folk of the farm, and training for the youngsters. The skills of breeding and selection, planning for the future.

Thor has shown me time and again that he can guide the practical management of resources, any resources, and lend his power in the execution of the resulting tasks. His strength supports us in dealing practically with the unexpected, with challenges and even disasters of all kinds, with scarcity as well as abundance. He leads us away from being helpless whiners, overwhelmed by life. He's a Can-Do God, and his children follow him in that. Anyone who wants to make a success of their practical, everyday life will benefit from working with Thor and his family members Sif, Thruðr, Magni and Moði.

The old Heathen poets don't talk about these ordinary down-to-earth things except to scoff at them, but the fact that Thor is called the farmer's God says a lot when we understand what farming is all about: rolling up our sleeves and digging down into the fertile soil of everyday tasks to make a good life out of what we have.

Sif: Kinship and Hospitality

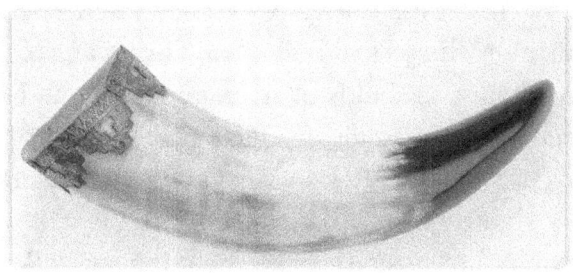

Well-preserved drinking horn found in a Swedish grave-site.

Sif's name itself means 'related, relative', connected to the plural Old Norse word *sifjar* meaning 'one's relations, family, kindred'. The German word *Sippe* means the same: kinship, consanguinity, family, relatives, kith and kin; it is also the word for a genus (one step higher than a species) in biological terminology. In German branches of our troth, Sif's name is Sippe or Sibbe. In Old English, *sibb* meant 'kinship, relationship, love, friendship, peace, happiness'—basically, the same meanings as the rune Wunjo. Proto-Germanic **sibja* meant 'one's own', a blood relation. Sib-related words indicating 'relationship' occur in all the old and modern Germanic languages.

There is a lovely adjective used of Queen Wealhtheow in the *Beowulf* poem: she is called *frithu-sibb folca,* the frith-sib of the folk (l. 2017). Heathen frith is the outgrowth of strong relationships; it is woven from the mutual trust and support that healthy interrelationships foster among us. I like to think of Sif as the frith-sib of all Heathen folk, related and relating to us all as a kinswoman and a leader in the kindly arts of weaving frith-relationships among us. Sif is related to other important Gods in our faith: she is the mother of Ullr and Thruðr, the wife of Thor, the stepmother of Magni and Modi.

Consider this: Sif is the Lady of Thor's hall Bilskirnir and of his entire realm, Thruðheim or Thruðvangar (meaning 'strength-world' and 'fields of strength.') The hall Bilskirnir is equipped with 540 daises; Odin, as Thor's proud father, boasts that it is the greatest of all halls *(Grimnismal* vs. 24). 'Daises' are slightly raised platforms where the tables and high seats of nobles are placed, while the common folk fill many more tables on the floor level. If Thor's hall has 540 such daises, that implies that there are a great many *more* tables for the common folk, the farmers, craftsfolk, and workers of all kinds whose patron he is.

This is indeed an enormous hall! And no wonder: Thor is the patron of a huge number of folk, far more than Odin is with his *einherjar*. And who has charge of hospitality and care for all these folk—for their souls in the afterlife? It is Sif, of course, no doubt helped by her daughter Thruðr. Thruðr is listed as one of the Valkyries who bear drinking horns to the *einherjar* in Odin's hall *(Grimnismal vs. 36)*, but in my perception she does not often do so there. She is more frequently found in the hall of her own family, Bilskirnir, helping with hospitality there along with many other activities she is involved with. Sif has charge of the care and hospitality offered to countless souls whose patron she and / or Thor, Thruðr, Magni, or Moði were during their time in Midgard. (I believe that the giantess Jarnsaxa, mother of Magni and Moði, prefers to remain in her own hall in Jotunheim and follow the Jotun ways there.)

My sense of Sif's great Hall is one of comfort, companionship, and plenty, where all souls are welcome. Their strengths, talents, and skills are encouraged in the afterlife. These folk, in ancient times, were fighters at need, but focused more on the skills of daily life that all of us depend upon. I believe that the spiritual gifts and goodwill emanating from all these skilled and hardy souls in Bilskirnir, along with the Holy Ones there, offer strength and support, courage and inspiration, for those of us still working our way through the many challenges of daily life in Midgard. These gifts, and our respect and appreciation for them, weave us all together in the kinship of the spirit, and there may be many of our own blood-kin in that great Hall, as well.

I find that the family of Sif and Thor is a close-knit one, and see them both as patrons of parenting, grandparenting, and family life. Sif goes even farther, helping us to weave and maintain frith and good relationships with our extended kin and our heart-kin (those closest to us, whether they are related or not), as well as with our neighbors and those we work with. Her gifts of hospitality, nurturing, kinship, and frith are of great value, and we should not hesitate to call upon her to help us with these important matters in our lives.

"Midgard Vikingsenter" reconstruction of a feasting hall in Norway.

Thor and his Family

The Thorlings

Thor with his children: Magni, Moði, Thruðr.

There is a kind of courageous, driving, powerful energy within us, and within other beings and the environment as well. This power was often called *mod*, but also called *mægen* in the ancient Germanic languages, and very often these terms were used together, to give a complete picture of a powerful form of energy that can be directed by our Mod-soul. These two terms come together perfectly in the names of Thor's and Jarnsaxa's sons, Magni (main, mægen) and Moði (mod-y, filled with mod), and are further enhanced by the name of Thor's and Sif's daughter Thruðr or 'strength'. Thor himself, of course, is the embodiment of mod, mægen, and strength as well. Let's explore this mystery of power just a little further.

There is a strange figure of a three-headed man shown on the Danish Gallehus horn, who is generally thought to be Thor. He is holding a long-handled implement, an axe or a hammer, and with the other hand holds a rope tied to a horned and bearded animal, presumably a goat.

Thor and his Family

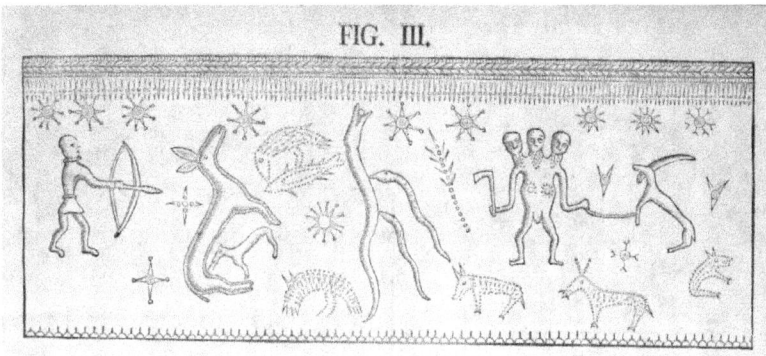

Three-headed figure from the Gallehus horn.

Here are my own thoughts about this figure. I do believe it is Thor, and that the heads on either side of the central one represent his sons, Magni and Moði, with their powers which arise from his own. I think many or all of the figures on the Gallehus horn(s) show indications of mystery cults or ritual patterns dedicated to various Deities, and that this three-headed figure represents one of those mysteries. It also points toward Thor's mystery of his ability to slaughter and eat his goats and then raise them to life again by hallowing their bones with his Hammer.

The strange depiction of him with three heads, in my view, indicates both the multiplication of his mod-and-main power, and the budding of his offspring or emanations, Moði and Magni. All of these: budding or growing mod and main, sacrificing (the goat) to his need, and then bringing dead bones to life by hallowing with his Hammer, are part of Thor's mystery. There is much to ponder here, as we seek to understand the full expression of mod and mægen, sacrifice and revival into life, and the great and complex powers of Thor expressed through his mighty Hammer.

Thruðr and her father Thor.

Meditations, devotions, magical workings, and other focused attention on Thor and his children are very fine ways to develop and shape our own mod and mægen energies. It's my opinion that modern Heathens would do well to pay more attention to the 'Thorlings' or Thor's children, not least because they were / are / will be Ragnarök survivors and thus among the divine leaders of the next cycle of the Worlds. The idea that 'mod, mægen and strength' are focused through them and into the worlds, both now and later, is not a trivial consideration!

This leads us to another point: the phrase 'mod and mægen' together was how the ancient Germanic scholars translated the Latin term *virtus* or 'virtue', specifically the kind of virtue that refers to 'special powers, outstanding potency' of things like powerful herbs and magical implements. This understanding implies that the triple Thorlings, Modi-Magni-Thruðr / Mod-Mægen-Strength, can be called upon to imbue something with power and virtue in this sense, including our own souls but also magical and healing items and spells, among other things.

This may have been an underlying meaning of the rune-inscription *wigi Thonar*, 'Thor hallow', on the 6th-century Nordendorf fibulae: calling on Thor not only to make the inscribed item sacred or hallowed, but also to fill it with virtue and power, mod and mægen, for some special purpose. (See Chapter 23, *"Wigi Thonar: The Powers of Thor's Hammer,"* and Chapter 21, *"The Powers of the Dwarves,"* for more about hallowing, mod, mægen, and 'virtue.')

Thor and his Family

Magnetic Power

One of the ways we can build and channel mod-power in our lives is, in a sense, to work backwards. Instead of trying to grow mod-power directly, we can grow it through a process of 'suction' or 'magnetism'. We do this by deciding where we most want to use our mod-power and then allowing our focus and dedication to these areas of life to pull our mod-energy and abilities in that direction. Once this magnetic power / energy starts flowing strongly, it helps to break up energy blocks and pinch-points that our life experiences and circumstances have created, which hamper our access to our own mod-power.

"Donar-Thor," by Max Friedrich Koch.

Thor and his Family

Thinking about magnetic mod-power leads us toward the similarity between 'magnet' and Magni Thor's son. The word 'magnet' comes ultimately from Magnesia, a region named after one of the demigod sons of Zeus Thunder-God, Magnes, who was considered the founding-father of the ancient Greek tribe which settled in that region of northern Greece. Magnetic ore was found here and was called 'the stone of Magnes.' *(Online Etymology Dictionary.)*

Here we have two powerful sons of the Thunder-Gods Thor and Zeus, with basically the same name, Magni and Magnes, associated with the word for magnetic iron. This leads us to a connection with Thor's mighty iron Hammer and its flows of power, and likewise with Zeus's great Thunderbolts.

Looking at the Thorling brothers Magni and Modi, we have the combined power of mod and main or mægen associated with the power of magnetism. For myself, these energies feel profoundly real and meaningful both within and around me, and draw me toward the Thorlings as powerful Gods to work with when seeking to understand and use such energies.

Móði represents and helps us channel our mod-power. Magni represents the magnetic force that can pull out mighty flows of that mod-power in a direction that we choose. Their sister Thrúðr, 'Strength', represents the strength of character and Will needed in order to direct these powers rightly. Móði is the 'substance' of Mod, Magni is the 'force' of that substance, and Thrúðr is the 'form' that shapes the expression of the substance and the force.

Thor himself ties all of them together: a God not only of might and main, but also a God of trustworthy character, of right and beneficial action, and a God whose actions are powerful and effective. All of them can support and help direct our efforts to grow and shape our powers of mod and mægen, character and will. Through all of them we can learn more about how these powers express themselves in Nature, people, and the many holy Powers of the Worlds.

Thor's Act of Compassion

Few of us, perhaps, would think of Thor as an example of divine compassion in our faith, but I suggest this is worth considering! It all depends on understanding how different beings—Gods, people, ancestors—express their compassion, and such understanding depends in turn on one's culture and expectations of compassion. I would say that elder Heathen cultures focused much more on compassion as practical action, as we see so often from the German Goddess Frau Holle / Holda for example, rather than on compassion as an emotional exchange of feelings.

Here is one non-obvious example of such godly compassion from our lore (from *Gylfaginning* in the prose Edda, Sturlason p. 38). In this tale, Thor stops overnight with a peasant family, slaughters the goats who draw his chariot, and shares their meat with the family. Unbeknownst to him, however, the son breaks a leg-bone for the marrow. When Thor waves his Hammer over his goats to restore them to life the next morning, he discovers that one of them is limping. Thor falls into a mod-fury—*Asmoði*, the 'mood of the Æsir'—and threatens the family in revenge. But he is not in a blind rage: when he sees the family's terror, he *sefadiz,* he shifts from the raging of his *Asmoði* state into the compassion and

Thor and his Family

calm of his sefa-soul and agrees to accept compensation rather than enact revenge.

The family offer their son and daughter to Thor as their compensation, and from our modern perspective this does not seem like a compassionate outcome. Look at it from the perspective of the society at that time, however. For peasant children to be taken into service with a great Deity would be the ultimate dream come true, an honor and benefit to the whole family.

Thjalfi gained fame and reward as a brave and trusty companion of Thor on his adventures, something he would never have achieved as a laboring peasant, no matter how hard he worked. His sister Roskva goes with them on their next adventure, but we don't hear more of her after that. I assume she eventually joins the household of Thor's daughter Thruðr, or his wife Sif, and gains the many advantages of greatly enhanced social status.

The 'compensation' Thor accepted was, in truth, a continuation of his compassion and his blessing for the family, as indeed was the original sacrifice and feast of his goats to feed a poor peasant family (as well as himself, of course!). Instead of slaughtering or cursing the family for their transgression, he improved their lives.

Thjalfi and Roskva, by Constantin Hansen.

Thor and his Family

"Sif" from Swedish Edda translation.

Love Songs of Sif and Thor

Here is a poem to honor the love between the Goddess Sif, who is often considered a Goddess of the grain, among other things, and her husband Thor, a God of thunder and lightning, whose energies ripen the grain for harvest. The harvest of ripened grain is their gift to humans ('bairns', in my poem), but also portends their seasonal parting, as the energies of Sif that are represented in the grain are cut down. She then sleeps under the snow until awakened again in the spring by Thor's thunder.

This poetic depiction of Sif gives only one aspect of her manifold being; many Heathens do not see her as a seasonal grain-Goddess, but in quite different ways. This symbolic perspective of her, however, is one that works well for a love-song! I believe, and experience myself, that our Gods can each take on many forms and meanings and should not be plugged into rigid categories, any more than people should be.

Winter: Thor's Lament
Your golden hair is shorn, my Sif,
Your head wimple-wrapped.
Robed and veiled in white
You dream the winter nights.
Frigid wind shifts snow-crystals
Hushing over hummocks,
Sounding like wind in your hair.

Winter: Sif's Dreams
Thor keeps troth,
His heart of living oak
Is solid and true,
Well worth loving.

Spring: Sif Awakens
Feels good to stretch and wake;
Rain is chill, but thaws the Earth.
I hear the first echoes
Of Thor's thunder over the mountains.
He's laughing now, it's good to hear him!
He's coming closer, I hope he remembers…

Thor and his Family

My shoots are young and tender,
Just a pinprick
Of green above the mud....
Thor, you lummox, you're doing it again!
You'll squash me flat–every spring
It's like this! Take it easy, love,
Abate your force. Couldn't we try
A gentle rain, for once?

Summer: Thor's Song
Land lies yearning under Sun's caress,
Grain glints and glistens in waves of wind.
I run my fingers through your hair
And hear your hushing whispers,
Hoarse with passion.
Ah! My Sif,
Even the wide plains,
Even Middle Garth's broad reaches,
Even Ase's Garth itself,
Cannot hold our love enclosed.

Summer: Sif's Song
I move beneath your hand,
A hand like no other.
Thunder pulses through your touch,
Heat lightning flashes,
Limning my bones with fire.
The storm's roar engulfs me,
I am swept away, I know not whither,
Nor care to know, Vingi-Thorr:
I am with you.

Thor and his Family

Harvest: Farewell

Thor: Golden my beloved, ripe under Sun's glow.
Buzz and drone of chafer's wings
Echo the honing of scythe on stone.
A last breath of wind through your hair, my Sif,
Ere wind's hush betoken
Your tresses' fall
Under the sickle's hooked gleam.

Sif: So bairns' blessing
Is love's bane, and love's gift:
Blessing, bane, and gift are one.

Both: Golden was love,
Gold will it be again,
While Wyrd wends.

7: Walburga and the Rites of May

Witches and Walpurgisnacht

First, some descriptions from Grimm's *Teutonic Mythology:*

"The Witches' excursion takes place on the first night in May...they ride up Blocksberg on the first of May, and in 12 days must dance the snow away; then Spring begins... Here they appear as elflike, godlike maids." (Grimm v. IV, p. 1619)

"(There) is a mountain very high and bare...whereon it is given out that witches hold their dance on Walpurgis night, even as on Mt. Brocken in the Harz." (Grimm v. IV, p. 1620)

"We know that our forefathers very generally kept the beginning of May as a great festival, and it is still regarded as the trysting time of witches, i.e. once of wise-women and fays; who can doubt that heathen sacrifices blazed that day?" (Grimm v. II, p. 614)

"We know that all over Germany a grand annual excursion of witches is placed on the first night in May (Walpurgis), i.e. on the date of the sacrificial feast and the old May-gathering of the people. On the first of May, of all days, the periodical assizes (Things) continued for many centuries to be held; on that day came the merry May-ridings, and the kindling of the sacred fire: it was one of the highest days in all heathenism. ...The witches invariably resort to places where formerly justice was administered, or sacrifices were offered. ...Almost all the witch-mountains were once hills of sacrifice, boundary-hills, or salt-hills." (Grimm v. III, p. 1050-1)

Grimm mentions that some (perhaps all) of the witch mountains were once the residence of Holda and her host.

"Down into the tenth and into the 14th centuries, night-women in the service of Dame Holda rove through the air on appointed nights, mounted on beasts; her they obey, to her they sacrifice, and all the while not a word about any league with the Devil. Nay, these night-women, shining mothers, dominae nocturnae, bonnes dames... were originally daemonic elvish beings, who appeared in woman's shape and did men kindnesses; Holda, Abundia, to whom still a third part of the whole world is subject, leads the ring of dancers.... It is to such dancing at heathen worship, to the airy elf-dance and the hopping of will-o'-the-wisps, that trace primarily the idea of witches' dances; festive dances at heathen May-meetings can be reckoned in with the rest.

To Christian zealots all dancing appeared sinful and heathenish, and sure enough it often was derived from Pagan rites, like other harmless pleasures and customs of the common people, who would not easily part with their diversion at the great festivals. Hence the old dancings at Shrovetide (beginning of Lent in February), at the Easter fire and May fire, at the solstices, at harvest and Christmas... ...to this day stories are afloat in Sweden of dances and reels performed by the heathen round holy places of their Gods: so wanton were they, yet so enticing, that the spectators at last were seized with the rage (wod), and whirled along into the revelry." Grimm notes that Heathen dancing and processions were demonized by frightening people into thinking that if they took part in them, they would be trapped into endless, exhausting dancing or into the "everlasting hunter's chase," the Wild Hunt. (Grimm v. III, pp. 1056-7)

The Roots of Walpurgisnacht

These are a few of the accounts of the festival usually called Walpurgisnacht (the night of April 30) and May-Day (May 1). Clearly, it was a festival of major importance in Heathen times, and continued to keep strong hold of the minds and feelings of the Germanic folk down to the present day or close to it. What are the Heathen roots of these customs and of the name of this night? What meanings might they hold for us today? I will attempt an answer to these questions here, using several older sources of information, including a lovely book by Ernst Ludwig Rochholz, published in 1870, which traces the Heathen roots of three German saints back to Goddesses of ancient times, including Walburga (Verena and Gertrud are the other two).

Rochholz makes much of the contrast between the light-hearted springtime rites on the first of May, featuring flowers, dancing maidens and children on the one hand, with the frightening activities of the witches during Walpurgisnacht, a night of bonfires, spells, witches and beasts, storm and hail. He asks, "What kind of a pairing is this, of the witches of the Brockenmount with a saint of the church, under one and the same name!" (p. 1) The purpose of his study is to seek out the connection between the two, stripped of its Christian ornamentation, which he believes originally resided in one being, "the worthy wholeness of a Germanic Goddess." (p. 1)

Saint Walburga

There actually was a Christian nun, later a saint, named Walburga who lived during the 8th century in Germany. The cloister which she ran as abbess was built in 760 and called

Walburga and the Rites of May

"Heidenheimer Kloster," namely "Heathen-home Cloister!" It was named after the town where it was located in middle Frankenland, which in turn was named after a "holy spring," Heidenbrunnen, where Heathens had been baptized. It seems likely to me that this spring had been holy long before the Christians came, as springs so often were in Heathen times.

Nothing noteworthy during Walburga's lifetime, nor her birth or death-dates, caused any association between St. Walburga and Walpurgisnacht. What apparently brought about the association of her with that date was that after her death, a miracle-working liquid or oil began to flow from the tombstone placed over her remains, which caused healings and was the reason for her canonization as a saint. Both the oil and the canonization occurred on the first of May. Later Walburga's body was broken into pieces and buried at different places—as far away as present-day France and all over Germany—so that other churches could get the benefit of the holy oil as well.

The church later tried to downplay the association of the oil and the saint with the Heathen-contaminated Mayday, but the connection remained in people's minds. If one looks at the accounts from Grimm, one may guess that in the minds of people who have not completely forgotten age-old Heathen wisdom, the association of the woman saint's miracles of healing and renewal with the day on which 'witches' (wise-women, Elf-women, Goddesses) cast out winter and called in the life-giving May, is not an unnatural one.

In Bavaria there is a very old Walburga's chapel that is said to be located on the site of an older Heathen temple. The chapel stands on its own hill, surrounded by linden trees. Hills, especially hills standing alone, are in Germany traditionally the dwelling places of Holda, Frau Holle, and other Heathen holy female beings later seen as witches. Linden trees have always been holy to Frigg and to the German Goddesses. Place names and chapels stemming from Walburga (many associated with linden trees, hills, and holy wells) litter the landscape in Bavaria, Austria, and other Germanic homelands.

"The greatest number of the oldest churches in lower Germany are dedicated to this same saint." (Rochholz, p.17). "Lower Germany" includes what are now the Netherlands, Belgium, Saxony, and other regions of northern Germany—regions where formerly the Goddess Nehalennia was widely worshipped. Quite a few modern Heathens have put forth the idea that 'Walburga' is simply Nehalennia renamed.

Museum display of altars to Goddess Nehalennia, in Holland. Note that many altars show her with a dog.

Walburga's Dog

Walburga's symbols, as shown in the oldest stone carvings in her chapels, are a dog and a bundle of grain. There is nothing in the abbess Walburga's biographies to account for portraying her with a dog, but there is much to show that German Goddesses were associated with the dog as their *Hilfstier* (helping animal). "Grey hounds accompany the three Norns. The fertility Goddesses Frau Harke, Frau Gode, and Frau Frick (Frigg) have always a hound beside them, and...Frau Berchte in Steiermark is called the 'poodle-mother' because of her dog" (Rochholz p. 20). The Goddess Nehalennia is usually pictured with a dog on her altars and votive sites. Speaking Walburga's name is a charm to tame fierce or even mad dogs.

In folklore, the dog has much to do with fertility, health and good luck. For example, Rochholz mentions superstitions about the need to feed a mysterious 'Windhound,' said to be left behind from the Wild Hunt, during springtide to ensure good weather for the crops. The Windhound is connected to fertility, good luck and plenty in the house and the farm fields, and in some places is called the 'Nourishment-Hound' *(Nahrungshund)* (p. 22). Rochholz recounts many other superstitions relating dogs with Goddesses of fertility. The Christian Mary and female saints are also frequently portrayed with dogs in German chapels, and there is a *Hundskapelle* (dog-chapel) in Innsbruck said to have originally been a Heathen temple. One must suppose that this attribute of a dog accompanying Heathen Goddesses was carried over into the Christian iconography of holy women, including particularly Walburga.

Walburga Chased by the Wild Hunt

"Nine nights before the first of May is Walburga in flight, unceasingly chased by wild ghosts and seeking a hiding place

from village to village. People leave their windows open so she can be safe behind the cross-shaped windowpane struts from her roaring enemies. For this, she lays a little gold piece on the windowsill, and flees further. A farmer who saw her on her flight through the woods described her as a white lady with long flowing hair, a crown upon her head; her shoes were fiery gold, and in her hands she carried a three-cornered mirror that showed all the future, and a spindle, as does Berchta. A troop of white riders exerted themselves to capture her. So also another farmer saw her, whom she begged to hide her in a stook of grain. No sooner was she hidden than the riders rushed by overhead. The next morning the farmer found grains of gold instead of rye in his grain stook. Therefore, the saint is portrayed with a bundle of grain." (Rochholz, p. 26-27)

"Wild Hunt," by Johann Wilhelm Cordes.

Walburga is here described as a 'white lady', joining her with many other sightings of 'white ladies' told of across Germanic lands. The 'whiteness' is attributed to a sheen of light: perhaps ghostly, perhaps holy, perhaps both. Elf-maidens are thus described, and Anglo-Saxon has a word *elfsciene* or 'elf-sheen', meaning 'shining bright as an Elf,' which is also used as a personal name. The description of Walburga's adventures also bears strong similarity to the harrying of the moss-wives or wood-wives by the Wild Hunt which usually occurs in the autumn and winter. Woodcutters are supposed to mark three crosses in the shape of a triangle on the stumps of trees they have felled. Inside the triangle (another 'magic' triangle) is the only place the moss-wives and woodwives are safe from being torn to pieces by the Wild Hunt. (See Grimm v. III, p. 929)

Of course in tales which mention this, the safety of the moss-wives is attributed to the crosses. Considering the Heathen nature of these spirits, however, it is tempting to envision the crosses, set in a triangular pattern, either as a triple Nauthiz rune protecting them in their need, or as a degraded form of a Valknut or a trefot, other Heathen signs of power. When not being chased by the Wild Hunt, woodwives are friendly and helpful beings who offer good advice and assistance in daily tasks, and repay favors done to them with bits of ordinary things (wood chips, splinters, grain, etc.) turned into gold. (See Grimm v. II, p. 484.) One can see the strong similarity between the moss-wives' plight and behavior, and that of Walburga in the tales mentioned above.

In Walburga's case, it seems that the Wild Hunt embodies the powers of Winter, trying to prevent the Spring from becoming established. Walburga apparently is able to take some sort of revenge for her bad treatment by the Wild Hunt, however. The Walburga-processions enacted around the villages and fields in Germany and France are supposed to protect the lands against strong winds and bad weather, giving her back her power!

Walburga's Symbols and Domains of Action

Of Walburga's symbols or attributes, the bundle of grain is obviously a fertility symbol and is typical of the Germanic Matron Goddesses or demi-Goddesses once worshipped all over Europe, including Nehalennia, as well as being a symbol of Goddesses in other Indo-European pantheons, such as Demeter and Ceres. The three-cornered mirror seems clearly related to the Norns and the Well of Wyrd: we can see the three corners of the foreseeing mirror as the three Norns, the mirror as the Well itself with the three Norns standing around it. The mirror is particularly a give-away: who ever heard of, or would want to make or use, a triangular mirror? It is not a convenient shape for viewing one's face, in the normal usage of mirrors!

The dog, the bundle of grain, the magical mirror, the spindle, the gold shoes and crown: none of these are likely attributes of the abbess of a Christian nunnery, nor is an abbess likely to have been dashing around the countryside at night, having adventures! The whole scene I quoted above about Walburga is impossible to attribute to the staid head of a nunnery. On the other hand, these symbols or attributes are highly typical of Heathen Germanic Matronae, Goddesses, and holy women. The spindle is the attribute before all others of the Norns, wise-women, idises, and other womanly wights associated with fate and fortune in the Germanic countries.

The use of the spindle and hand-spun thread for May-Eve spells of women's magic is described by Rochholz and by Grimm. Love-oracles using the spindle and thread, and other means, were said to be sent by Walburga herself. Again, sending love-oracles seems an unlikely activity for a nun, but a very likely one for Germanic Goddesses and Idisi or Disir.

Walburga and the Rites of May

Walpurgistide was also the time to shame lazy farmers into working harder, by making a straw doll named Walburga and presenting it to any farmer who had not yet ploughed his land by that day (Rochholz, p. 40). This is quite reminiscent of the well-known chiding and punishment (for example, their yarn being snarled and fouled) that women receive from Heathen Goddesses such as Berchta and Holda during Yuletide, if their own work has been skimped.

Here's a modern straw doll or harvest-doll, apparently hanging from a clothesline. This is still a popular art-form in farming communities of many countries, after the harvest is in.

None of these attributes, activities and symbols can be argued to have anything to do with a Christian abbess and saint, but have everything to do with Heathen Goddesses and holy women, who have always concerned themselves with fertility and food, love, life, death, and hidden knowledge. Thus it is in the highest degree likely that attributes associated with a Goddess celebrated at May-even during Heathen times were later grafted onto Walburga, the Christian saint whose holy day is celebrated on the first of May.

Walburga and the Rites of May

King and Queen of the May

Witches' spell-fires and shining-white Goddesses in flight are not the only stirring events occurring during this holy tide. Much ado takes place during May-Day itself, still celebrated with folk-festivals today in Germany, Holland, England and other European countries. During several years that I lived in Bavaria in the 1980s, I never saw a town without its May-tree set on top of the unique craft-poles that are erected by each town and village. On the craft-poles are hung metal figures representing all the crafts that are pursued in that town and available to the public. May-trees are often affixed to the tops of these tall, slender poles—quite a challenge!—and stand there throughout the year until it is time for them to be taken down and burned, and the next May-tree erected. England is also famous for its May festivals, including Maypole dancing and processions of the King and Queen of the May.

May-Day festivals traditionally included a fierce battle between the forces of Winter and those of Spring. Usually these battles were led by the May-King, a young man chosen for his strength, beauty and charisma, and garbed in his 'armor' of greenery. He and his troops would skirmish against the horde of Winter, and then return in a festal procession, accompanied by the May-Queen and other ladies, to engage in dancing, feasting and singing the many folk-songs associated with this holy day. In some cases, it might be the beauteous May-Queen herself who ousts the Hag of Winter. (Rochholz's chapter on May-fests provides many details on May-day customs.)

Whatever of various forms it might take, however, the keynote of the May-Day festivals is energy: the energy of youth and new life, sexuality and mating, of fighting and the chase, dancing and leaping; of ridding oneself of the old and worn-out and eagerly grasping the new.

A Sampling of Walpurgistide Customs

Here are a few of the very many customs, rites and charms associated with Walpurgisnight and May-Day:

- All worn-out household items such as brooms, cloths, and wooden implements, should be burned each spring in the Walpurgisnight fires.

- Washing your face with dew right at sunrise on May-Day will give you special powers of sight, in particular, the power to know who your future husband will be.

Walburga and the Rites of May

(Folklore says nothing about knowing your wife, but my husband can attest that this works for men, too. One May-Day morning, many years ago, he felt it was time for a change in his life, time to settle down. He went out at dawn to his front lawn (in front of a secluded old farmhouse in the countryside), which was covered with dew. Being the man he is, he didn't just wash his face in the heavy dew. He lay down on the grass and made a 'dew angel', the way children make snow angels by lying in the snow and spreading legs and arms back and forth. At that time, he and I were simply friends. He didn't 'see my face' while making the dew angel, as folklore attests, but this act of his set in motion a magical influence on both of us. A few weeks later, on Midsummer's Eve, our relationship changed from friendship to romance. And one year later, on Walpurgisnacht and May-Day, we celebrated our own Heathen wedding complete with bonfire, Maypole dance and many old folklore games and customs. So he and I claim that the dew-bath can work, and that Walburga's loving influence and the powers of May-Day haven't waned!)

- Put out a slice of bread liberally spread with butter and honey for the Windhound, to protect your land from bad weather and ill-fated crops. This offering is called the "Ankenschnitt;" it's an appealing rite for those of us who live along Tornado Alley in the USA!

- It is customary to dance, jump, spring and leap around during these festivals, either at the Walpurgisnight fires or during the May-Day revels. Especially, the mistress of a household should leap over her broom at some point during this time. (The broom is held crossways and leapt over—one does not need to leap the height of a standing broom! Elderly or childbearing housewives may wish instead to step over the broom laid on the ground.) Farmers believed that their grain would grow as high as they could leap at Walpurgistide. (Here in the Midwest, home of the tall corn, this would make for either disappointing corn-crops, or very impressive men!)

- Life-size (or smaller) strawmen are made and 'loaded' with the ill-health and ill-luck of the old year, then burned in the fires on Walpurgisnacht.

- For those alert and with the eyes to see, this is an excellent time to catch glimpses of Elves, swan-maidens, landwights and other nature-wights, as well as other beings one might prefer not to see, such as night-mares.

- It was for many centuries the custom to offer a plentiful meal and beer to all comers to Walburga's chapels at this time. Rochholz maintains this was carried over from Heathen customs of generously feasting the folk at this holy tide. The Walburga-feasts were apparently a potluck, where folk were expected to bring a food offering to share. Hold a potluck yourself!

- Men might find it good to ensure that they are caught up with the work needed to maintain their homes and land, to avoid the embarrassing presentation of a Walburga-doll from some enterprising Goddess or her earthly delegate!

What Does This All Mean?

As often when we go to the old folklore-based sources, what we end up with is a big jumble of fascinating bits and pieces. We are left wondering what to make of it all in a religious sense, and how it might have meaning and relevance to the practice of Heathenism today. I shall make an effort to address that question, with regard to what is called Walpurgisnacht and May Day, and offer some suggestions and personal

Walburga and the Rites of May

viewpoints about the deeper meaning of this holy tide and the Goddess who rules it.

First let us look at the major elements associated with Walpurgisnacht:

- processions and gatherings of 'witches' upon famous witch-mountains, which may be assumed to be demonizations of former Heathen holy wights, wise-women, and hallowed sites;

- divination, spellcraft, oracular activities, and other sorts of witchcraft;

- bonfires, which are set upon sites of significance for both Godly and human activites;

- forcible casting-out of Winter, illness and that which is worn out by the May-King and/or Queen and their green-bedecked and licentious troops, bringing in their wake marriages and fertility of crops, beasts and mankind;

- dancing, merry-making, and loosening of the usual rules governing sexual behavior;

- blessing-processions, with sacred objects and offerings, around fields and villages, bringing fertility and protection from bad weather;

- a 'lady clothed in white' who brings fertility, occult knowledge, and protection, but who is herself besieged by the forces of tumult, death and chaos.

There is clearly a rich lode of material here which, when combined with the many folk-customs, can be mined for ideas about May-Day celebrations and rituals in our time. One can easily find a basis for anything from a solitary, mystical rite, to a women's magic-working, a lovers' tryst, a camping trip and perhaps a bonfire on a mountain (if fire-hazard is not high), a hospitable dinner for family and friends (with the hostess leaping her broom, for entertainment!), or a large, uproarious festival, depending on one's inclinations, circumstances, and resources. What is clear from the lore, however, is that this was indeed a major and significant Heathen holy tide and should be observed as such in one way or another.

Valborg, the Swedish version of Walpurgisnacht.

Returning Life

Though I think it is fairly clear from the lore I have outlined above, I will summarize here what seems to have been the underlying significance and meaning of Walpurgisnacht and May-Day. First, it is the time when the deathly cold, decay, ill-health and dreariness of Winter are driven out, to make room for newly-growing life and all that pertains to it: mating between humans, and beasts wild and tame, fertility of the fields, health and vitality, and the greening and blossoming of the land. Youth, beauty, sexuality, and strength are celebrated.

Then, all must be protected from the return and reconquest by Winter's woeful forces (definitely a possibility in northern climes!), requiring magical and religious rites of warding and hallowing. The driving out of Winter and the warding and hallowing might be done secretly and mysteriously by gathered witches and their flickering flames on the mountain-tops, or by the May-King and Queen and their doughty horde, or most likely by both: the witches by night and the May battle-troops and processions by day.

These days, there are many Heathens living in regions and climates quite dissimilar from the climate of Northern Europe. These Heathens generally adjust the dates for seasonal celebrations, for example, switching Walpurgisnacht and Halloween / Disablot in the Southern Hemisphere so these holidays are aligned with the coming seasons of Summer and Winter. I would also suggest, for Heathens living in areas which have no distinctive Winter and Summer seasons, to align Walpurgis-tide celebrations with the coming of the most fertile season in your region. For example, the coming of the monsoons, or the season when most of the fruits in the area are coming into bloom.

A Between-Time of Magic

Since this is a turning-tide when the season is not quite one thing or another—a 'between-time,' it is very suitable for occult divination and spellcraft: a time to take advantage of the thinner veils between the worlds and the fact that our minds are temporarily focused away from everyday affairs and onto the magical energies of Nature's spring tides. This is a time for looking into that which is coming into being, for seeking deep roots of life-knowledge and life-mysteries, for love-magic and spells of growth and change, conception and birth.

A Springtime Goddess

Finally, and most obscurely and mysteriously for us, this holy tide seems to have been associated with a Goddess, probably one who bore different names in different places. Very likely, the holy powers and nature of 'St. Walburga' were originally aspects of one of the Germanic Goddesses, such as Nehalennia, Nerthus, Holle / Holda, or Berchta. The branch of Heathenry called *Urglaawe* considers that Walburga is an aspect of Frau Holle, and has many observances similar to those I have described here for their celebration of Walpurgisnacht (Schreiwer p. 66).

For myself, with my focus on Anglo-Saxon Heathenry, I like to think that Walburga the Goddess is not greatly different from the Goddess Eostre (Anglo-Saxon) or Ostara (German). In my personal devotions I see Walburga and Eostre as sisters, though I have no basis in the lore for doing so.

One aspect that feeds into this belief of mine is that the holy tide of Eostre, in Heathen times, was not precisely on the day of the Spring Equinox, as Heathens generally celebrate it today. Eostre's holy tide was not a day, but a month: *Eostremonath,* which began on the night of the first full moon after the Spring Equinox, and ended one moon later, in late April.

The meaning of this, for me, is that Eostre's tide stretches from early spring into late spring, coming to a close just as Walburga's tide begins to flow into the world, in late April. It is as though two sisters, riding their respective tides of power, are reaching out to one another across the divide between bright and dark, airy and earthy. Though Eostre's companions are the shining Elf-women while Walpurgisnacht is celebrated for its dark witches, I think originally there was little distinction between the two.

Eostre-tide and Walpurgistide both celebrate the power of returning life, both its dark, mysterious, blood-deep side, and its bright, shining, blossoming side. They cannot be separated. Christian fears, mythology and superstition have separated the 'white lady,' the supposed St. Walburga, from the darkness of the Wild Hunt, and have set her as a charm against ills such as bad weather and mad dogs, often thought to be caused by witches. Yet on her own holy night, it is the supposedly dark witches who have power, who gather in ancient places of sacrifice to do what is needful to be done, even when the folk no longer consciously remember that is the case. In reality, there is no separation here between the dark and the light, life growing out of death and decay, brightness arising from danger and fear, sacrifice given for fertility.

I see Ostara and Walburga as being closely similar Goddesses of spring and all that spring bears with it: the bright and the dark, the festal and the mysterious, youthful beauty and age-old wisdom. I see them accompanied by shining Elves and old wise-women, and by the often-described companions and worshippers of Holda / Holle and the other Germanic Goddesses. They rule the whole of springtide, from the first Summer-findings of robin and violet and the spring Evennight, up to the gateway of Summer and the Godly powers that there hold sway.

The Name of the Goddess

In the name 'Walburga,' we are dealing with a folk myth containing several apparent conflicts. Factually speaking, Walburga was an historical Christian abbess. According to folklore, 'St. Walburga' is a white lady with magical attributes, closely similar to the other Germanic 'shining-white ladies' whom we know as Heathen Goddesses, Elf-maidens, Disir, Matronae. Walpurgisnacht has been seen for many centuries as a night of witches and occult powers. I hope I have shown here how all those pieces can fit together and what they mean in a deeper sense. The one remaining mystery, to me, is: what about the name itself?

I really hesitate to call a Heathen Goddess by the name of a Christian saint! Yet the name itself and its overtones in the term 'Walpurgisnacht' have been blessed by folk-tradition with a set of nuances and subtle meanings that can clearly be seen as genuinely Heathen. My personal solution to the dilemma here of what to call the Goddess and her holy tide is simply to accept and use one of the variants on the name 'Walburga.' I do not want to use that exact name since it belonged to an historical Christian, but neither do I want to abandon tradition and call the Goddess something completely different, not even 'Ostara' although I think they are closely related. Ostara belongs to the beginning of spring and to its shining, airy, Elf-like nature, while 'Walburga' has become associated with the more witch-like, dark and earthy rites of Walpurgisnacht, of spring moving into the earthiness of summer, in spite of her 'white lady' image in folklore.

So, I make a small change and call the Goddess Wælburga, using Anglo-Saxon spelling and pronunciation. The meaning of this name, Wælburga, picks up on the dark nature of the bright/dark Eostre/Wælburga pairing, since the name means 'burg of the slain.' Considering the divination and spellcraft activities of Walpurgisnacht, and the great assistance that can be given in these by the souls of the dead, using the name Wælburga seems especially appropriate. Her name also gives me the satisfying image of Wælburga being herself a refuge of the dead: the dead resting in the care of a Goddess who also brings springtide and new life. What could be more beautiful?

An alternate spelling, 'Wælbyrga,' would also emphasize this imagery, with its meaning 'burial-mound of the slain.' Mounds are an ideal place to conduct many kinds of witchcraft and occult activities, as well as serving as the refuge of the dead, and as something like a miniature 'hollow hill' of Holle / Holda and her host. Seeing these aspects as being part of Wælburga's nature brings her even closer to the other Germanic Goddesses: Nehalennia, Holle, Berchta and the rest. The modern Heathen sect of *Urglaawe* indeed considers Walburga to be an alternate form of the Goddess Frau Holle. These Goddesses, too, rule fertility and new life, yet also guide and guard the dead in their care. All of them fit well with Rochholz's description: "the worthy wholeness of a Germanic Goddess."

However this Goddess's name evolved, I believe that now Wælburga / Walburga is quite comfortable with the name that has grown up around her and her holy day during the last thousand years and more. The historical accidents, apparent contradictions and confusions surrounding her name are all simply the way things usually do come about, in a wyrdly natural, organically mythical and folkloric sort of way! Her original name may be a mystery, but she herself certainly has not suffered that fate. It simply remains for us to care enough, about her and the portion of Heathen Godlore and holiness that she represents, to delve beneath the apparent confusion into the true heart of who she is. This is a deed of wisdom and troth that all our Gods and Goddesses expect us to achieve, for each one of them.

8: Eostre / Ostara

"Ostara," by Johannes Gehrts.

In my song below, I address the Heathen Spring / Dawn Goddess as 'Ostara,' because it is the most familiar. For myself, I like to call her by her Anglo-Saxon name, Eastre or Eostre.

The Anglo-Saxons honored her by naming an entire month after her: *Eostre-monath,* which began on the first full moon after the spring equinox. This timing coincidentally overlapped with the calculations for Easter (which falls on the first Sunday after the first full moon after the spring equinox, in the Western church). This is how the Christian holiday came to be named after a Pagan Goddess in England (Easter) and Germany (Ostern). In all other countries, even in Scandinavia and Holland, this holiday is named after some version of 'passover' or 'paschal' tide, because the crucifixion and resurrection occurred during the sacred time of Passover in the Jewish calendar. Only in the ancestral languages of English and

Eostre / Ostara

German was the devotion to the Spring and Dawn Goddess and her holy month so strong that the name of her month was attached to the holy day: Easter in English, Ostern in German.

These names are both derived from words for 'east', relating to dawn and springtime. The name Eostre is cognate to the Greek Goddess of the Dawn, Eos. Ostara is the German version of her name. There's a long tradition in some places in Europe of climbing a hill or mountain before the sun rises on Easter morning, to greet the dawn on that day; I did that myself when I lived in Bavaria in the 1980s, though I was unaware of modern Heathenry then. I like to think this is a continuation of Pagan practice: greeting Ostara on the mountain-top as her holy springtime month begins.

It is also meaningful to address this Dawn-Goddess by her reconstructed Proto-Indo-European name, *Hausos*. She has many other names in other Indo-European pantheons, some of them closely related, like the Greek Dawn-Goddess Eos. All these names refer to the East and the Dawn, and the associated season of Spring.

Though I have not found solid proof of this, I like to think that the fertile Hare, who runs wild and free with March madness at this time of year, was the sacred animal of Eostre and Ostara (it is called the Oster-Hase in German). Hence the 'Easter Bunny', whose behavior is a good deal more sedate and child-oriented than is the wild Hare with its spring frenzy of fighting, mating, and mad dancing!

As we celebrate Ostara, let us honor Eostre's power to bring renewal and fertility, to release us from the constraints of winter and set free our urge to create, to celebrate, to renew our lives. Hail the Spring and the Dawn: Hail Ostara!

Eostre / Ostara

Ostara's Dance: A Song

Ostara comes in rushing swiftness, dawntide gold,
Her glowing brightness, cool and clear, we now behold!
She glides between the shimmering stones
With gentlest step, our lithe maiden glowing:
With blessing treads the mountain's bones.

Her flashing gaze, her soul's clear main, make bright the air,
No Elf-queen mighty, full of grace, could be so fair!
She glides between the shimmering stones
With gentlest step, our lithe maiden glowing:
With blessing treads the mountain's bones.

With floating grace upon the sward the Elf-maidens come,
To spin about the Springtime Queen, their souls' sweet home.
She glides between the shimmering stones
With gentlest step, our lithe maiden glowing:
With blessing treads the mountain's bones.

Ostara, Lady, come to us, your folk do call,
Your springtime gifts, your blessing give, to one and all!
You glide between the shimmering stones
With gentlest step, our lithe maiden glowing:
With blessing tread the mountain's bones.

Sung to the tune of a Dutch carol "King Jesus hath a garden full of diverse flowers."

Eostre / Ostara

About the song: Years ago, before I knew about modern Heathenry, I experienced a beautiful dawn scene in the Alps. Wisps of white mist rose from wet grass and twined in the dawn light and breeze as though they were dancing, while the rising sun shot pearly gleams through the mist and reflected off boulders and rocks. This scene stayed in my memory, and years later when I wished to write a song for Eostre, this memory inspired me. I was also inspired by the lovely Anglo-Saxon word *ælf-sciene* or elf-sheen, describing the shining beauty of the Elven-kind. The wisps of rising mist, pearl-shot by the sun, seemed to me to be elf-sheen maidens dancing in the dawn light, gathering around their beloved Lady of the Dawn. This was the beautiful scene that led to my song "Ostara's Dance."

"Meadow Elves (Ängsälvor)" by Nils Blommer.

Eostre / Ostara

In Honor of Eostre

Lady of Light, Spring, and Growth

Here are a few verses from a longer poem by Algernon Charles Swinburne (1837-1909), an English poet. The poem, Atalanta in Calydon, *is in honor of Atalanta of Greek mythology, a huntress, swift runner, and devotee of the Goddess Artemis. I have used these verses for years as inspiration for my own devotions to Eostre / Eastre / Ostara / Hausos, our Goddess of dawn, spring, growth, and fertility.*

I imagine the references to her bow and arrows in the poem as the rays of light that first strike over the horizon in the east, and Eostre's 'prey' being the shadows and cold of winter. The swift running of her feet over the land leaves behind her the energy of fertility and growth, soaking into the soil. Frozen streams and rivers break up into floes of ice, rushing and booming through ravines. Wind roars and sings through the mountain passes. Animals come out from their dens and burrows to see what's going on and seek their mates. Birds return, calling on the wind. All is energy, light, movement, growth! Hail to you, Eostre!

> When the hounds of spring are on winter's traces,
> The mother of months in meadow or plain
> Fills the shadows and windy places
> With lisp of leaves and ripple of rain.
>
> Come with bows bent and with emptying of quivers,
> Maiden most perfect, lady of light,
> With a noise of winds and many rivers,
> With a clamour of waters, and with might.

Eostre / Ostara

Bind on thy sandals, O thou most fleet,
Over the splendour and speed of thy feet;
For the faint east quickens, the wan west shivers,
Round the feet of the day and the feet of the night.

Where shall we find her, how shall we sing to her,
Fold our hands round her knees, and cling?
O that man's heart were as fire and could spring to her,
Fire, or the strength of the streams that spring!

For the stars and the winds are unto her
As raiment, as songs of the harp-player,
For the risen stars and the fallen cling to her,
And the southwest-wind and the west-wind sing.

For winter's rains and ruins are over,
And all the season of snows, and sins;
The days dividing lover from lover,
The light that loses, the night that wins;

And time remembered is grief forgotten,
And frosts are slain and flowers begotten,
And in green underwood and cover
Blossom by blossom the spring begins.

Excerpted from Atalanta in Calydon, *by Algernon Charles Swinburne*

9: A Tale of Nanna and her Kin

Valkyrie, by Arthur Rackham.

Mani

Once upon a time—a time that is all the time that ever was or will be—there lives among the Holy Powers of the Worlds a lord among lords. As with all the great Powers, he has many names: *Mani* the Moon is one of them. *Nokkve,* he is called, as well: Captain of the Ship of Heaven; and *Gevarr,* Warder of the Atmosphere; and *Nef,* the Mist-Dark One. Each night he sails his shining ship over the holy way of Nokkve's Path, granting the gift of light to Midgard below and Asgard above.

A Tale of Nanna and her Kin

The Holy Ones of Asgard look down through the airy floors and meadows and rivers of their realm at night, and see the light of Nokkve's ship reflecting up to them. The denizens of Midgard are blessed with its light shining from above. Nights and months are counted by the changing light of Metod, the Measurer of Time. Two of the eldest Dwarves assist him in this work: Ny New-Moon and Nidi Moon-Dark.

Among the lesser powers of the world are the *Heiptr*, fierce spirits which chastise those who turn to ill deeds during their time of life in Midgard. The Heiptr use bundles of thorns called *limar* to thrash evildoers, waking them up to their erring path and giving them the chance to turn and tread rightly again. Nokkve the Captain, Gevarr the warder of the ether that surrounds Earth's atmosphere, also has charge of the Heiptr-spirits. As he captains the silver Ship of Heaven on its proper course, so he directs the Heiptr to urge humankind onto the paths of worthiness. As he wards Earth's blanket of air from harm, so he seeks with his Heiptr to ward his folk from the harm of ill deeds. As lord of the Heiptr and the limar-switches they use, he is known as *Eylimi*—lord of Limar-Island, which of course is the Moon-Island floating in the sky. Many tales are told, in many lands, of the old man in the moon with his bundle of thorns on his back. Eylimi shows himself there on the moon, shining in the night sky during the time when evildoers are most tempted to go abroad: a warning to his folk to walk the paths of goodness and avoid the vengeance of his Heiptr.

Sol

Not alone is Mani. Another shining light dwells in the sky: Sol, the Mother-Sun, who rules the days and the passage of the years. She and Mani are the children of Mundilfari, lord of the World-Mill, which keeps the earth and the tides turning, all of Hvergelmir's mighty rivers flowing, and all the lights of Heaven rotating on their paths through the worlds. So bright and hot is Mani's sister Sol that the High Powers had to place the shield named Svalin between her and the Earth, to prevent Earth from burning away.

As with other holy brothers and sisters in the tales of our faith, they love and wed each other. Light to light they are drawn—the Captain of the Moon-Ship and the Wain-Rider of the Sun--and of them are born two daughters. Like them, their daughters have many names, but one each will do for now, the names their parents gave them, foreknowing their daughters' deeds. The elder is called Sinhtgunt, and the younger, Sunna, the Daughter-Sun, who will one day take her mother's place after the end and the beginning of things.

Young Nanna

Bright and brave are these two young girls, and they wax and grow in the delight of their parents' love. In Sol's great chariot they race across the sky each day—laughing, their hair whipping in the wind—while their mother urges onward the mighty Horses of the Sun. At night the little girls curl in each other's arms, rocking in the cradle of the Moon-Ship, while their father—his hand strong and sure on the tiller—wards their rest and sings to them the silver songs of the moon.

Sinhtgunt is born with a warrior's great heart, full of protective love and courage, and as she grows she earns the name *Nanna*—the Brave One, the Daring One. She travels with the Valkyries, learning from them the skills of the warriors of Heaven and the wisdom of the Swan-Maidens: wisdom of runes and magic and the hidden powers of life. She rides a great steed whom she loves like a brother, dressing him in harness of shining silver and grooming him until his midnight hide shines with silver gleams. He is as great-hearted as his mistress, and together they ride the paths of the night sky. When he shakes his head, frothing drops of dew fly from his bridle onto the earth and bring fruitfulness everywhere they fall.

Skoll and Hati pursuing Sol and Mani, by John Charles Dollman.

But not all in Heaven's fields is made for delight and play. Always, behind the warding and the love and laughter given the girls by their holy parents, lie the shadows of the great Sky-Wolves. As little girls, Sinhtgunt and Sunna enjoy but do not know the reason for their mother's speed in her swift Sun-Chariot, and their father's utmost care in steering his Ship of Heaven. Always behind their golden mother runs the giant-wolf Skoll, longing to devour her, knowing that—one day—he will succeed. Behind their father's ship that tosses on the billows of Heaven runs the giant-wolf Hati, jaws slavering, desiring only to bring his destruction. Mani and Sol ward their little ones from fear and danger and let them grow up in unshadowed delight.

Nanna, Warrior-Maid

But the time comes when the warrior-maid Nanna opens her eyes and sees her parents' danger. Though the maidens love both their parents dearly, Nanna is closest to her father while Sunna's heart leans toward her mother. In her roamings through the night sky, Nanna sees fierce Hati pursuing her father's ship, ever straining to reach it. And for the first time, she notices the grim lines that mark her father's face, the tension in his hands as he sets the sails and clenches his fist on the tiller of his ship. His sharp eyes peer ahead through the dangerous waves and billows of the etheric skyscape he navigates, never daring to glance behind, but clearly Mani knows his pursuer is there and strains forward to outrace him. The nightly chase is not over until the Moon-Ship sinks through the waves of the sea and sails into the harbor of Varin's Bay in the west of great Jormungrund—the primal plane of being that underlies Midgard and Asgard, where the oldest of the Holy Powers have their halls. There, the Moon-Ship and the Wains of Sol and the Goddess Night and her son Day all have their landing in the safe harbor warded by the brave Varangians and their chieftain Billing. There, the powers of the sky can take their rest.

"Valkyrie," by Peter Nikolai Arbo.

A Tale of Nanna and her Kin

Nanna's heart fills with love for her father and the care he has always given her, and her heart leads her to ride as a guard for him and his holy ship in their struggles across the sky. Thus she takes the place foreseen by her parents when they named her Sinhtgunt: "she who battles her way night after night." With the great bow that is her favorite weapon, she takes upon herself the facing-backwards that her steersman-father dares not do, and rides her black steed behind the stern of the silver Moon-Ship. Struggling through the ship's wake and the pulsing billows of the etheric sky, she plies her bow and slows Hati's pursuit, though she cannot stop it. Nanna's stallion, with the same courage as his mistress, plants his heavy hooves and trumpets a challenge to Hati the Wolf each time Nanna turns to loose her arrows at him. Nanna's swift arrows fly toward Hati, then drop as falling-stars through the airs above sleeping Midgard.

Threatened by the fierce defense offered by Nanna and her steed, Hati is forced to run further behind the Moon-Ship than before. As time passes Nanna's faithful love is rewarded by the easing of the grim lines on her father's face. Sometimes she is able to leave her stallion to run behind the ship, while she sits with her father on the ship's bench and shares with him the tales and songs of their folk. Sometimes, there, Mani and Nanna are joined by Mani's foster-son Hoðr, who shares their tales and merriment. But all the while, the seeds of love for Nanna grow in Hoðr's heart, although she sees them not.

Not all Nanna's time need be spent warding the Moon-Ship, since the Moon is not always in the sky. She often has the chance to enjoy herself sparring and riding with the troops of Valkyries. Thus it comes about that she and her sisters-in-arms are riding around the rim of Asgard one morning on patrol. And there Nanna sees a young God, gleaming white and gold, who sits upon a green mound with his hands clasped around his knees watching them go by. Nanna pulls her horse to a stop, letting her companions pass by, her gaze drawn to the God as his is to her. She knows who he is, but they have never spoken face to face. "Balder," she utters—just that one word—and pauses, as the shuttle of Wyrd's loom echoes in the distance.

Balder

When Nanna speaks, Balder feels that for the first time he truly knows his name and who he is, deep within his heart and soul. In the eyes of each, Nanna and Balder, are reflected love and goodness and courage, and the shining light of the fields of Heaven. As Nanna is a Moon-Dis, sharing in the powers of the Moon, so is Balder a Sun-God.

"The Sun God," cast iron fire-back.

Within himself he distills and concentrates the essence of Sol's *hamingja*, as though he is a magnifying glass collecting the rays of the Sun and reflecting those rays out into Asgard and Midgard and all the holy Worlds. Warrior and judge he is, noble and brave and great-hearted, the greatest in goodness of all the holy Gods. At that moment of awakening, like calls to like: Moon-Dis to Sun-God, courage to courage, love to love.

"You've spoken my name, maiden, and made me know it for the first time in fullest truth," Balder tells Nanna that morning, standing face to face on the green mound of Heaven. "I say that you are my name-giver, and ask you: what gift will you give me for it?"

Nanna smiles and turns her head aside for a moment in thought. "Over on Solfell, the cliffs of the Sun, lie many swords. One of them is the best of all, inlaid with gold. A ring is on its hilt, strength of mind in the middle, terror on its tip, for the one who seeks to own it. On its boss is a serpent that chases its tail."

"And is that all, maiden—fine gift though that is? Have you more to give me?"

He smiles at her and she smiles back in mischief.

"A horse you will find there, too, Balder—a horse of might and magic. When you choose it so, the stamping of your horse's hoof will bring forth a spring from the earth, a gift to those whom you love and ward. In Midgard will be many springs and wells that are named for you, and whole tribes of men as well. Is that enough for you?"

"You know it is not enough! For now I will take your gifts gladly, maiden, but the day will come when I will seek more from you."

"That, we shall see!" she says, smiling over her shoulder as her stallion canters away.

A Tale of Nanna and her Kin

Hatafjord

Balder finds Nanna's gifts and makes good use of them in the battles he fights of light against darkness. There comes a time when he and his troops sail to Hatafjord, led by Balder's great ship Hringhorn, to battle with giants and evildoing men. On the rim of the fjord's cliff Balder sees the giant-wolf Hati, chieftain of Hatafjord and foe of the Moon-God, standing in his giant-form to lead the battle. There Balder strikes Hati with his spear of light, sorely injuring him.

Overcome with rage, Hati's wife and his daughter Hrimgerd, strong with the powers of the ocean's fury, seek to wreck Balder's ships with wave and storm. All night the ships are tossed high on the waves and fall smashing down into the wave-troughs while water washes over their decks to gulp down the sailors. Hidden shoals and rocks threaten them, and Hati's wife lays herself down as a barrier in the sea for the ships to run aground. But to the amazement of all, the ships survive this attack, and the morning light brings calm. Standing on the promontory where her father was struck down, Hrimgerd the giantess taunts Balder's exhausted men, and demands wergild of Balder for her father's injury. The wergild she wants is a night with Balder, to beget his child, but he refuses.

Stung, Hrimgerd accuses Balder: "I know you'd rather have her—the one who watched over you in the harbor last night. That sea-golden girl surpassed me in strength when she landed here from her father's ship. She alone is stopping me from destroying the Prince's men."

Balder's lieutenant calls out to her: "Hrimgerd, answer the Prince now: was it just one girl who protected the lord's fleet, or many traveling together?"

Hrimgerd answers, "Three times nine maidens were there, but one rode in front of them, the shining girl in her helmet. The horses tossed their heads and frothing dew fell from their manes onto the valleys; onto the mountain forests fell fine grains of hail. They bring good luck to mankind, but to me they are hateful."

Wedding

Balder's heart lifts high when he hears these words, and he knows the time has come to seek what he wants from Nanna. He goes with bridal gifts for her, for Mani and Sol and all of Nanna's kin. And so the strands of wyrd that each were born with are wrapped around each other, no longer separate, but intertwined until the world's end and beyond. As Sun and Moon come together in Nanna's parents Sol and Mani, so again they meet and love in the persons of Balder Sun-God and Nanna Moon-Dis.

Arthur Rackham.

Thus they are wed, and never are there two who love each other more than they. Together they fight the battles of the light, and together dwell in bliss in their castle Breidablik in Asgard, offering hospitality to all who come. Balder's parents

Odin and Frigg take delight in their son's dear wife and the gifts of hamingja, wisdom and faithful love that she brings him. Nanna's parents and sister give their blessing to Balder, knowing his kinship with them as a God of light. The kinfolk all grow in friendship, and special friendship there is between Nanna, her mother-in-law Frigg, and Frigg's sister Fulla. Even Hoðr, Balder's half-brother and Nanna's foster-brother, does his best to wish them well, though his heart hurts within him. He loves them both, and there is no cure for his pain except his own courage and endurance.

Among the many pleasures of Balder and Nanna are the expeditions they take with their kinsfolk, riding through the beautiful fields and wolds of Asgard and Jormungrund, and visiting humankind in Midgard. Often they ride together: Balder and Nanna with Sunna her sister, Frigg and her sister Fulla, and Odin their patriarch. And on these trips it comes to pass as Nanna foretold to Balder: Balder's magical horse stamps his hoof, and a life-giving spring appears as Balder's gift to humankind. Because of this, many springs and wells in all the Germanic lands are named for him, often in Balder's name-variant of Phol or Fal. On one such occasion, Balder's horse wrenches his foreleg. But the galdor-magics of Odin and the four Goddesses quickly heal the injury and leave the horse's wonderful powers intact.

Forseti

Balder is a judge—the most right-minded and merciful of all, and many beings from the different worlds seek him for his wisdom. But in his very perfection lies his greatest failing. Most beings are imperfect, a mixture of light and dark. The bright light of Balder's wisdom and justice is too strong for their eyes, too strong to find a place in their lives. The very perfection of his wisdom and judgements make them impossible to implement in the rough and tumble of life in the complex worlds of Earth. Thus it is: the perfect judgements of Balder fail through their very perfection, until the fine son of Balder and Nanna grows into his own strength and wisdom.

In Forseti his father's piercing brightness is tempered and blended with strands closer to the earthly lives which reach out to touch the Gods. Where Balder's justice is too high for mortals to reach, Forseti's skill in touching mankind at their own level allows his well-tempered wisdom to take root in their hearts. It is said that no one leaves the presence of Forseti Lawgiver, son of Nanna and Balder, without a fair and workable resolution of the issues that brought them there.

Balder's Dreams

Thus life continues among them, until the time comes for another strand—spun by Wyrd long ago—to make its appearance in the pattern. Among all the Worlds—Asgard and Vanaheim, Midgard, Jotunheim, and all the other worlds—the wind begins to blow more chill than once it did in the morning of time. Something strange is mixed in the air, and a tremble of change is felt. Balder dreams uneasily. Dvalin and Dain the ancient Dwarf-fathers dream dark dreams as well, and unrest is felt among the all the Holy Ones. Odin and Frigg seek the secret paths of wisdom, and along with Wyrd they weave hidden strands—bitter and sweet— out of the very fibers of their hearts.

All beings, fearing an inchoate threat to Balder, swear holy oaths to Balder's mother Frigg, that never will they bring him harm. All beings, that is, except for one: the soft-stalked mistletoe, that grows high in the boughs of the mighty oak. Its voice is so small and soft and secret that it is never heard nor missed among the mighty choruses of love being sung for Balder.

One being, only, among them all hears the voice that isn't there, and tracks it down. One being, Loki, plucks a twig of mistletoe and takes it to the mightiest of the ancient smiths. The smith once was a friend of the Gods and worked with them to make many beauties of the Worlds. But great offense has come between them and now he nourishes hatred in his heart. His names are known, and his story is known, but they come in another tale too long to tell here. Suffice it to say that in malice is the soft sprig of mistletoe plucked, and with malice and mighty magics it is wrought into a razor-sharp dart, thirsting for holy blood. With mightier magics yet, it keeps—for all its sharpness—the outer seeming of a simple twig of mistletoe. Loki hides this magic arrow next to his heart, cherishing it and waiting for his chance.

Odainsakr

Meanwhile, in the golden heart of Jormungrund the Primal World, under the central root of the Great Tree in Mimir's holy realm and guarded by Delling, the bright Elf of the Dawn, stands in hidden peace *Odainsakr*—the Field of the Undying. Once three loving Gods shaped Ask and Embla from two trees, and Ask and Embla in turn gave birth to men and women. From among these first men and women in the Age of Gold, during the morning of the world, the Holy Powers chose out Lif and Lifthrasir, and other men and women of untarnished fame and goodness of heart. These people the Powers named the *Asmegir*—the descendants of the Æsir—and they gave them the realm of Odainsakr, to live there protected from all ill and harm until the end of this cycle of the Worlds.

After Ragnarök, Lif and Lifthrasir, the other holy men and women and their children, will people the new Earth that rises, cleansed of ill, out of the girdling sea. But until the time we speak of now—the time when the chill wind of change is felt in the other Worlds—the Asmegir have been alone, without the company of any Holy Ones. Though the most pious of all humans, they have had no one on whom to lavish their love of holiness. Now, with this wind of change that blows chill in the other worlds, blows a warm little wind of change into hidden Odainsakr. A messenger comes to the Asmegir, telling them to prepare for their greatest joy which is soon to come. And so they do, these wise Asmegir, and their hearts beat high with happiness while those in other worlds sink with dread.

Hoðr's Blindness

There comes an evening then, among the blowing winds of change in the world of the Gods, when Balder's half-brother Hoðr walks through the circling woods on his way to a Yuletide feast and sumble. In the twilit woods he comes across a shadowy troll-wife, riding on a great wolf with serpents as her reins.

"Come with me," she calls to Hoðr, "and be my lover. You will never know such love as mine."

But Hoðr is repelled and rejects her invitation.

"So be it, then," says the troll-wife. "You'll pay for it, when the time comes to make your boast in sumble." Cackling, she rides away in the darkness on her wolf-steed.

Hoðr dismisses the incident from his mind and continues on to the feast with his comrades. Afterwards, the holy boar of sacrifice is led around the hall, while each take their turn to lay a hand on it and drink their sumble-pledges. When Hoðr's turn comes and he lays his hand on the boar, a strange blindness of thought comes over him. Gone is the shield of loyalty and courage with which he protects himself and his kin against his forbidden love for his brother's wife Nanna. Blindly, Hoðr touches the great boar and raises his horn in sumble-pledge. Blindly then he speaks, absent his will and his sense, and his boast is this: that he will wed Nanna, his brother's wife. Thus are the words spoken in holy sumble, on the oath-boar, and cannot be unsaid.

The cursed blindness lifts from Hoðr then, and he is sick at heart. In bitter repentance, he journeys far to find his brother Balder and warn him of what he has done. Balder gives Hoðr warm welcome when he arrives.

"Welcome, Hoðr! What news do you bring? Why, my brother, have you left your lands and come alone to meet me here?"

And Hoðr answers him in bitterness of heart: "A terrible crime has come upon me. I have chosen that bride of yours with the sumble-horn."

"Do not reproach yourself!" his brother replies. "For both of us, Hoðr, what's said in sumble must come true. Evil dreams have spoken to me and to the Dwarf-fathers; I know not what fate awaits me. Your boast may turn out to be for the best, after all, when hidden wyrd becomes known."

"You're saying, Balder, that I deserve goodwill from you? It would be more fitting for you to bloody your sword on me, than to grant frith to me, your enemy."

A Tale of Nanna and her Kin

But Balder tries to comfort his repentant brother, telling him that he suspects the troll-wife who cursed Hoðr to be Balder's own fylgja, warning of his death. Such is Balder's shining courage and his acceptance of his unknown wyrd, that his brother is comforted for a time, and drawn to join Balder and the other Æsir at their feasting and games.

Mistletoe

Most of the Æsir there are in great spirits. Having obtained—they think—the promise of all things not to harm Balder, their fears are gone and their hearts are high. Laughing, they launch missile after missile at Balder, and joyously they applaud when each missile brings him no harm. But Hoðr, his dread returning, sits in a dark corner and closes his eyes. His heart trembles within him. He starts when he hears a soft voice in his ear, greeting him with friendly words, and when he opens his eyes it seems to him that darkness still remains before him.

"Who is that speaking to me?" he calls, startled.

"It is only I—Loki. I noticed you were not joining in the fun here and am sorry to see it. You seem to be in low spirits. Come, cheer up and join in with us!"

"No…..no," answers Hoðr, shaking his head. "I have no heart for such games; I wish they would leave off playing."

"Come now, Hoðr–that's no way to behave at the feast of the Æsir. That's no princely mood you have, but the quivering of a thrall. Come–there's no harm in it–join the fun!"

"No, I have no wish to do that, and anyway I brought no weapon with me. I have nothing to throw, and don't want to throw anything. And it seems very dark in here to me, very dim—why is it so ill-lit?" The shadows growing in Hoðr's heart seem to veil his eyes ever deeper in darkness.

"Death of Baldr," by George Wright.

"Look," says Loki in friendly chiding. "I have here this little twig of mistletoe. What harm could such a thing possibly do? Come on—take it and give it a toss at Balder. You can't be the only one here not having fun, sitting off in a corner and grumping. What will everyone think of you?"

Loki continues his skillful persuasion until Hoðr rises uncertainly and turns toward Balder.

"It still seems awfully dark in here to me," he says to Loki. "I can hardly see to aim, anyway. This whole thing is foolish." And he goes to sit down again.

"No, no!" Loki encourages him. "Really, it isn't dark–there's plenty of light to aim. Here, I'll help you–I'll just stand behind you and guide your hand in the right direction. We can't have it said that Hoðr the Warrior, alone of all the Æsir, has no heart for games of weaponry!" And he laughs loudly.

With ill-grace, Hoðr lets Loki help him toss the mistletoe. The little twig strikes Balder straight on, and everything in all the Worlds comes to a momentary halt as Balder, bleeding from the heart, sinks down to the floor in the throes of death. And with him sinks Hoðr's heart as well, so deep in dread and grief it seems he cannot breathe. All his blindness is gone now, and he sees only too well the red flow of blood from Balder's heart, and beautiful Nanna fallen weeping across his bloody chest.

"Be you hale and whole," says her husband tenderly. "Strengthen your heart, my love. This will be our last meeting in this world. I beg you, bride—do not weep! Listen to what I say. Share your bed with my brother Hoðr, who has always loved you, and live in love with the young prince."

But Nanna answers him, "I said in my dear homeland, when Balder chose me and gave me rings, that I would never, if my lord died, fold a prince of no fame in my arms."

With his last breath, noble Balder tries to soothe his wife and persuade her to take comfort in his brother's love after his death, but she will have none of his persuasion.

A Tale of Nanna and her Kin

Baldr's Death, by Lorenz Frølich.

As she rises from Balder's body, her gaze catches the eyes of Frigg and Odin, staring down darkly at the body of their son. But hidden behind the darkness is a strange spark of light, shining through their tears and grief, that Nanna does not understand. Then Odin and Frigg both look at her, look at her very strangely, and for the second time in her life Nanna hears the shuttle of Wyrd's loom weaving.

Balefire

A shadow of darkness sweeps over her then and she leaves that place, never to enter it again. She bridles and saddles her black steed, arms herself as a Valkyrie, and rides into the night sky crying wildly and strangely upon the wind. None can catch her, not even Hoðr who rides after as though he would break his heart to reach her.

Nanna's wode-ride.

Several days she is gone, and neither knows nor cares what is done in Asgard then. It is only when she sees and smells the beginnings of the smoke from Balder's balefire that she returns. There she sees Balder laid out in splendor on his great ship Hringhorn, surrounded by gifts, launched onto the sunset sea. Nanna rides her black horse onto the flaming ship, dismounts, and lies beside her husband, joining him in death as the balefire wraps them round.

A Tale of Nanna and her Kin

Balder's ship Hringhorn becomes his funeral pyre.

The Hidden Halls of Peace

Nanna awakens to a sweet scent of flowers, and a gentle wind blowing around her. There beside her lies Balder; his eyes are open and he is smiling at her with all the love in his heart. Balder takes her hand and pulls her up, looking around them as they rise. And there at a slight distance, full of joy yet not wishing to intrude, they see the shining faces of the Asmegir and the flowering fields and halls of Odainsakr, all bedecked in brightest welcome for the two of them. At last the Asmegir have a God and Goddess among them, to share with them the holy love and wonder that can grow between Gods and their folk when their hearts and souls are open to one another.

A Tale of Nanna and her Kin

Nanna and Balder are settled in high contentment, feasting with their folk the Asmegir, when a messenger comes to call on them. Almost unheard-of is it, that anyone who does not belong in Odainsakr is allowed to enter the brightness that lies behind its high, protective walls. All taint of strife, evil, illness and decay must be kept out of that holy place so it may be safe and whole when its time comes to be the life-source of the new worlds.

But for this once, Hermod the messenger of Asgard is allowed to speak briefly with the holy couple. He has come, he says, to see how they fare in their new life, and bring comfort back to their kin in Asgard. Nanna and Balder assure Hermod that all is well and more than well with them, and Hermod can easily see that for himself. Before he leaves, Nanna gives him beautiful gifts to take back with him, made by the skilled Asmegir. Lovely, fine-woven linens she sends to Frigg her mother-in-law, understanding now the mingled darkness and brightness that she saw in Frigg's eyes as Frigg faced the wyrded death of her son, knowing what would come after that for him. And Nanna sends beautiful golden rings to her friend Fulla, Frigg's sister.

Balder gives Hermod the magical arm-ring Draupnir to return to his father Odin, who had laid it on Balder's bale-fire. "Tell my father," says Balder, "that I thank him with all my heart for his gift of Draupnir and the generous funeral-gifts he gave me. But he must know, now, that such a ring as this does not belong in Odainsakr, and must be returned to the other worlds to follow what is wyrded for it there."

Hermod takes the gifts and good wishes of Balder and Nanna, and with a longing, lingering glance behind him, departs from Odainsakr, never to return. But he is not the last one from Asgard that they see. Not very long afterwards, another one comes to join them in that place of the undying, to live and love and thrive until the new world comes. Höðr, Balder's beloved brother and his slayer, Nanna's foster-brother and would-be lover, joins them after he is slain in vengeance by Vali. The love that ties the three of them together is there freed from its pain and trouble, and lives on to give them all joy and contentment.

Thus they wait through the long, slow, peaceful days, while outside the walls of Odainsakr the World-Mill turns time and tides through the ages of men and Gods, and the winds of the world shift and change, whispering of Ragnarök.

~~~~~

A Commentary on Sources

A thorough discussion of sources and interpretations for the mythological tale told above would require a full-length essay. There is so much contradiction, so many seemingly disconnected bits and pieces, missing links, and confusing or apparently 'makes no sense' material associated with the primary sources for the myth of Nanna and her kin, and then on top of that, so many modern interpretations of the lore to choose from, that the subject of sources and interpretations is not a simple one. In addition, there is the issue of criteria: what is the 'vision of mythological truth' against which one tests, and rejects or accepts, various accounts and interpretations of the myth? I certainly have such a 'vision' myself, which shaped my retelling of the myth, though it can and has been shaped in many different ways.

Here is a list of the primary sources and interpretations that I have used.

A Tale of Nanna and her Kin

1. The source I have relied most heavily on is Viktor Rydberg's volumes of *Teutonic Mythology: Gods and Goddesses of the Northland*. I have found Rydberg's interpretations of the following mythological aspects to be convincing enough to work well as a tale:

- the identity of Sinhtgunt (a Goddess mentioned in the 10th-century German Second Merseberg Charm) with Nanna, and all the material about Nanna's father being the Moon-God in different forms;

- the information about Odainsakr and the Asmegir, and the residence of Balder, Nanna and Hoðr there;

- the World-Mill and Mundilfari its keeper;

- information about Jormungrund, the primal world, which incorporates Hel, Vanaheim, Alfheim, Jotunheim, Niflheim, Odainsakr, the three roots of the Tree and the Wells they stand over, and many realms and halls of the ancient Powers of the Worlds.

(Rydberg is often criticized by other scholars for what are considered his labored efforts to tie all the elements of Norse myth into one interconnected whole. I won't get into that argument. But from the standpoint of a storyteller, I find some of his insights intriguing and inspiring. They lead in fascinating new directions for pursuing a vigorous Heathen tale-telling tradition, which is, after all, what all of our lore is based upon: tales, folktales, sagas, fairy tales, and more. Scholarship is informative, but tales are inspiring, and it is for this reason that I most appreciate Rydberg's ideas.)

2. *The Second Merseburger Charm:*

>   Phol and Wodan fared to the wood,
>   Then was Balder's foal's leg wrenched.

> Then galdored Sinhtgunt and Sunna her sister,
> Then galdored Friia and Volla her sister,
> Then galdored Wodan, as well he could,
> Be it bone-wrench, be it blood-wrench, be it limb-wrench:
> Bone to bone, blood to blood,
> Limb to limb, as if they were glued.
> (Barber, p. 65.)

When we look at this, an Old High German charm written down during the 10th century C.E., we see a set of Deities listed: Phol (likely a German version of Balder), Balder, Wodan, Sinhtgunt, Sunna, Friia and Volla. All but one of these Deities are known in Norse lore, named there as Balder, Odin, Sunna, Frigg, and Fulla. The unknown one is Sinhtgunt, but if we accept Rydberg's suggestion that she is Nanna under another name, then what we see pictured in this charm is a delightful family outing in the woods. Balder rides with his father Odin and his mother Frigg, his wife Nanna / Sinhtgunt, his sister-in-law Sunna, and his aunt Fulla. When his horse is injured, the whole family pitches in to help.

3. I agree with Rydberg that the "Lay of Helgi Hjörvardson" in the *Poetic Edda* seems to incorporate some very significant, and otherwise missing, pieces of Balder's and Nanna's myth. Not that Helgi is necessarily intended to be Balder in every aspect—there are clearly aspects of Helgi's tale that do not mesh with the Balder myth—but it does appear that the poet who composed this poem attached pieces of the Balder myth to it. In fact, some parts of this poem which make the least sense in the context of Helgi's tale (which is considered by modern scholars to be a confusing jumble of fragments hard

to weave together), make the most sense in the context of Nanna's and Balder's tale.

Many of the dialogues I've used in my telling of the myth were adapted from this poem, with Helgi (whose name means Holy One) being identified with Balder, the Valkyrie Svava with Nanna, prince Hedin with Hoðr, and other characters by name in the poem, who also seem for various reasons to belong to the myth and bear the same names in the myth. The latter include the giant Hati and his kin, and Svava / Nanna's father Eylimi.

In particular, I think the poem provides some very interesting motivations for people's actions in the Balder / Nanna myth, that otherwise, in other tellings of the myth, do not make a lot of sense; and the poem also fleshes out some of the myth's characters and events very nicely, in ways not found elsewhere.

4. Other sources I have used include Snorri Sturlason's prose *Edda,* Saxo Grammaticus' *History of the Danes,* and Jacob Grimm's *Teutonic Mythology.* From a subjective viewpoint, I have used much thought, meditation and prayer, to try to attune my telling of the tale to the desires and the essential realities of the Holy Ones who are represented in the tale, to the best of my ability.

A final note: Although it is perhaps a bit awkward stylistically, I have deliberately used the present tense in my telling of the tale, rather than the usual convention of using the past tense. I try, in this way, to capture the mythological essence of timelessness—the sense that each stage of the myth, while it follows a certain time-structured sequence, nevertheless endures in a timeless, ever-present reality which

A Tale of Nanna and her Kin

we can touch with our understanding, and celebrate in our religious ceremonies and devotions.

10: Syn: The 'Just Say No' Goddess

The face of this sculpture holds an expression of determination that I associate with Syn. Her medieval veil symbolizes her self-possession and her denial of intrusion into her personal space.

Here is what we are told about the Goddess Syn, who is listed among the companions of Frigg. *"Syn: she guards the doors of the hall and shuts them against those who are not to enter,*

Syn: The 'Just Say No' Goddess

and she is appointed as a defence at assemblies (Things) against matters that she wishes to refute. Thus there is a saying that a denial (syn) is made when one says no." (*Gylfaginning 35* in the prose *Edda*, Sturlason p. 30.)

This makes her the Goddess of defense attorneys and public defenders, among other things. It also makes her a Goddess to call upon when our identity has been stolen, or false accusations or rumors are circulating about us: her power of denial is what we need here.

I call Syn the 'Just Say No!' Goddess, who ensures that we keep our healthy personal boundaries strong, knowing when and to whom and to what we must "say no" in order to preserve our integrity, dignity—and our relationships. She 'closes and wards the door' whenever this is necessary for our safety, privacy, and peace of mind.

Simek assumes that Syn guards the doors of Frigg's hall Fensalir, specifically (p. 309), but we can regard her as a door-warden in general, a vitally important role these days. Syn defends against invasion of privacy and personal rights, whether this is done in person, over the internet or telephone, or any of the many other ways our privacy is invaded. The constant bombardment we all suffer from—advertising, influencers, politicians, the lot—creates disorder in our thoughts, our emotions, our homes, our families and relationships, in our country and in the world. We need divine help just to shut the door from time to time, to have a peaceful space to nurture ourselves and our relationships.

Following on this, Syn is a very helpful Goddess when we practice meditation, helping us to close the door on extraneous thoughts and scattered emotions, to reach the still space where her companion Vør holds sway, the Goddess of

Awareness. I see Syn as a patron, or matron, of our Hugr-soul, our Fylgja, our Vørðr, and other spirit-beings who ward our inner self from dangers of the physical, social, and metaphysical worlds and beings.

Syn is an important Goddess for the modern world, and I'd like to see her power grow. The more we call upon her and work with her, and the more involved she becomes in Midgard today, the greater her power will grow to help us create safe and sacred spaces for all our needs in Midgard.

*Syn wards the doors for us
and keeps our innermost spaces inviolate,
if we so wish.*

Syn: The 'Just Say No' Goddess

Here is a prayer to call upon Syn. You can change the plurals of 'us, we, our' to 'me, I, my' if you like. But it does no harm to pray on behalf of others as well as yourself when you speak this prayer.

A Prayer to Syn

Syn, grant us wisdom
To know what should be denied,
To discern what should not enter
Into our cherished spaces of heart and home.

Syn, grant us courage
To stand against what is wrong,
To deny the easy paths of harm and waste,
And tread the ways that lead to hard-won blessings.

Syn, grant us grace
To understand our own deserving:
The spaces of our Being are sacred;
All that enters therein must be worthy,
Or remain outside the door.

11: Heimdall

*"Heimdall at the Bridge of Heaven,"
by Emil Doepler.*

Heimdall: Warder of the Atmosphere

There is one called Heimdall;…he is great and holy. … He lives in a place called Himinbjorg (Heaven-fortress) by Bifröst. He is the Gods' watchman and sits there at the edge of heaven to guard the bridge against mountain-giants. He needs less sleep than a bird. He can see, by night just as well as by day, a distance of a hundred leagues (around 300 miles). He can also hear grass growing on the earth and wool on sheep, and everything that sounds louder than that." (p. 25, Sturlason.)

Heimdall

Heimdall's hearing, by Emil Doepler.

Here I celebrate Heimdall as both the warder *of* the atmosphere, and the warder *in* the atmosphere. As Heimdall wards the bridge to Asgard, he also wards the boundary between the Earth and the Sky or the Atmosphere. If we envision some of the giants as embodiments of harmful influences, then Heimdall can be seen as the one who helps to prevent those harmful influences from impacting Earth's atmosphere. Pollutants of many kinds, particulates, and heat itself, travel from the Earth into the atmosphere. Humans are responsible for large parts of this, as are also natural processes that can be viewed as Jotnar and their actions.

Heimdall

Heimdall alone cannot prevent all of this from happening. He is a *watchman*, a warder. He cannot defend against hordes of giants, or pollutants, all by himself. What he does is raise the alarm: alerting the Gods, or alerting us, that danger approaches. Then, it is up to all of us, Gods and humans—and perhaps Jotnar too—to gather together and respond appropriately to the danger.

I suggest that Heimdall has expanded his already-amazing sensing capacities, as described in the *Edda* passage above, into a far greater range of action: all of our high-tech remote sensing capabilities! And in particular, all of the capabilities that warn of dangerous influences and conditions. For example: weather satellites, satellites that sense groundwater and surface water supplies, ocean temperatures, drought and stressors on forests and crops, pest invasions, extent of deforestation and wildfires, sea level rise, glacier retreats, and many other 'eyes in the sky'. And ground-based sensors, too, such as those that warn of stresses and movements within the earth, setting up conditions for earthquakes, tsunamis, and volcanic eruptions. These are Heimdall's 'ear or hearing in the Well.' There is even a new computer system in Europe, intended to help manage climate-related emergencies, that is named HEIMDALL.

As warder of the boundaries, Heimdall also deals with limitations—not only the boundaries between us and dangerous phenomena, but also the boundaries that limit our own disruptive and dangerous actions. Sometimes, humans can be more destructive than Jotnar! Humans don't take kindly to limitations, but they are necessary for balance: for ecological and natural balances, and also for balance within our complex and widespread social systems, and our individual behavior.

Heimdall

All of the remote-sensing capabilities I described are extensions of Heimdall's ability to 'see for a hundred leagues and hear the growth of grass and wool on the sheep.' Heimdall's warding of the boundaries and demarcation of border and 'no-go' zones are relevant to us as humans, as well as to Jotnar and the dwellers in Asgard.

But none of Heimdall's amazing abilities to discern and demarcate and warn of danger will do much good, unless we pay attention to these warnings and take appropriate action. As the Gods take counsel with each other, and with other beings, when faced with intimations of Ragnarök, so also should we humans take counsel with each other, with Deities and landwights, ancestors and other beings, and find the best path forward under the threatening conditions of climate change and other environmental impacts on our treasured Earth.

I suggest that Blots, prayers, calls, meditations and symbols dedicated to Heimdall can help us take the steps that are necessary here. We need clear sight—the ability to observe accurately, and clear thought, to develop an objective view of what is actually happening. We need wisdom, courage, determination, to develop, implement and support remedial measures and different ways of doing things, in response to the dangers. We need to adapt, where we cannot immediately remediate. We need to help one another around the world, recognizing that there are no boundaries to the harm that is happening, nor to the needs that are arising for humans and other beings as well.

Heimdall sounds the call, and all should answer: living humans and ancestral powers, Holy Ones, all the wights and powers of Nature and the Earth. Let us not be blind in the face of his penetrating Sight, nor be deaf to the bone-deep roaring of his mighty Gjallarhorn!

The Gifting of Heimdall: A Tale

This is a tale, my imagined 'prequel' to the Rigsthula, *a poem in the Poetic Edda. Rigsthula is an ancient poem that tells of Rig-Heimdall's travels and deeds in Midgard. My story begins with Heimdall's conception and ends where Rigsthula begins. Here, I weave together some of the many ideas that have been proposed over centuries about Heimdall's parentage. I thank the members of the Devotional Group which I briefly led, for the information and inspiration I've gained from them and that has fed into this story. Our group drew the conclusion that Heimdall actually finds human efforts to understand his mysterious parentage rather amusing, and has no intention of enlightening us about it! In addition to the entertainment value, we think Heimdall appreciates that his mysteries stimulate creative work in humans, like the story here and many others.*

Rolling waves, turning under, turning over, turning around. Foam and froth on the surface, deep, sinewy currents writhing underneath. Salt, stinging and invigorating: the sea-cold draft of life. Shards of light through the water: sun-dazzle, moonbeams, lightning flashes, *wuldor*-furls in multi-colors hanging in the northern skies, shimmers of eerie light from the depths, foxfire gleams in the tumbling waves. Rolling, churning, over and over.

Like butter in the churn, the churning waves roll up a tiny mote of being. Back and forth, back and forth it rolls. It gathers salt, the savor of life. It gathers sun-dazzle and moonbeam, lightning, sky-light, sea-light, dawn and dusk, all as refracted prismatic patterns in the water, and rolls those prisms of light into itself. It gathers flecks of amber, floating on the waves, and rolls those, too, into itself. This tiny being begins to shimmer with its own prismatic light.

Songs of power weave about the little one, sonorous echoes of wind and water. Whale-songs, seal-songs, seabird songs, songs of the sea-elves, echoing like distant horn-calls, calling souls into otherworldly matter. The infant being vibrates to the power of the eerie calls, the rushing waves, the whistling winds, the plangent chanting of the wave-maidens as they cradle it and roll it in the churning waters. Its inrushing souls bring many powers with them.

"Heimdal and his nine mothers" by W. G. Collingwood.

Day by day this being grows, and takes on the Hama, the ensouled shape, of an infant God. Brilliant with multi-colored light, he at last attains the perfection of form that is needed for birth into the Worlds. The time comes for him to leave

Heimdall

the watery womb of the nine wave-mothers who have churned and rolled him into being, and be born onto the land.

Each wave-mother in turn takes him in her arms to cradle and to kiss goodbye, then passes him on. Himinglæva kisses him, and Bloðughadda; Hefring and Kolga. Dufa kisses him; Uðr, Hronn, Bylgja and Bara give him salty kisses. One by one they roll him toward the misty shore, until the ninth wave lays him at last upon the sand. The daughters of Ægir turn away with echoing cries of farewell and plunge into the deep. The baby, alone upon the gritty shore, gasps in his first breath of air, filled with önd, and lets out a vigorous wail.

It's a strange place, this world where he has landed: shallow and flat, not rising far above the sea. Swathed in misty clouds, drifting thinly. Still, almost silent, except for a strange creaking sound in the distance, and heavy vibrations on the ground like giant footsteps. The creaking and the footsteps draw closer to the baby, louder in the damp air. Soon, a long, pole-shaped shadow appears through the mists: the handle of a gigantic mill—the World-Mill itself, being doggedly propelled by nine Giantesses. Their heavy stamping jiggles the baby, and he ceases his wailing momentarily, gazing around, but soon starts up again.

Heavy steps come closer, shaking the Earth. Gjalp and Greip stamp; Eistla and Eyrgjafa and Angeyja dig their toes into the sand and push. Ulfrun and Imðr and Atla chant in deep tones. Jarnsaxa perks up her ears and calls on the others to stop.

Hearing the wail, the Giantesses pause in consternation. A baby crying! Such a thing must be impossible! There was no way a baby could arrive on their shores, nor any way for them to produce a child themselves, while they were engaged in their years-long stint of steadily turning the World-Mill.

Heimdall

Peering through the mists toward the sound, they discern a brightness through the mists. There—that is where the sound is coming from.

The World-Mill must not cease its motion: the turning of the Earth and the Stars depend upon it. Jarnsaxa and Eyrgjafa leave their posts to find the babe, while the other giantesses continue turning the Mill.

Baby Heimdall with Jarnsaxa.

Heimdall

And there he is, shining white, with flickers of rainbow colors lighting the air around him. Wailing and alone and hungry, newborn to the Worlds. Jarnsaxa picks him up and cuddles him as they return to the others. The giant-women's eyes light up as the babe is passed to each of their embraces, walking along in rhythm with the World-Mill.

"Our child," they cry.
"A gift from the Sea!"
"He lights the world with his brightness! See him shimmer!"
"Our young tree, straight and strong; he will be known as our descendant, come from our roots."
"We name him Heimdall, world-shimmer, tree-pillar, bow of the heavens!"

Atla searches out precious herbs and seaweeds, and Ulfrun enchants them with her rune-galdors. Eistla brews them in the cauldron, and the giant-women each drink of this magical *alveig*. Soon, rich milk flows from their breasts to feed the babe.

Nourished on the bounty of his nine great mothers, young Heimdall quickly grows tall and strong. He cares for their flock of sheep, bounding along like a young ram himself, while his mothers push the World-Mill. He carves the horn of a big old ram, slaughtered for the pot, into a blowing horn, and maddens his foster-mothers by blowing it incessantly. His lungs and chest grow stronger with this exercise, and he develops a mighty voice.

But Heimdall is not always noisy. The strange, otherworldly island where they live is so still, surrounded by sea and air. Except for the giantesses, Heimdall, and their sheep, nothing else disturbs the silence there, nor treads the grasses that tremble in the wind. Heimdall likes to sit and listen to the silence: the growing of the grass, the distant creak of the Mill, whispers of the wind. He sends his hearing out across the Sea, farther and farther, as he grows year by year, and his senses become more powerful.

Young Heimdall wonders about his world.

A young man now, tall and strong and shining, he stands often on the misty shore, straining to hear more clearly the faint sounds he senses from across the Sea, borne upon the wind.

These are not sea-sounds; he knows those. Not island-sounds, nor wind-sounds, nor the sound of his foster-mothers at their mill-work. These are whispers, grunts of effort, groans of strain, faint laughter, calls and shouts, the lowing of strange beasts.

It begins to dawn on him: there are more worlds out there, more than this misty island and the World-Mill. Heimdall goes to his mothers, questioning his own understanding of the world around him. Jarnsaxa answers him.

"My son, you are right. There are other worlds out there, worlds that we came from, worlds where Æsir and Vanir, Alfar and Dwarves live. Worlds of Jotnar and Humans and other beings. Soon our turn at the World-Mill will end. We will return to Jotunheim, and other giantesses will come to take our place. All of us must leave here, and your worlds, my son, are not the same as our world. You must go elsewhere."

Imðr tells him: "We are your roots. But you are the Tree, growing tall above the ground, growing into Worlds we do not know."

Eyrgjafa says, "You must build yourself a boat of driftwood, and entrust yourself to the Sea from which you came, my son. Soon the time will come for us to part."

Heimdall gathers driftwood, borrows Jarnsaxa's great iron knife, and carves the logs to fit snugly together. He carves wooden pegs to fasten them and caulks the seams with gum boiled from fish scales and bones, and the roots of herbs. He knows nothing of sails and oars, and his boat possesses neither.

The time comes for the parting of the ways. Torn between his reluctance to part from his foster-mothers, and his curiosity about all the strange sounds he can hear from the distant horizons, he stands uncertainly on the shore, looking

Heimdall

from one side to the other. His foster-mothers step forward one by one, embracing him and giving their blessings.

Heimdall finally turns away from them, toward his tiny boat bobbing in the gentle waves. He pushes off from the shore, then steps into the boat and kneels down, looking ahead over the horizon.

As the flat island of the World-Mill drifts out of sight behind him, he hears a gentle singing and splashing around the boat. Faces and floating hair appear in the water, white hands reach up to the rim of the boat. Fascinated, Heimdall watches as the boat is surrounded by the wave maidens singing to him.

"We are your mothers!" they sing. "Remember us, remember our song. Remember the cold, vital, surging sea from which you were born!"

And Heimdall does. He is overwhelmed with a surge of memory, memory of the restless sea, the soft foam, the echoing calls of sea-beasts, the gentle embraces of his wave-mothers. Overcome, he lies back in his little boat, gazing at the sky, and drifts into a long sleep, as the wave-maidens guide his boat on its journey across the sea.

Heimdall dreams. He dreams of a great Tree, with a Wellspring at its roots, and strangely shaped fruits hanging from its boughs. Heimdall climbs that Tree to gather the fruits, but when he reaches the first fruit, he sees it is not a fruit, but rather an angular shape surrounded by a round, empty space. He puts his face to the space and feels a cool moisture, as though he is peering through a waterfall. As the moisture spreads around his head, his mind is overwhelmed with meaning—the meaning of that angular shape hanging in empty space, and the cosmic powers that it bears. The meaning condenses into a seed, embedded in his Hugr, and he knows it is a rune, a whisper of mystery.

During his long sleep as his wave-mothers push his boat across the sea, Heimdall harvests all the rune-fruits and turns them into seeds of wisdom stored in his Hugr, ready to sprout at his wish and his need.

After a timeless time, the little boat crunches up onto a pebbly beach. Alerted by the unusual noise, Heimdall awakens. Splashing waves and eerie song draw his attention to the sea and his wave-mothers, who are bidding him farewell. He stands at the rim of the water, his arms held out toward them, and gives them his thanks and farewell.

As Heimdall turns away from the sea and begins walking inland, he notices that he has grown taller and stronger; he is a full-grown, full-bearded man now. How long had he been sleeping in the boat, as it crossed the unknown seas that separate the worlds?

He feels like a new being, a man, a God, full of gifts and knowledge unknown to him until now. Dreams and songs have nurtured his growth while he slept. Seeds have been implanted in him and are growing rapidly in the air of this new world, ready to be shared with others. He needs another name to celebrate this change.

Heimdall shakes his head and keeps on walking as he muses on this. After a timeless time, he comes upon a farmstead where he sees a few animals, and small muddy fields of crops and vegetables. Heimdall walks up to the turf-covered hut, knocks on the doorpost, and glances inside where he sees a middle-aged man and woman seated by a fire in the center of the hut. They look up at him, and call out "Welcome, traveler! Please come in and tell us your name."

"Call me Rig," he says, and steps over the threshold.

Heimdall

…..If you want to know what happens next, open your copy of the Poetic Edda and read the Rigsthula, the Tale of Rig.

Rig-Heimdall is given hospitality in the cottage of Ai and Edda, and responds with his blessings. By W.G. Collingwood.

The song on the next page can be sung to the tune: "The Angel Gabriel from Heaven Came" (Basque carol).

Heimdall

Heimdall's Call: A Song

Great Warder of the Bridge, he stands foursquare,
The Ase with icy eyes and gleaming hair.
Sounds of life he senses with hidden ear,
    For Gjallarhorn is calling:
    Heed ever the soul-deep song!

The son of nine great mothers, Heimdall wise,
He fathered sons of Man in hidden guise.
He lights the path of wisdom into our ways,
    For Gjallarhorn is calling:
    Heed ever the soul-deep song!

Bright Heimdall bars the bridge against all ill;
No force in all nine worlds can bend his will.
Our breast with steadfast strength he always fills,
    For Gjallarhorn is calling:
    Heed ever the soul-deep song!

Rig's main calls to our mind and to our Mod,
His song awakens heavy heart and mood!
His rainbow glows against the darkest cloud,
    For Gjallarhorn is calling:
    Heed ever the soul-deep song!

Hail Freya's champion and Loki's bane,
Bring gift to offer at his holy fane,
That Heimdall's might may wax and never wane,
    For Gjallarhorn is calling:
    Heed ever the soul-deep song!

At the coming of Ragnarøk, a golden-combed rooster named Gullinkambi will crow to call the Einherjar from Valhalla. Here we can see Gullinkambi joining Heimdall in his efforts to alert the Worlds.

12: Earth-Mother, Nerthus

"Nerthus," by Emil Doepler, showing the annual procession of the Earth-Goddess Nerthus's image around the countryside, as described in the Roman author Tacitus' book, Germania, *written during the 1st century CE.*

Earth Blessing: A Prayer

Here is a modernized and Heathenized blessing-invocation to the Earth-Mother that I adapted from the Old English Æcerbot, suitable for Spring seasonal ceremonies such as Ostara / Eastre, Earth Day, Wonnezeit, Mayday, etc.

Earth-Mother

Earth Blessing

Eastward we stand, asking for the grace of life!
We ask the famed lords,
We ask the mighty rulers,
We ask holy heaven-realm's warders,
Earth we ask, and high heaven,
And heaven's might and high halls,
That we may, with this prayer, by the gifts of the Gods,
Fill the Earth with strength through our firm faith,
And beautify her green meadows,
That all may have weal in Earth's realm.

Erce, Erce, Erce, Earthen Mother,
Give forth life that is waxing and thriving,
Increasing and full of strength:
Trees and plants, beasts and birds,
And all beings of Earth and Waters.
Grant, ye Holy Ones of heaven and earth,
That Earth's life be warded against all foes,
And defended against every ill
Sown by bale-workers throughout the land.

Be thou hale, Earth, Mother of all!
Be thou growing in holy embrace,
Filled with food for the use of all,
Full acres of food for every living thing.
Brightly blooming: be thou blessed!

Earth-Mother

Notes on the Earth Blessing

Word-notes: *weal* means 'well-being'; *bale-workers* (baleful ones) are those who work harm and destruction; *hale* means healthy and whole.

Historical note: The magico-religious charm called the *Æcerbot* or 'acre-remedy', along with extensive instructions for the accompanying day-long rituals, has been preserved since Anglo-Saxon times in a Christianized form. The roots of both the words and the ritual are clearly Heathen, however, and the focus of it is more 'magical' than 'religious', especially when all the ritual actions are considered.

The intent of the original ritual was to heal agricultural land that was not bearing well, perhaps due to the curses of sorcerers and witches. In my much-shortened version of the invocation here, I've turned the focus to modern 'bale-workers', praying to protect the land from pollution and destruction. The original focused on growing crops for human consumption; here I interpolate a few words to include non-human children of the Earth as well as human. I like to use this version as a prayer to honor Earth Day.

Earth-Mother

Erce, Eorðan Modor

Eorðan Modor: Earthen Mother.
("Earth Goddess" garden sculpture installation.)

"Erce Earthen Mother": 'Erce' is a mysterious being, the focus of much scholarly discussion. This is further confused because all translators I've seen translate Anglo-Saxon *eorðan modor* as 'mother of Earth'. Does Earth have a mother? Who is she? I translate *eorðan modor* completely literally as 'earthen Mother, mother made of earth,' in the same sense as 'an earthen berm or an earthen pot'. Hence, Erce is the Earth Mother, which simplifies things considerably. The name, or invocation, of Erce could stem from a number of sources; there is much scholarly discussion but no firm conclusions. I'll add a bit to the discussion here!

According to the online dictionary *Wordsense.eu, erce* is the vocative form of *eorcnan*—the 'vocative form' meaning the way that you would call or invoke someone using that word or name. *Eorcnan*, in turn, means 'true, genuine, holy.' So if you wanted to call a being whom you consider true, genuine and holy, you wouldn't say *eorcnan*, you'd say *erce*.

A related word in Anglo-Saxon is *eorcnan-stan*, a precious stone, a gem. (I assume this is where the Anglo-Saxon scholar J.R.R. Tolkien got the name Arkenstone for the great gemstone in his book *The Hobbit.*) Turning to the Gothic dictionary we have the word *airkns* or *airknis* = 'good, holy, sincere,' and the feminine noun *airknitha* meaning 'goodness, genuineness, sincerity.'

Going back yet further in time, we can find the Proto-Indo-European root *er-* which has two meanings. One meaning is 'earth,' and shows up in the Germanic languages in earth-related words. The other meaning is 'to move, to set in motion,' and forms the root of Germanic words relating to 'being or existence,' like our pronoun 'are'—'you are,' meaning 'you exist'. (Watkins p. 24).

All of these meanings: 'true, holy, goodness, earth, to move, to set in motion, to be, to exist' would be logical attributes for a fertility / earth Goddess whose powers are needed to stimulate growth and procreation. It seems to me that these possible meanings and roots of her name are correct, and I take them as indications of this Earthen Mother's nature.

It isn't clear how this name should be pronounced, but I have my own view of this, too! Normally in Anglo-Saxon words, if 'c' is followed by 'e' then the 'c' is pronounced 'ch.' There are some exceptions, which we can roughly guess at by looking at how the word's descendant is pronounced in modern English, specifically the name of the full charm or prayer 'æcer-bot' in Anglo-Saxon, 'acre-remedy'. Modern

English 'acre' has a hard 'c', and we assume that the A-S word did, too.

What about *erce?* Normally this would be pronounced 'air-cheh', based on the spelling, but that would not be the case if the word / name is derived from *eorcnan,* which is pronounced with a hard 'c'—*ey-ork-nan.* This results in the pronunciation as air-keh, with a hard 'c'. There's another clue that points in this direction as well: an obscure German Goddess named Herke *(Hair-keh),* which sounds almost the same. Jacob Grimm wrote about the German Goddess Herke or Harke, saying that the tales and beliefs about her were very similar to those of Frau Holle, Frau Berchta, and Frau Freke (Frigg) (p. 253, vol. I).

Going back to the Proto-Indo-European roots, the oldest form of the root *er-* meaning 'to move, to set in motion' had an initial 'h': *her-*. With a generous interpretation, here we have roots of the *erce* and the *herke* versions of the name. I believe that Erce / Erke and Herke are names for the same Goddess, an ancient Germanic Earth-Goddess who sets in motion the processes of life growing from the Earth and living on the Earth. She is our Earthen Mother of many names: holy, good, and true.

Earth-Mother

Nerthus: A Poem

A poem in honor of the Goddess of the Earth, she of many names: Nerthus, Erda, Erce, Hludana, Fjörgyn, Rinda, and many more.

Nerthus, Erda
Your might and main
Are spent for our gain
From field and hearth
From orchard and garth
The signs of your grace.

Of you we are born
To you we return
In blood and bone
In tree and stone
You leave us your trace.

Ground of the world
Your beauty unfurled
In meadow and glade
In sunlight and shade
We see your face.

Nerthus, Erda:
Mother of all
Give heed to our call
For always we turn
Toward your fullness we yearn:
Our holiest place.

"Earth Mother" by Edward Burne-Jones.

Matrons and Disir

13: Matrons and Disir: The Heathen Tribal Mothers

Altar to 'Matronis Aveaniabus.' According to Simek, this is the same as the Matronis Aufaniabus, who have more than 90 altars dedicated to them. They are located mainly in Germany, in the heart of the Matron cult area, and date from around 164-235 CE. Sometimes the altars are addressed to a singular Goddess (Dea, Sancta) Aufanie, whose name may mean 'generous ancestral mother' from Gothic ufjo = *abundance.* (Simek p. 23.)

Matron Worship in Germanic Lands

A belief and trust in protective maternal Deities seems to have been strong among our Heathen forebears for many centuries, at least as strong as their belief in the Æsir and Vanir more familiar to us today. The earliest written records of these beliefs begin during the first century C.E. and predominate in the lands of the continental Germans. The core areas of the Matron Cult were in ancient Germania, eastern Gaul, and northern Italy, but it reached as far as present-day Scotland,

Matrons and Disir

Frisia, southern Spain and Rome. More than 1100 votive stones and altars to the *matronae* or mothers have been found to date, over half of which are dedicated to beings with clearly Germanic names; the others are of Celtic origin or are unclear whether Celtic or Germanic. The Germanic folk and the Celts apparently shared this belief, as with a number of other similarities between the beliefs of these peoples.

Matrons (two of them headless) holding symbols of abundance, including fruit. The small animal seems to be a puppy, or perhaps a piglet?

More than simple votive stones have been found, however: in some areas there were large cult centers, temples and monuments, especially along the Rhine. Some of the largest were in Pesch, Nettersheim, and Bonn. The temples, monuments and votive stones show that the following were important to the worship of the mothers:

-burning bowls of incense

-sacrifices of fruit, fish, and pigs,

-imagery of fruit baskets, plants, trees, babies, children, cloths for wrapping babies, and snakes.

Images of the mothers generally show them in a group of three, though occasionally two or one are found; usually at least one of them holds a basket of fruit, and often a baby is held. Often all of them have clothing and hairstyles or headscarves indicating their matron status, though sometimes the middle figure is shown dressed as a maiden, with her hair loose.

Interestingly, many of the votive stones and monuments were dedicated by Germanic soldiers and sailors, legionaries in the Roman Empire, rather than by women, though frequently the stones were set up on behalf of the soldier's entire family or his clan. Many times, though, it is clear from the inscription that the soldier inscribed it for his own sake, asking the mothers for protection, health and wellbeing, and perhaps luck in battle, or often thanking them for having already provided it.

Indeed, many of the monuments and stones were thank offerings for what the mothers had already given, indicating the mothers' obvious ability to respond to their believers prayers! Apparently the worshippers made vows to the matrons, to set up a stone for them if the mothers granted their prayers. One inscription says: "To Alatievia (the 'all-divine one'), on her own command, from the physician Divos. (Simek p. 6.)

The worshippers then fulfilled their vows by having these stones set up, leaving us their many records of this flourishing faith over the course of four centuries. Since those who set up the stones had learned to write in Latin, as soldiers and sailors of the Roman Empire, the inscriptions are in Latin and the matron names are latinized, even though the folk who set them up were Germanic or Celtic. All of the examples given here are names thought to be of Germanic origin.

The primary functions of the mothers, as shown in the inscriptions, were to help in time of need, to protect, to watch over a family or clan, to help in fertility and childbirth, to heal, and to give protection in battle. In addition, many of the inscriptions appear to be to water Goddesses or spirits, who have the name of the river or spring in which they reside. These were perhaps being propitiated by believers seeking safety in traveling on the water, a good harvest of fish, or protection from drought or flood. In the case of spirits of springs, folk would have wanted to make sure the spring did not dry up.

The names of the mothers are multitudinous; more than 100 different clearly Germanic names have been found to date. Frequently the names are those of clan-mothers or folk-mothers, as can be seen in examples of inscriptions to the 'Swabian mothers,' 'German mothers,' 'paternal Frisian mothers,' and the 'mothers of the paternal family of Kannanef.' Others—Goddesses or spirits of places—are named for the river or spring where they live, such as the Renahenae of the Rhine, or for the town or area they watched over, like the Albiahenae matrons of the town of Elvenich.

Frequently the mothers are named for their attributes, such as giving and protectiveness (Gabiae, Friagabiae, Alagabiae) or the powerful ones (Afliae). In the case of the Ahueccaniae, the first element of their name is thought to relate to water, and the second element to Anglo-Saxon *wiccian:* to make magic and to Middle High German *wicken:* to prophesy, creating a very interesting combination! The Alaferhviae, depicted together with trees, are thought to derive their name from an Old High German word for tree or oak; other matron names also seem to have a linguistic connection with trees/oaks. The Audrinehae probably means 'the friendly powers of destiny,' showing a connection with the Lesser Norns. These are just some examples of name-derivations; there are many more. Quite often the derivations of their names are obscure.

In the general area of the largest cult centers, as many as 360 monuments name the same three sets of matrons: the Aufaniae, Suleviae, and Vacallinehae; in addition are stones which mention only one of the three. The matrons Vacallinehae have at least 130 inscriptions dedicated to them alone, with another 150 fragments that may have been theirs as well. The name Vacallinehae is probably based on a place-name; thus these mothers were probably the protectresses of the folk who lived in that particular area. More than 90 inscriptions to Aufanie have been found, who appears to have been a single Goddess rather than a collection of mothers as were the Vacallinehae. Aufanie was often named as 'Goddess Aufanie' or 'holy Aufanie,' making her divine status quite clear, while other times she was titled 'matron Aufanie.' One interpretation of her name, based on a Gothic derivation, is 'generous ancestral mother.'

About 40 inscriptions are dedicated to the Suleviae matrons; these inscriptions have been found scattered all over Europe and tend to be more informative about the matrons than most votive stones are. These inscriptions show that the Suleviae were considered guardians of the private, domestic sphere, guardian spirits of the household.

Probably the most well-known Goddess with matron-like functions is Nehalennia, worshipped primarily in the northern continental Germanic regions. About sixty inscriptions and votive altars or stones to her have been found. As depicted on her votive altars, her attributes are a basket of fruit, frequently a ship or an oar, and a dog. She is thought to have been, in addition to a fertility Goddess, a patroness of seafaring (most likely for peaceful purposes such as fishing and trade), and a Goddess of the dead. These attributes are common to the Near Eastern Goddess Isis as well; it is possible that the references to Germanic worship of Isis by the Roman writer Tacitus could have applied in reality to Nehalennia. Some scholars also think Nehalennia could be another name for the Goddess worshipped as Nerthus by the Angles and other Germanic tribes, whom Tacitus describes as Terra Mater, Earth Mother. *(References for the Matrons, matron cult, and individual matronae by name are found in Simek alphabetically.)*

Altar to Nehalennia: note that she is stepping into a canoe-shaped boat. The word 'NVARINUS' on the plinth is likely a version of 'navarinus' or 'navalinus,' meaning 'shipyard or chandler' (seller of ship supplies). Thus, she is addressed as 'Nehalennia Navarinus,' patroness of shipyards and chandlers. Here are also her typical symbols of dog and fruit.

Matrons and Disir

General Conclusions about Matron Worship

The many inscriptions to the matrons, their descriptive names along with images from their stones and temples, allow us to extract several general conclusions out of their great variety of attributes.

1) The matrons and matron-like Goddesses were widely worshipped among the Germanic peoples over a period of at least several centuries. My suspicion is that they were worshipped long before we have written records of them, and that the written records only began showing up during the heyday of the Roman Empire with its cadre of fairly literate soldiers and other functionaries of Germanic origin. In other words, I don't think that the widespread worship of matrons, and Latin literacy, just happened to coincide at once; I think the practice of worshipping matron Goddesses was around for a long time but did not leave traces until the common folk learned to write inscriptions to them on stone, or could afford to have it done for them.

2) The matrons had a number of functions, including especially protectiveness, help, and gift-giving; fertility, health, children, wise rede or foreseeing, and other gifts.

3) They were associated with certain natural features, in particular rivers, springs, and trees.

4) Individual towns, regions, tribes, clans, families, and households frequently had their own dedicated matrons.

5) Matrons were worshipped by all sorts of folk: women and men, common folk and leaders, soldiers and civilians; they had a very broad base of worshippers.

6) People seemed to regard the matrons as being very personal, local and close to them. The inscriptions are often addressed to 'my' or 'our' matrons. It seems likely that folk considered the particular matrons they worshipped to belong to them, their family, their native place, rather than seeing them as distant, Olympian figureheads out of the reach of mortals.

7) People seemed to put a great deal of trust in the mothers, and judging by the number of thank-offerings for prayers answered, the trust was well-founded.

Hans Schöll in his book *Die Drei Ewigen* (The Three Eternal Ones) traced the continuation of three German Goddesses through the Heathen era and far into the Christian one, appearing later as saints, princesses, or just three sisters. He primarily used the evidence of the many recognizable variants of their names: Ambet, Gwerbet, and Borbet. (There are several matron names that I think could be related as well: Ambiamarcae, Ambiomarcis, Berguinehae, Borvoboendoa.) What is particularly interesting is the very local nature of people's understanding of these Goddesses or maidens. Pretty much invariably, the martyrologies, folktales or anecdotal sources specify that Ambet, Gwerbet and Borbet lived right over there, pointing out some local place; are buried here; up there on the hill is where their father the king lived; there is where they were martyred as saints; and so forth—even though sources in distant parts of Germany and Austria said the same things about their own localities. The sources seemed unaware that other German folk knew of these feminine beings, and assumed the three maidens belonged to them, were their own local Holy Ones.

Many of the characteristics and images of Ambet, Gwerbet and Borbet are identical to those of matrons, and so is their local, personal nature. Schöll has done us a great favor tracing them in all their guises through Heathen and Christian times, and has shown how strongly belief and loyalty was held by the folk, in spite of Christianization.

To this evidence may be added the centuries of belief, in the Germanic countries, in well-maidens, river-maidens, wood-wives, and other protective feminine beings associated with the same natural features as the matrons were, though these beings suffered the same process of demonization as all other Heathen holy ones did.

I wonder, too, whether the common Christian folklore and folksong theme of the 'three Marys' does not also relate back to the matrons. The three Marys were supposedly Mary the mother of Jesus, Mary the mother of John the Evangelist, and Mary Magdalene, which comprise a trio of two motherly or matronly figures that one imagines with covered heads, and one unmarried, maidenly figure with long, loose hair, as the images of the matrons so often show. According to folklore, the three Marys often appear to people in need of help or wise rede, or occasionally when a death is pending, just as the holy Heathen womanly beings do.

Moving North....

The cult of the Matrons, judging by the age of the inscriptions, began to die out among the continental Germans by around the fifth century C.E., presumably due to the growing hold of Christianity in these regions. As it happens, this is also the time when England was first settled by the Heathen Saxons, Angles, Jutes and other tribes, including Frisians and Franks. The early English historian Bede, born in 673 C.E., mentioned in his writings that the still-Heathen Angles celebrated sacrificial feasts at the beginning of the year, at Yuletide, in honor of the Mothers. He wrote *modraniht, id est matrum noctem,* namely *"modraniht,* it is the night of the mothers." It is important to note that both the Anglo-Saxon word *"modra-(niht)"* and the Latin *matrum* are in the plural, not the singular. (Simek p. 220; Bede *De temporum ratione* 13.)

Some modern Heathens celebrate this holiday primarily as 'Mothernight,' conceived of as being the night the year is born, the solstice tide. This is very beautiful imagery, and certainly a most fitting way to celebrate this event. But we should not lose sight of the fact that the Anglian holy tide described by Bede was very clearly the 'Night of the Mothers, what would in Scandinavian countries be called the *Disablot,* Disting, or festival of the Disir, the familial soul-mothers. It is also clear that, since the festival is described as a sacrifice, it was intended primarily for the deceased mothers more than the living ones: the mothers who have gone through and past death to become sources of wisdom and soul-might for their living folk. Thus, while indeed it makes perfect sense to celebrate the solstice with the imagery of Mothernight, and honor today's living mothers, there is no question that the soul-mothers of one's kin are the ones who should receive highest mindfulness and honor on this holy night.

Simek in his *Dictionary of Northern Mythology* substantiates this understanding of the meaning of Mothers' Night and draws the linkages between the Anglo-Saxon observances and those conducted on the continent and in Scandinavia:

"Thus it corresponds to other Germanic Yule-tide festivals;... The Modraniht *as a Germanic sacrificial festival should be associated with the Matron cult of the West Germanic peoples on the one hand, and to the Disablot and Disting already known from medieval Scandinavia on the other hand and is chronologically to be seen as a connecting link between these Germanic forms of cult."* (p. 220)

It seems we have a fairly continuous thread with which to follow the Heathen Mothers through historical time, starting in the Germanic countries of the continent at the beginning of the Common Era, leaping to the isle of England just as records began to dry up on the continent, picking up in Scandinavia in later times with the sagas and other references to the Disir, and then going underground in the form of folklore once Christianity had taken hold in the Germanic lands.

The Disir of Scandinavia

The Mothers are most familiar to today's Heathens as the Disir, our understanding of them coming primarily from the Scandinavian sources. Though the sagas are not considered by scholars as necessarily historically accurate on every point, nevertheless it seems very likely that their references to the *Disarsalr* (Disir-halls) and the frequent references to the *Disablot* sacrifices at harvest are historically correct. Note that in Scandinavia, the most common festival of the Disir took place at Winternights, during mid-October after the harvest had been gathered and the winter slaughtering was taking place. This is in contrast to the Anglo-Saxon Mothers' Night celebration at Yuletide, with respect to the date, but the characteristics of the festival seem otherwise to have been very similar.

"Disarblot" by Malmström.

In addition to the Disir-halls, stones or piled stone harrows were also dedicated to the Disir. One can see the continuity between the Matrons' Roman-era temples, cult-centers, votive stones and altars, with the later Disarsalr and harrows, even though inscriptions were seldom associated with the Scandinavian establishments. Indeed, six hundred years after the heyday of the continental Matron cult, we find a description in Saxo Grammaticus' *Gesta Danorum* of what he called a "shrine of the norns, with images of three seated nymphs" in Scandinavia, that seems closely similar to

Matrons and Disir

archeological finds of Matron temples on the continent. (Simek, p. 207)

It seems that in later Scandinavian times, the connection between the Mothers and specific places or natural features (rivers, springs, trees) had faded or weakened, though it was not completely absent, while the ancestral connection remained very strong. The one indication I have found that clearly links the Disir with the land or features of the land are references to *Landdisasteinar*, or stones of the land-Disir (see Simek, p. 186). The land-Disir were apparently believed to live in these rocks, and it is not clear (to me, at any rate!) whether they were seen as nature spirits, ancestral spirits, or both together. Nevertheless, this is one more commonality between the Matrons of the continent, who clearly functioned as both nature-spirits and as protective maternal ancestral spirits, and the Disir of Scandinavia. Certainly folklore would be a worthwhile route to try to trace more details of the continuity between them.

Besides the close and clear-cut connection with many natural features and regions, another thing lost when the cult of the Matrons went underground on the European continent is the richness of descriptive names for the Matrons found in the hundreds of inscriptions we have. Scandinavian Disir are almost never named. Two notable exceptions are Thorgerd and Irpa, very powerful Disir of the clan Hlaðr in Halogaland, who were fully-trusted by Jarl Hakon. These Disir had an elaborate temple of their own and fought beside their kinsmen in battle by appearing in the sky shooting darts of hail from their fingertips. *(Njal's Saga 88, Saga of the Jomsvikings,* and *Skaldskarpamal.* See Simek pp. 326-7.) But these two are very much the exception rather than the rule, and the usual pattern seems to have been worship of 'the Disir' as an undifferentiated group, who also appeared as anonymous individual Disir in dreams to give warnings or sometimes threats to kinsfolk. They are recognized as Disir, but not named as individuals or as groups, in contrast to the continental Matrons.

Scandinavian lore, then, shows that the strongest feature of the Disir is their ancestral connection to their families and folk, and they seem to have played a very strong role in everyday life and faith, as they did earlier in history as well. It is my subjective impression (I have not tried to count the references!) that there are more frequent references, direct and indirect, to *Disablotar* than there are to Blotar for any of the Æsir or Vanir in the Scandinavian literature. Disir helped in childbirth, gave rede and warnings to their kin, protected them, brought luck, aided them in battle, and gave strength to the family line:

Matrons and Disir

"...the idises act, not only as shapers of the family line, but as embodiments and transmitters of its ørlög and the whole spiritual complex associated with it. A family, or aett, which is mighty of soul will have mighty idises who look upon its bairns with a kindly mood and give the best of gifts; but if the heritage carries an ill ørlög, the idises will bring that down upon the children of the line." (Gundarsson, p. 108)

The sagas also show the dark side, where the ill-will of the family's Disir bodes death for a family member, a sign that his luck is at an end. Even Odin acknowledges the peril of the Disir's ill-will; he tells king Geirrod, just before he kills him, that "I know your life is over; the Disir are against you" (*Grimnismal / Grimnir's Sayings*, vs. 53, Poetic Edda).

Sometimes the association of the Disir with their kinsman's death seems related to the Disir's anger or their wish for a sacrifice, or a serious loss of luck, whereas in other instances it seems they simply appear in order to invite their kinsman home with them. (I refer to men in these sentences because I am not familiar with anything in the sagas that show whether the Disir treat their kinswomen in the same way, or differently.) This darker side of the mothers is not apparent from what I know of the continental Matrons, though indeed one would not expect to find votive offerings to the dark side of the mothers, so perhaps it was there but we do not have records of it. On the other hand, it is also possible that the authors of the sagas exaggerated the darker side of the Disir in order to heighten the drama of their stories.

An interesting twist to the dark and light aspects of the Disir show up in a few tales where there is a struggle or contest between light and dark Disir over one of their kinsmen, which is interpreted as a struggle between the kin's ancient Heathen

Disir and the newer Christian Disir who are coming into being as their kinfolk's faith is converted. The Heathen Disir, the dark ones, win and gain the death of their kinsman Thidrandi because the strength of the new Disir is as yet too weak to compete with them. One interpreter of events describes the cause of Thidrandi's death this way:

"I expect that your Disir which have followed this old faith have now learned of this changing of customs (Christianity) and that they shall be forsaken by their kin. Now they must not have wanted to have no share from you before they part from you and they must have this (Thidrandi) as their part. But the better Disir must have wanted to help him and were not able to do so as things stood." (This event is described in Kristni Thattr, Olaf's Saga Tryggvasonar, in the *Flateyjarbok.*)

Clearly, a Christian slant is being placed on these events, and possibly the whole occurrence was made up or reinterpreted for purposes of dramatic storytelling and Christian proPaganda. But the overall sense that Heathen Disir would be disturbed and hostile over the coming of the new faith was surely an accurate one. They were losing their link to their kin; surely this more than anything else would bring out their dark side.

Heathen Disir Today

My own experience with the Disir has shown me that they do indeed have a passionate attachment to folk of their own blood and those adopted into their kindreds, and will hunt us down through the coils of time and space in order to keep or renew the bonds of relationship. When their offspring move toward Heathenism again, this seems to act as a clarion call to the ancient Heathen Disir of our lines, and they will home in on us with all the might of their beings. I have noticed that they are especially interested in and intent on Heathen weddings, childbearing, and adoption, not surprisingly since the family line depends on these activities.

We can expect the Disir to bring with them the same gifts they always have: help in time of need, wise rede and foresight, protection, luck, fruitfulness, and motherly care. In addition, they carry the ancient ørlög or orlays of our family lines, the layers laid down by ancestral deeds and by the Norns which shape what we are and what we shall become. As I see these orlays, they are tangled, snarled and raveled by the changing troths and beliefs of the generations. The Disir long to smooth out the raveled ends of our kin-orlays and reknit them to folk of firm Heathen troth and thews.

In keeping with the principles of our faith, the mothers expect to give gifts and receive them in return; our failure to accept their gifts and our failure to return gifts are equally offensive to them. They do indeed have dark sides, and they have been living in the dark, underground, for a long time. It is time for us to bring them out again into the light and warmth of our family hearths, reknitting our bonds and troth with them, giving them back the honor of their own names, accepting them as our ancient kin and as our link not only to the might and main of our family lines but also to the magic and power of nature that the earth-rooted Heathen mothers once mediated for us.

Next Yuletide, light a candle and set a place at your table for your Disir or Idesa on Mothernight (the eve of the Winter Solstice). If you have enough chairs, designate one of them as theirs for the feast, and perhaps drape it with a decorative cloth. Welcome them hospitably to your table and your hearth! Set their place with your best tableware and leave out a dish of good food and drink throughout the night for their feasting. Among the kinds of food they like are porridge with milk, or a milk pudding or cream soup, and for drink, ale, cider or mead. They also like fruit, and smoked fish (you can buy small tins of smoked herring at your supermarket). The next day, leftover food should go to the family pets or be set out for the wild creatures; the drink should be poured on your outdoor harrow or at the roots of a tree. (Don't forget, also, to set out such a feast for all your departed kinfolk, not only the Disir, sometime during the season of Yuletide.)

You could also tie up small gifts for them and hang them on your Yule Tree. As their gift to you in return, ask your Disir to make themselves known to you and stand by you during the coming year, that you may face the demands of the world with the might and wisdom of your kin at your back.

14: Hallow-Streaming: A Meditation on the Mothers

*"Holda, the good protectress," a German Goddess.
By Friedrich Wilhelm Heine.*

This is reading is offered as a meditation for Hallows-Tide, Disablot, Mothers-Night, Yuletide, the holy tides of Frau Holle, Holda, Berchta, Fricka and others. It is especially dedicated to the German Goddesses with their Yuletide processions to gather up lost souls, and to the Matronae. The focus of this meditation is on the Soul-Mothers and their care for the souls of all beings; it can be used in whatever way and whatever time one chooses to be mindful of them. If you wish, you can put into the text the name of the holy tide you are celebrating, particularly at the beginning of the last paragraph. For example, instead of "Now, at the turning of the Tides of Time..." you can say "Now at the turning of Hallows-Tide / Yuletide / Mothers-Night / Hollenfahren, etc.".

At the Turnings of the Year the great Tides of Life and Death, Moon-drawn, inexorable, wash across the quivering Worlds.

The restless souls rush forth from the lost places and the lost songs: a drumming deep within the Earth, curls and lashings of tumbled winds and waters, flowerings of flames, out from the Otherworlds into Midgard and from Midgard forth into Worlds beyond our knowledge. Each soul, each wight, living or dead, is a needle drawing a thread of power, stitching the Worlds together: needles of silver and of stone, of iron, antler, bone.....

And now the great Spirit-Mothers of all beings come, each calling to her own lost ones: Mothers of clan and tribe and solitary folk, Mother Dog and Mother Wolf, Mothers of Whale and Wren, of Oak and Corn, the shining Sow, Auðhumla herself calling the souls of cattle and kine. Come home, come home, to kin and hearth, to den and nest, to moonlit meadow and rolling wave, to burrow and branch and starlit pool. Come fleeing out of life and into other life, come gather might and main with us before returning to the fray.

And so they come, wights and souls of humankind and beasts and all beings: terrified and trembling, stoic and dignified, fulfilled, starved, exhausted, slaughtered, devoured, enraptured they come, stumbling or sure-footed, each to their own Train of Souls, following the Voice they know, each trailing strands that weave the Worlds together, warp and weft of hallowed power. The warp is threaded by the Dead and the weft by the Living, changing places in an endless rhythm of Being, humming across the Worlds.

God and Wight, Human and Beast, Tree and Herb: attuned to one another we pour the passion of our love and need for one another from cup to cup, Well to Well, from life to life and need to need, and the Worlds thunder and quiver with this mighty flow.

Now, at this turning of the Tides of Time, awaken! Listen and remember what your souls already know. Open to the surges of memory and mystery that move through your being. Know your own attunement to the flows of power streaming across these blessed, ever-renewing, all-hallowed Worlds.

"Dancing Fairies" by August Malmström.
One can imagine this scene as the spirits of the dead seeking refuge with the Mothers.

Tapestry weaving of a tree with animals.

15: Werthende: Song of Becoming

Werthende (Verðandi in Old Norse; Werthende is the name translated into Anglo-Saxon) is one of the three Wyrdae or Norns, who ward the Well of Wyrd and nourish the great Tree of the Worlds. She rules the domain of Becoming: the very instant of time when a being or a deed ripens from the layers Wyrd has laid and springs forth to lay new layers and respond to Scyld's tuggings, faint or strong, upon its thread of life. I see Werthende dressed in red here, because she bears the blood of new life coming into being. Her name is pronounced WARE-then-deh, or VARE-than-dee.

Werthende: Song of Becoming

Red the threads of Werthende's weaving,
Blood of birth and life brings she.
Her needle's point, a world unfolding:
The endless Now of budding deeds.

The wave of Time moves on unmoving,
Just as a wave moves not the Sea.
All flows past that point of shaping:
What is becoming, what should be.

Pierced with knowledge no words capture,
Thread on which worlds hang like pearls,
The soul is strung, that seeks to venture
Within the Well's green-shaded furls.

Cupped in moss, the deepest wonder
Of all that is, lies hidden here.
Drops of dew, the Tree's deed-plunder,
Fall through boughs like sweat and tears.

A mighty maid, come from the East-lands,
Gowned in red sits spinning there,
With sisters two; their threefold shaping
Weaves a web both dark and fair.

And over all, the great Tree arches:
The shape of all that has been won.
Life flows through its limber branches:
Thread that Werthende's hands do spin.

Note: There's a little oddity in the last line of this poem, where the rhyme would be better this way: "Thread that Werthende's hands have spun." I make a gentle vow to Werthende that when I speak to her or about her, I speak only in the present tense, to honor her status as the Norn of the present moment of coming-into-Being. The final line of the poem causes a tiny jerk of attention to Werthende's foundation in the present moment: never past, never future, never 'perfected' in the sense of completed and finished, always budding into the perpetual Now.

More on Werthende's / Verðandi's Domain

I think that the domains of the other two Norns, Urdhr and Skuld, are both quite complex and multifaceted, but that Verðandi's is more straightforward. Her name means 'Becoming / coming into being.' Hers is the point of the needle, the edge of the knife, the imperceptible moment when something moves from 'not-being' into 'becoming.'

Once the 'becoming' has 'become,' has been completed, Skuld attaches strands of shild / debt / obligation to that which has become. This is a metaphor for the action of causality, of cause and effect. Skuld's name comes from a form of the word 'should,' and implies that 'given this thing / event / action / being / situation which has now come into being, this is what 'should' result from it.' It now rolls over into Urdh's domain of 'what-is,' what has happened, been accomplished and completed, entered into Being. It is tethered lightly or strongly to Skuld's domain of 'what should be,' depending on many complex factors, and those tugs from Skuld's tethering threads create the function of causality. In the meantime, the next instant of Becoming arises and moves on, into the same pattern. That very moment of Becoming is Verðandi's / Werthende's domain.

I like to picture Werthende both as a midwife into Being, and as the gatekeeper of the quantum realm! A *potentiality* arises in the quantum realm and is 'called to' or 'attracted to' Werthende. This potentiality could manifest as a deed, a person, a situation, an object, a thing or event of any kind. She then midwifes its birth into the domain of Time and Being as we know them. It's as though the potentiality of a deed, a situation, a being, a moment of Time itself, is the 'soul' of that thing, and she calls this soul into its 'body,' which is its reality in this Space-Time where it is enacted into being. It is then given a wyrd—that is, it takes on its role in causality—and is embedded into the solidity of 'what-is,' Urðr's domain. Werthende remains at the gateway of the quantum realm, midwifing the next births into being.

16: Perkwus: The Tree of Life and Soul

"The Tree," painting © Laurie Inn.

Trees are so important to historical Heathen belief and practice, as well as to other branches of historical Paganism, that entire books can—and have—been written on the subject. Here I will follow a few among the many tree-related threads that are woven throughout this fabric of our troth— threads which I have followed in my study, writing, and practice for many years. These threads all lead from, and to, the great Tree of Life, of which we are all a part.

Perkwus: The Tree of Life and Soul

Here I've interspersed a few verses from a long poem by Algernon Charles Swinburne called "Hertha," first published in 1871. The name Hertha is an alteration of Nerthus, and in this poem 'Hertha' speaks as both Earth Mother and as the World-Tree, combined together. All of the verses quoted here are from this poem, except for the Havamál verse as noted.

Gods, Soul, and Trees

Perkwus: This is the reconstructed Proto-Indo-European (PIE) word for the **oak tree**, and it is linguistically closely related to several other words and names important in Heathenry. There is the PIE Thunder God, *Perkwunos, whose name survives in the names of the Slavic and Baltic Thunder God, such as the Baltic Perkunas. It also survives in a Norse word for a Heathen temple: *fjarghus*, where *fjarg* is a plural word meaning "the Gods," collectively. Thus, the Fjarghus is the Gods' house, all the Gods together.

In the singular, this word *fjarg* shows up in the names of ancient Norse Deities of whom we know little: Fjörgynn, the father of Frigg, and Fjörgyn, the mother of Thor. 'Fjörgyn' also means 'the earth,' known as the mother of Thor, while the masculine Fjörgynn is thought to be related to thunder. I believe that these Deities are a brother-sister pair of spouses, as Njorð and Nerthus may have been at one time. (See discussions in Mallory & Adams pp. 407-8 and 582; also deVries vol. II pp. 274-5. Wikipedia has a brief but useful discussion on Fjörgyn and Fjörgynn.)

Fjörgyn and Fjörgynn can be regarded as the Germanic 'descendants' of the PIE thunder God, Perkwunos, based on the linguistics of their names. I think that Fjörgynn is an ancient Germanic version of a Thunder-God, and that Fjörgyn is the powerful Earth-Goddess known by many names across time and space. Their powers are expressed through various aspects of nature, but the emblem and the special channels of their powers in the Midgard realm are the oak tree, fir, and pine, and by extension trees generally.

Njorð and Nerthus are powers who focus on the fertility and plenty that humans strive to gain from the earth and from the sea, and the frith that one hopes for this prosperity to bring. Fjörgyn and Fjörgynn focus, I believe, on the powers of earth and air as they express themselves through the wilder spectrum of activity: storms, lightning and thunder; mountains, rocks and cliffs; deep forests, woods and wildlands.

Where dead ages hide under the live roots of the tree,
In my darkness the thunder makes utterance of me;
In the clash of my boughs with each other
Ye hear the waves sound of the sea.

Table 1 on the next page shows the related set of Proto-Indo-European words that lead to these conclusions about Fjörgyn and Fjörgynn: words relating Gods, trees, mountains, and life-soul together.

Perkwus: The Tree of Life and Soul

Table 1: Gods, Earth, Sky Powers

Language	Life-Soul	Earth / Deity	Thunder / Deity
Proto-Indo-European	*perku	--	*Perkwunos Thunder God
Proto-Germanic	*ferhwa	*fergunja=mountain	
Old Norse	fjör	Fjörgyn (Earth Goddess) Fjörgynn (father of Frigg) fjarg ("Gods," plural form) fjarghus (Gods' house, temple)	Thor Thunder-God, son of Fjörgyn Earth-Goddess
Old Prussian Lithuanian, Latvian Old Russian	--	--	percunis = thunder Perkunas Thunder-God Perunu Thunder-God

Anglo-Saxon	*feorh*	*fyrgen* = forested mountain	–
Old Saxon	*ferah*		
Old High German	*ferah*	Firgunnea = 'ore mountains'	
Middle High German	*verch*	virgunt = forested mountain	
Gothic	*fair, fairhw*	*fairgunni* = forested mountain region	–

(* The asterisk is used before Proto-Indo-European (PIE) and Proto-Germanic words to indicate that these words are reconstructed using linguistic science. There are no written records of their language going back to the time before the Indo-European peoples split off from one another.)

I realize that in the texts which come down to us, and that are important in modern Heathen belief, Thor is the son of Odin and Fjörgyn. I think that in the dim and misty past, though, he may have been the son of Fjörgyn and Fjörgynn, and that they, in turn, were morphisms of Perkwunos. Interestingly, this would make him the brother or half-brother of Frigg, and Odin's brother-in-law rather than his son. Even as attested in known Heathen lore, Frigg and Thor would be at least cousins, if not siblings, if Fjörgynn Frigg's father and Fjörgyn Thor's mother are siblings as their names would indicate.

In any case, here we have several progenitor Deities who are linguistically connected with trees, and especially with the oak tree, which is considered to 'draw' lightning, or God-power, to itself. Let's follow the implications further.

Trees and Souls

Table 2: Trees and Life-Soul Words

Language	Trees	Life-Soul
Proto-Indo-European	*perkwu* = oak	*perku*
Proto-Germanic	*ferhwa* = oak	*ferhwa*
	furhwon = fir	
Gothic	*furh-jon* = fir	
Old High German/ Old Saxon/ Old Frisian	*fereh-eih* = oak *foraha* = pine	*ferah, ferh, ferch, verch*
Lombardian	*fereha* = oak	*ferech*
Old Norse	*fjörr* = tree *fura* = pine *fyri* = fir	*fjör* = life-soul, pith *fjörr* = living being
Anglo-Saxon	*furh* = pine	*feorh, ferhð*
Modern English Modern German	fir tree *Föhre* = pine	--

Table 2 shows closely related words for trees and for a specific soul, called *ferah* in Old Saxon, *fjör* in Old Norse, and split into two words, *feorh* and *ferhð*, in Anglo-Saxon. Ferah is a term for the life-force that makes humans and other living beings alive, and its meaning is expanded in different directions that are relevant to this life-soul, including meanings of 'mind (Anglo-Saxon *ferhð)*, wisdom (Old Saxon *feraht)*, human beings (Old Saxon *firibarn)*, living beings (Anglo-Saxon *feohrcynn),* and 'the folk' or the community of people (Old Saxon *firihi).*

The connection between trees and the human spirit runs deep. Paul Friedrich notes that "phonologically unimpeachable" Indo-European cognates for the PIE word **doru,* meaning 'wood, tree,' include words like 'truth, loyalty,' and Norse *tru* meaning 'belief.' (Mallory & Adams p. 598.) Trees are examples of steadfastness and faithfulness, outliving humans and holding their place through storms and disasters of all kinds. They were considered as guardians and warders, such as the *vårdträd* (warding trees) and *tuntre* (farmstead trees) in Scandinavia (Dowden p. 70). In fairy tales and sometimes in actual practice in Germany up until recent times, the *Lebensbaum* (life-tree) or *Schicksalsbaum* (fate- or wyrd-tree) was planted when a child was born, and the fate of the tree and the fate of the child were considered to mirror each other. Many other close, 'personal' relationships were considered to exist between specific trees and human individuals and communities (Erich & Beitel p. 466-7).

I am that which began,
Out of me the years roll;
Out of me God and man,
I am equal and whole.
God changes, and man,
And the form of them bodily;
I am the soul.

(Tree-trunk carving of the German Goddess Frau Holle.)

A different kind of warding function is shown by the Yew in early Germanic culture: not only were bow-staves preferentially made from yew, but also judges' staffs and other ritual implements were made of yew (Mallory & Adams p. 654), as well as yews being planted to ward graveyards up until present time in England. All of these reflect various ways of warding the wellbeing of the community.

There is also the implication here, supported by a vast number of religious and folklore practices, that the qualities inherent in specific trees continue after they are cut and the wood used for human purposes. Michael Bintley's book *Trees in the Religions of Early Medieval England* discusses how these understandings carried over from Heathen into Christian practice in early England. Among the most remarkable features was how early English Christians not only revered the Christian cross, but personified it in art and poetry as a tree-being with thoughts and feelings of its own. The famous Anglo-Saxon poem, *Dream of the Rood*, exemplifies this, where the entire poem is 'spoken' by the wood of the cross itself ('rood' is a word for the cross). Would the Germanic peoples have had more trouble accepting Christian symbolism if Jesus had died in a different way, not hanging on a wooden cross or 'tree'? It's an interesting question to ask!

This personification of trees and the recognition of intimate links between trees and persons implies that they share something soul-like, which I believe to be the Ferah soul. In my understanding, this soul expresses itself differently in humans and in the species of other living beings, but it shares the same substrate of the Ferah life-force.

Here I offer a story about these connections between Gods, primal trees, and the coming-into-being of humans.

I've taken the liberty of retelling the familiar myth of the shaping of Ask and Embla from logs or trees, by including in my story these insights about the connections between Gods, life-souls (Ferah), trees, humans, Earth, thunder and lightning.

A New Tale of Ask and Embla

Trees, rooted in Mother Earth, attract lightning bolts, Sky-God power. And so, one mythic day, Thor rode the clouds above a forest in his beloved Midgard, while from Asgard three mighty brothers set forth in that direction, all coming at last to a strand between the forest and the sea. This slender strip of no-man's-land stood between Land and Sea, Midgard and Otherworlds, Matter and Spirit.

"Two Trees," unfinished painting by Asher Brown Durand.

Together the Gods came across two trees there, trees with great Ferah-spirits of their own that drew the Gods' awareness like magnets. Raising his Hammer, the Hallower of Midgard gave the life-releasing blow, striking one tree on the fore-swing and the other on the back-swing.

The trees-becoming-humans stood there between Mother Earth and Father Sky, between negative and positive poles of power, and felt the God-mains flowing through them in brilliant surges of actinic light.

And so the Ferah-souls within these trees burst forth as flames and were transformed into Ferahs of new beings, human beings, different but akin to the ancient spirits of the woods. The Sons of Borr gave their great gifts: breath and spirit, wode and speech. They clothed these transformed Ferah-spirits with the human shape, the Hama, so they would not be naked spirits in a world of tree-clothed wights. Human Hamas are so skillful and powerful that Ask and Embla, as Odin remarked, felt like heroes when they had been so clothed!

> *(Odin said:)*
> *My clothes I gave, along the way, to two tree-people.*
> *They thought themselves heroes when they had clothing;*
> *The naked person is ashamed.*
> (*Havamal* verse 49, in the Poetic Edda, my translation.)

At Ragnarök, human souls will take shelter within the beleaguered Tree. Then, at the beginning of the new cycle of time, Lif and Lifthrasir will come forth as flames of life from the sheltering wood, just as their forebears Ask and Embla did, so many generations before.

Trees and the Community of Life

As you can see by referring to Tables 1 and 2, there are a number of words that derive from trees and the soul-words *ferah, feorh, fjör,* etc, that refer also to living beings, human beings, and their collectives. An example is the Anglo-Saxon *feorhcynn,* the 'kindred of the feorh,' of humans and of living beings generally. Old Saxon *firihi* means 'the folk,' and *firibarn,* 'child of ferah', refers to human beings. Old Norse *fjörr* refers to a 'living being,' including trees. Other related old Germanic words refer to forested regions, where the forest is a community of trees and other living beings.

Perkwus: The Tree of Life and Soul

These exposed roots show how the roots of separate trees mingle together underground, communicating with each other through mycelia and chemical signals. We too, as members of the Feorhcynn, and in a sense the spiritual descendants of trees, have hidden roots embedded in metaphysical layers of nature. We can learn to sense through these root-organs, and to communicate through them in nonverbal ways.

A forest is not simply individual trees standing around in the same area. Tree and plant roots intermingle with each other underground, and interact with all the myriad of soil organisms, including fungal mycelia which facilitate complex biochemical communications and interactions among the trees and other living beings of the forests. (See Sheldrake's book *Entangled Lives;* also the discussion of cultural 'entanglement' or 'meshing' between human minds, bodies, and 'things,' in particular trees and wood, in Bintley pp. 18-20.)

To speak of *ferah / feorh / fjör* is to speak also of this community of life, the *feorhcynn,* consisting of *ferah-*ensouled living beings in many different forms interacting with, and depending upon, each other in ways both overt and subtle.

In Heathen times and beyond, trees, groves and forests were used to mark places of communal worship and assembly, and these trees were highly revered. One of the ways that Christian missionaries and kings tried to destroy Heathen and Pagan worship was by cutting down these trees, including the enormous Donar-Oak at Geismar, and the famous Irminsul, a wooden pillar or tree-trunk revered by the Saxons as the support of the world. (Dowden pp. 70-71, and 118-119.)

Though not occurring in a Germanic context, the tale of how Martin of Tours tore down a Pagan temple and the pine tree beside it is notable. The Pagan villagers stood by without significant protest while their temple was destroyed, but the attack on the pine tree that grew next to it was strongly resisted, and according to the accounts of Martin's activities, this happened more than once (Dowden p. 76). I suspect that the pine trees were there first, and were the primary focus of worship, while the temples played a supportive and practical role in sustaining that worship. Note that the preponderance of cases where sacred trees were attacked involve either oak trees or pine trees, both named in Proto-Indo-European by *perkwus-related words.

Perkwus: The Tree of Life and Soul

Destruction of the Irminsul, by Heinrich Leutemann.

Perkwus: The Tree of Life and Soul

Della Hooke in her book *Trees in Anglo-Saxon England* describes a fascinating recent find in Norfolk, England, resulting from coastal erosion. A huge oak-tree had been *uprooted* (not cut) in the spring of 2049 BCE, and set upside down, with the roots upwards and the upper part of the tree buried to support this position. This was surrounded by a stockade of split poles that were made from another enormous tree some 22 feet in diameter. All of this must have entailed a great amount of work, especially for neolithic peoples and their tools. Hooke has some interesting speculations about the purpose of this establishment, and its similarity to aspects of Hindu, Persian, Saami, and other ancient myths about the Tree of Life (pp. 15ff.). Whatever meanings it may have had, it's clear that this was one of the many expressions of community religious and symbolic practices relating to sacred trees.

The tree many-rooted
That swells to the sky
With frondage red-fruited,
The life-tree am I.
In the buds of your lives is the sap of my leaves:
Ye shall live and not die.

In Closing

It is no wonder that ancient Heathens, and ancient Pagans generally, chose to worship in groves and forests, assemble for meetings under great trees, shape tree trunks into god-posts and other sacred images, have specially honored beams and doorposts in their buildings, use kennings and names of trees to describe and name people, and tell many myths and stories

Perkwus: The Tree of Life and Soul

about the relationships between trees and humans. Like trees, the roots of our being are entangled with each other and our environment. Like trees, people are nourished and sustained by Gods of earth and sky. Like trees, we are sometimes struck by lightning / God-power, and if we do not burn to death, then we burn with life as conduits of God-power into the world.

Great Yggdrasil is the backbone of the multiverse; the Irminsul pillar-tree unites earth and sky; Iðunn sustains the Gods from her magical apple tree. Donar-oaks and other mighty Midgard trees sheltered assemblies and ceremonies of the folk through time immemorial. Ancient Greeks traveled many miles to hear Zeus Thunder-God whispering his oracles through the Oak of Dodona. Trees played the same central role in the worship and communal practices of Celts, Slavs, and Balts as they did with the Germans. The religions of the Pagan Indo-Europeans, past and present, would not be what they are without the holy presence of the trees.

I bid you but be;
I have need not of prayer;
I have need of you free
As your mouths of mine air,
That my heart may be greater within me,
Beholding the fruits of me fair.

Perkwus: The Tree of Life and Soul

Sunlight slanting through the solemn, silent forest shows us that even the greatest cathedrals with their stained-glass windows and carven columns are only pale reflections of the oldest temple of all. Beyond the logic of evolutionary science, which is true in its own way, the human spirit knows its kinship with the trees.

Note: The tables and portions of the text in this chapter are taken from the chapter "Born of Trees and Thunder: The Ferah Soul," in my book Heathen Soul Lore Foundations: Ancient and Modern Germanic Pagan Concepts of the Souls.

Part II. Wights

Part II. Wights: Heathen Otherworldly Beings

"Troll becoming a hill," by JNL.

Part II. Wights

My portrait of our housewight, Elmindreda, working at her task of spiritual cleansing of our home.

17: Landwights and Human Ecology

Living things such as trees, and landscape entities like lakes and mountains are the meeting places, users and transformers of Earth, Sun, Moon, and other celestial energies, both physical and metaphysical. Each physical entity possesses at least one soul or spirit that involves itself in this work, along with all the energy transformations and interactions performed by its physical body. The landscape is further populated with many kinds of metaphysical beings which we can, for ease of reference, group together as "landwights."

Natural rock-face formation in Colorado.

There are also Landwights that encompass the soul of a place, whether a large region or a small homestead. These were called the *genii loci* by the Romans. I like to capitalize these latter Landwights to distinguish them from the smaller, free-roaming landscape wights of many kinds.

All of these embodied beings, indwelling souls or spirits, and non-embodied beings interact on all levels with the great souls and bodies of the Earth, Sun, and Moon, creating together a nested set of physical-spiritual ecosystems in which we are each a small part of the greater whole. In times and places not overly dominated by high-tech humans, the majority of the interactions and energy transformations occurred within a relatively well-defined area, which was an interactive part of larger and smaller areas within and around it. These interactions and interdependencies are studied by the science of ecology, which has many branches. Here I will say a word about the branch of systems ecology and its relevance to understanding the interactions between landwights and humans.

Systems Ecology and Eco-dynamics

Systems ecologists study ecosystems at different levels and look at the mass balances of matter and energy that flow into and out of an ecosystem, and particularly at the productivity of the system itself: how it uses, retains and maintains that energy and matter. A stable ecosystem will take incoming energy from the Sun, and incoming resources such as flows of surface and groundwater, wind-borne pollen, seeds and insects, migrating animals and plants, and use these inputs to build an ordered, structured system characterized by interactive layers of complexity and resilience. In the process, the ecosystem creates itself as a unique entity, nested within larger and smaller scale ecosystems with which it interacts in a relationship of mutual interdependence. Though a given ecosystem usually blends at the edges with other systems, it has a unique, distinguishable character. If it did not, it could not be identified as a particular ecosystem.

Landwights and Human Ecology

A raw, newly developing ecosystem, such as occurs after great destruction like a wildfire or a hurricane, lacks complexity and internal structure of producers (plants), consumers (animals, insects), and mediators (microorganisms), and lacks the complex flows of energy and matter that knit together a mature, stable ecosystem. It requires more outside resources such as immigrating plant and animal species, and is fragile and easily disrupted. A mature, stable ecosystem generates most of its own biomass and biodiversity, maintaining complex internal layers and flows of energy and matter.

With this information in mind, I want to look at certain aspects of the eco-dynamics, if you will, between humans and Landwights, and look at the differences between past and present in industrialized parts of the world. A key element is the difference between the sources of energy and matter used by human settlements in the past and the present.

In less-industrialized human settlements, most of the materials, and especially most of the energy, were generated within that particular human-landscape ecosystem. Energy sources used by humans included their own strength, draft animals, locally grown wood and other fuels, local wind and water power, and the food they grew for themselves and domestic animals. Matter and energy which was no longer of use to humans remained in the system to be recycled through natural means: manure, waste, ashes, and indeed, the dead as well.

I mean no disrespect to the dead by this reference, but want to point out the importance of returning the human dead to the local land. Many, perhaps most, traditional cultures world-wide, including our own, have understood the very close connections between the human dead and the elves, landwights, even certain housewights thought to be the soul of the original founder of the homestead. Everything that existed in such settlements, including human bodies and souls, was understood to be part of a naturally recycling system, an essential process that created the hamingja, luck, fertility and well-being of the whole system. I consider that forms of luck and metaphysical power like hamingja, mægen or megin, and various kinds of luck as types of energy that contribute to the overall processes of a well-functioning Human-Landwight-Nature ecosystem.

Local humans returning to local land. Note that the word 'human' is related to 'humus,' meaning organic matter in the soil. 'Green burials' are recommended for this purpose!

Humans profited by the smooth functioning of the system, and so did the various wights involved: wights of the house and the farmstead, and wights of the landscape. A key factor here is the local sourcing and recycling of most of the matter and energy within the system.

"Landwight," paper collage ©Creel Lancaster. The wheels or balls that the Landwight is raising from the ground represent earth magic and earth power which the Landwight cycles through the system.

Sourcing and Cycling Resources

Now let's look at a modern American town, not even a bustling metropolis, but just a medium-sized generic town. How much of the materials and energy used by this town are self-generated, produced locally? And how much of what humans call waste is safely and naturally processed and reused in some way within that same system? I'm sure you know the answer as well as I do: very little of any of the above! I won't take up space here, going into details which any aware person can list for themselves, but will focus on a few points related to our theme.

Our energy sources are mostly from fossil fuels: oil, coal, gas, either used directly or converted to electricity. These fuels are formed from the bodies of plants and animals that died millions of years ago, and in most cases are transported from far away before they reach our generic town. Thus the primary fuel source is far distant from the local ecosystem not only in spatial terms but in time-span as well. And not only that, but it is distant in terms of biological relatedness to the plants and animals, and the wights, of the region where our town is located. The majority of materials the town uses, even food and in some cases water, are also imported from distant regions.

Now let's look for a moment at what happens during transition from a natural area into a built-up area, taking a development project such as a housing or mall area as our example. When the physical manifestations, like trees, rocks, animals, streams, are interfered with, damaged or destroyed by broad-scale human activities, the destroyed entities are breathed back into the Soul of the Earth, as they were breathed out into manifestation. There, they continue to occupy an inner landscape, of which the outer, physical landscape was the manifestation before it was destroyed.

These landscapes, inner and outer, continue to be connected, but in a much less effective, more chaotic way, once they have been destroyed or displaced from their outer location. The flows and exchanges of matter and energy, both physical and metaphysical, that had been mediated, enhanced and directed by wights at many levels are now confused and disrupted. Natural physical entities such as trees, rocks, and water bodies, no longer dwell on Earth's surface to be bathed from above and below by the energies of Earth, Sun and Moon, and all the physical and metaphysical ecosystem work they did no longer takes place in a material way. Instead of the building-up and maintenance of an ordered system, entropy gains a hold and causes decline or collapse of the manifold ordering powers of ecosystems and their indwelling, guiding wights.

And what replaces the ecosystem processes that the wights and the living natural beings mediated? Humans still use energy and materials, more than in the previous, more natural system, but at the present time these are sourced and processed in a very different way, as I discussed above. Now, complex human systems are developed to mediate energy and material processes, such as currency systems, transportation systems, economic activities, socio-political institutions and processes. All of these have their own life, their own importance and roles, and they shape our lives as modern humans. But in these systems, there is no understanding of the role of wights, no attempt to recognize and cooperate with them, and insufficient recognition and respect for the role of physical ecosystem processes, though the latter is thankfully changing.

Impacts on the Landwights

All of these factors have a very damaging effect on the landwights of all kinds. The destruction of physical animals, plants, landscape entities like lakes and forests, and their ecosystems is clearly a matter of primary importance, something that many people are able to recognize without any reference to landwights. But of equal importance, I believe, are two factors I've discussed here: the almost entirely non-local sourcing of the energy and materials that give life to our current industrial system, and the lack of interaction between humans and wights. These two factors are interrelated, because if people do not feel dependent upon their own region for food and other needs, there is little incentive to engage in practices that mutually benefit landwights and humans. There are many actions that can benefit the wights even when humans are not consciously aware of this, but they all have to do with human recognition of our dependence upon the land and our love and respect for it. Protecting the land, as in parks and refuges, is of great importance. But here I am talking about something in addition: *the active co-participation of humans and wights within a landscape to create and maintain the needs of life.*

Seen in this light, the benefits of the current world-wide movement toward sustainable relocalization, still in its infancy, take on even more importance than is already recognized by those who espouse it. If our hypothetical town begins to use more solar and wind power, for example, that is a human-technology way of taking up the role that natural entities played in the local ecosystem that humans replaced. Some towns are trying local currencies, usable only for goods and services provided by locally-owned vendors; of no use to global giants like Walmart or Exxon-Mobil. Farmers Markets and Community Supported Agriculture (CSA) initiatives provide locally grown foods, home-made items, wool, and other goods. Craft guilds are starting up again, along with the Slow Food movement, backyard food gardens, small-scale hydroponics, and many others.

Landwights and Human Ecology

All of these initiatives are of great importance and benefit for many reasons. Unrecognized by most, among those reasons is the re-creation of conditions where landwights and humans can beneficially interact again, both working together to facilitate the local flows of energy and matter that they mutually depend upon. Though it would be better if this were a conscious effort, it's unrealistic to imagine that that would be the case with very many people. Even so: ecosystems function with or without conscious understanding of these functions by humans, as long as humans are not actively destroying the systems. This is because we humans are part of the system, not outside of it; the system does not depend on our conscious understanding of it.

At least, that was the case in the past. Now, with human population and standards of living moving toward the edge of the Earth's carrying capacity, more consciousness is required of humans if there is any hope of staying in balance with this carrying capacity. In heavily populated areas, we can't go back to everyone burning wood or producing all their food in backyard gardens. Even renewable energy sources like solar, wind and hydropower come with significant environmental and socio-economic price tags. Compromises have to be made, and can only be wisely made when we are well informed and aware of the complex systems, natural and human, that are involved. For those few humans, and I pray they become more year by year, who are aware of the integral role of the Landwights as powerful children of the Earth, such wisdom needs to include our conscious communication and participation with the wights.

Communication with Landwights

There are many ways to commune and participate with the landwights, and a number of good books and essays exist on the subject. Following as many suggestions and guidelines of the relocalization effort as you can and choose to is highly recommended! There are many resources for this online. Here I will just suggest a few things that can be consciously directed toward your personal relationship with the landwights. If you have a yard or garden plot, spend time tuning in to the land and the wights before you begin any work there. It may take awhile, but try to develop a sense that you're not alone in this endeavor! The wights may have requests for things to do or refrain from doing on your land and may have good advice for successful growing. I don't hear them talk, though some do, but I keep myself open to impulses, intuitions, fleeting thoughts, a sense of what would be the best thing to do here. Sometimes you may receive useful guidance in dreams or trance-working.

In an apartment home, growing houseplants and treating them as lovingly and respectfully as your harrow or altar helps to tune you to the local wights. In either case, if you can grow something edible or drinkable, even if it is just some herbs in a flowerpot, that is dedicated while growing to your local landwights, and then mindfully eat it or drink it as an herbal tea with a portion set aside for the wights, this will help build your connection as well.

One of my favorite ways of fostering long-term communication is through the use of flower essences and other essences or waters. These are super-simple to make: simply place a few flowers from your land or a natural area near you into a bowl of spring water, place it in the sunshine for an hour or two, then drink it as a sacred drink. Some people like to place the water in moonlight rather than sunlight, or do both. Scruffy little weed flowers, dandelions, ground ivy, anything non-poisonous: often the most insignificant seeming flowers are the most powerful. Just go where you're drawn, except you need to be sure they have not been sprayed.

Since I often prefer not to actually pick the flowers, sometimes I will shake the rain or dew off living flowers into a bowl of water instead. This is good to do in protected areas where you are not supposed to pick flowers. You can also set the bowl down near a clump of flowers and leave it for awhile to absorb the energies without harming the flowers. Another approach is to use a washed stone or twig you have found to make the essence, rather than flowers.

Blessing-water

Even simpler, but just as meaningful, is to place a bowl of prayer-water either in your yard, in some natural area where you will spend an hour or so of time, or if that is not possible, in your home among your house-plants. Prayer-water or blessing-water is made by taking a bowl, if possible one that is beautiful or especially meaningful to you, filling it with whatever water seems right to you, holding it in both hands and then slowly and deeply breathing upon it three or nine times.

Before you breathe, prepare in your mind the prayers, wishes, blessings, thoughts or communications you want to breathe into the water. As you begin, speak the dedication for the being to whom you direct your communication, in this case to Landwights specifically or generally. Then speak your prayer once, or speak the first part of a longer prayer, and breathe upon the water. Speak again, either repeating the prayer for more power, or following with the second part of it. And again, for a total of three or nine times.

Then put the bowl down in the best place you can and stay near it or go for a walk around the area. This is to allow the Landwights time to respond by placing their responses and energies in the water. When you feel this has been done, thank the wights, pour about half the water on the ground or in the flowerpots as their share, and drink the rest. Then spend a little more time absorbing the joined thoughts and energies, yours and the wights, that were placed in the water. Writing the results in your journal is a good idea.

Done over time, these kinds of activities will strengthen the communication and bonds between you and the wights, and strengthen your respective souls as well. The use of prayer-water or blessing-water is also excellent for communing with Deities and ancestors, blessing and healing people, places, wights, animals and other beings. If you wish, you can add some mead, herbal tea, or other sacred brew to the water, but the water itself is important: it is a child of the Earth, energized by the Sun and Moon, as are the wights, and it should play the major role here. Water is not a passive medium, but an active participant in the communion, a bearer and enhancer of the sacred energies.

Our Homestead Landwight

I'll close by sharing two of my own experiences of the landwights, gained through spaeworking (trance-working). One is a description of The Landwight (definitely capitalized!) of our own homestead, Wynnwood. Though it seems like a "he" to me, I have never yet seen him in any anthropomorphic or animal-like form. Instead I see him as an energy shape, formed like a giant spindle wound with yarn that reaches half below the ground and half up into the air. Below the ground, a long strand of yarn energy reaches down toward the core of the Earth, the wight's navel-cord to Mother Earth. At the top of the spindle another long cord reaches up in the atmosphere, with a tuft of fine filaments at the end that wave and move constantly. I see this tuft as the organ that connects the Wynnwood Wight with the Sun, Moon, and other celestial bodies. The periphery of the spindle encompasses our land

and a little beyond it, and the yarn and spindle are in constant motion. Sometimes this energy will billow and writhe just under the surface of the ground, creating in spae-sight something like a giant animal shrugging its shaggy coat which is the surface of our land with its trees, shrubs, small pond and all the life on it.

I perceive this Wight as a powerful being, containing within himself me, my husband, our dogs living and dead (including the burials of elderly dogs of our extended families—we're up to eight spirit-dogs now that are members of our Wynnwood Wild Hunt), our house and blacksmith workshop, our pond and well, trees, birds and many wild animals, as well as the lesser landwights associated with all these. Our Landwight feels like an exuberant, whole, self-aware and self-rejoicing being, and seems more so than he was when we moved in more than twenty years ago. Perhaps that is because my own perception has grown more clear over time, or perhaps he has been strengthened and more clearly defined by our Blots and other interactions with him.

Thundering Across the Prairie

Here's the second vision of landwights I'd like to share. I saw myself at sunset, walking a small maze I had made, and as I did so many small landwights, about knee-high, rose up through the ground and joined me. They were too full of energy to walk the maze for long, though, and soon we were racing together over the vast prairie landscape.

As we ran and generated energy, they grew until our sizes were reversed, with me being knee-high to these wights the size of small giants. Exuberantly they thundered in random criss-cross patterns across the land, faster and wilder;

outpaced, I had to draw back and just watch. Buildings, towns, roads, were faint shadows in their wake, while the native tall-grass prairie grew higher and thicker all around them. All the twilit night they dashed about in my vision. Then as the sun rose I saw in the shadows of the land vast herds of bison moving slowly, and flocks of birds rising high in the sky.

The whole experience reminded me of folktales about the spirit-followers of Frau Holda and the other German Goddesses, the Wild Hunt, the ride of the Valkyries, and other energetic troopings of wights that bring life and fertility to the land.

Children of the Earth

My experiences and perceptions of the Landwights lead me to believe that the native landscapes and beings of our world continue to live within the womb of the Soul of the Earth, even after massive damage on the physical plane. The Landwights have access to both worlds, the seen and the unseen, and have the unique ability to knit them together energetically. This can only work to the benefit of all beings. But we need to be their partners in this work. We, too, are children of the Earth, Sun and Moon, living within their great, living souls, and we need to play our own vital role as part of this great physical-spiritual ecosystem.

Ing-Frey's Blessing

From time to time I ask all the Deities with whom I interact what they would like to have me do for them. With Ing-Frey, I am honored and delighted by the task he sometimes asks of me: to join him in blessing the smallest Landwights. In meditation, he asks me to sit with him in a forest glade in the gloaming, with the shadows of dusk creeping out, fireflies and moths flittering about, and the moon rising over the trees.

A crowd of very small Landwights gradually appears around us, their shapes and features blurry and animal-like, hard to distinguish in the twilight. To me, they look a bit like upright hedgehogs and other small animals and birds, but I don't know what they look like to each other. Some of these wights, with their babies in their arms, come forward one by one and lay the tiny creatures in my cupped hands. Ing-Frey's power of life billows around us all, but sometimes he chooses to channel it to these Landwights through me, rather than directly. I don't know why he chooses that, but I absolutely love holding those tiny lives in my hands and filling them—and me—with Ing-Frey's blessing.

"Tomten," by John Bauer

18: Renewable Energy Installations as Jotun-Shrines

This iron sculpture titled "Zauberlehrling" ('sorcerer's apprentice') looks like a dancing power pole. It definitely captures the idea of a Jotun-shrine!

A Human-Jotnar Switch

Our human-technological collective can now be considered as powerful and baneful as the most powerful of the Jotnar were considered to be in ancient times. In traditional Germanic thought, humans and human activities were viewed as 'ordering' powers, while the Giants were considered chaotic and destructive. But whatever the truth may be in that belief, it no longer holds. Human activities that could be viewed as harmless and even environmentally well-balanced become less so as human populations and technological capacities increase.

If the Jotnar were considered to promote chaos while humans and Deities promoted order, something has now turned around in that equation. In our efforts to promote 'order'—social order, economic order, global order, public goods—we have loosed chaotic forces of climate change, ecosystem destruction, pollution, extinction, disruptions and breakdowns of social and cultural patterns around the world. "We" being human beings as a collective, along with our technology, resource use, and generation of wastes.

On the individual human level, there is an innocence to this—the same innocence as animals and all living beings have. The basic things we want are natural, not evil: food, shelter, safety, health, children, kindreds, social groups. But when our numbers, our desires, and our resource consumptions multiply, we begin to tip large and complex earth-systems increasingly out of balance. The Jotnar naturally react to this; they are the children of Earth, in so many mythologies around the world. Taking another view, they are the inherent powers of the Earth projected into active forms that exist on the energy-levels of Nature.

We are enabling and provoking massively powerful Jotunn activity by our collective human activities: Jotunn activity seen in the warming oceans, changes in the global patterns of atmospheric and oceanic currents impacting our weather and climate, hurricanes, wildfires, drought, extinctions, ecosystem collapse, pest invasions and epidemics affecting humans, animals, crops, ecosystems, and all the resulting social disruptions.

"The Giant," painting by Francisco Goya.

In these ways, *we* are the sources of chaos and disruption in the natural life and living processes of Jordhr / Nerthus, while the Jotnar can be seen as mighty forces that work, albeit violently, toward rebalancing an increasingly chaotic natural world. Our actions trigger theirs, their actions trigger ours, and the whole situation escalates. On one level, it's almost like a dreadful contest between the human collective and the Jotnar as to who can bend the processes of nature more powerfully towards their will and their side. We can see the results all around us.

Renewable Energy Installations as Jotun-Shrines

Another Look at Jotnar

Let's take a closer look at this situation, beginning with the nature of the Jotnar. Who are they, what are they like? Here are some of the traits that humans have perceived in 'Giants', according to Germanic and many other cultures around the world.

1. They are excessive and overreactive, temperamental and powerful beings who unleash great, destructive energies into the world.

2. They are ignorant, thoughtless, seemingly even stupid. They just react, and don't think things through.

3. They are greedy and go after what they want, careless of the consequences.

4. They are focused on their own concerns. They may not perceive the impacts their activities have on humans, and even if they do, they don't care.

5. They multiply, and Deities like Thor and his brethren in other pantheons constantly have to fight them and keep their numbers down.

Hmmm.....do these traits maybe apply, in a collective sense, to some other beings we know? *Is it possible that the Jotnar might perceive these same traits in HUMAN BEHAVIOR???* (Gasp! Clutch pearls!) Let's walk over to the other side, turn around, and see what the view looks like from there. Keep in mind that we are talking about human behavior *collectively* over great spans of time and space.

1. Humans engage in fights, conflicts, raids, warfare, oppression, often for the most inexplicable and senseless reasons like 'glory' (whatever that is), pride and prestige, disagreement about some philosophical principle, one-upmanship, or taking offense at something. They also blow things up a lot, even when they're not mad.

2. Humans tend to think in the short-term, don't focus on long-term consequences. What they want now is of greater import than what will result from that, a long time in the future.

3. Humans have 'needs', they are always wanting this and needing that. They are never satisfied.

4. Humans are very human-focused, and in fact very focused only on their own social entities like family, friends, local interests, and people they feel connected to. They are not very willing to see, admit, or adjust to the impacts their actions may have on anything outside those circles.

5. Humans multiply, and the forces of Earth and Nature, personified as destructive giants, wights of illness, plagues of pests, and other energy-wave-forms that the Earth extrudes, are needed to keep their populations and impacts in check.

Is it possible that we and the Jotnar are kindred beings, with so many of the same traits? There's another story about where humans came from: not a story about trees and Embla and Askr, but a story about an Earth-born God called Tuisto / Tuisco, who produced Mannus (Mannaz), who then produced the founding fathers of the tribes. (Tacitus p. 63.)

A stone sculpture of the Anglo-Saxon God Tiw / Tyr.

There's lots of very enjoyable scholarly and Heathen discussion about this being and the meaning of the name, which probably relates to "two" in one way or another. Some have likened Tuisto to Ymir, said to be hermaphroditic, with Tuisto thus being male-female twinned together, which would make a lot of sense as a progenitor. Others see a connection with Tiw or Tyr, and with the word 'twist', also related to 'two' but with the sense of 'two things in opposition to each other,' Tiw as a God of conflict as well as a Sky-Father. There are many possible connections of this myth with names and myths in other Indo-European branches, and a number of them involve twins. (You can read a brief overview here: https://en.wikipedia.org/wiki/Tuisto)

Without getting too far into the weeds, I'm just going to pick out some strands and relate them to my thesis here. Let's bring together a hermaphroditic Ymir and a twinned Tuisto, born of Earth or of the icy-fiery cosmic powers that gave birth to Earth, and suggest they are twin progenitors of Jotnar and humans, respectively.

The difference in our human perception of their birth and their natures suggests the possibility that these beings were 'twisted' into opposition to each other from the beginning. Ymir arises from ice, one of the primal cosmic polarities, and something that is by its nature dangerous to humans. He-she is seen as something monstrous and primal. Tuisto is born from Earth—recognized as our Mother (occasionally Father) in so many mythologies—and is seen as someone divine and kindred to us. Yet, in this view, they are twins, twined and twisted together, for good and for ill.

This leads us to the idea that we and the Jotnar are more akin than we may realize. It also suggests that any solution or adaptation to the Earth-disruptions we all face now may need to be a joint effort among our two 'tribes', working in concert rather than fighting against each other. We need to create grithsteads / places of truce, and frithsteads / places where we interact frithfully and fruitfully with each other. Here is an idea about one form that this joint effort could take: regarding renewable energy installations as Jotun-Shrines, and as grithsteads (places of truce) or frithsteads (places for peaceful interactions) where humans and Jotnar can work together.

Jotun-Shrines

If we hope for the elemental Giants to tone down the impacts of their energies on our human world, one approach is to provide them with other outlets for it. The one I'm proposing here is renewable energy installations, which I will call REIs, for convenience: wind turbines, hydropower dams, solar arrays, geothermal, wave-energy harvesters, the lot. Even nuclear plants, which I'll discuss more, later, although they are not 'renewable.' Now clearly, most humans on this planet are not going to approach REIs in this way! This means that 'enlightened' Heathens, and perhaps other Pagans and Animists too, need to be the facilitators and ambassadors in this effort. The approach that I envision is simple in concept, but may be complicated in practice, depending on how creatively we pursue it.

Let's start with this: what is a shrine? In essence, it is any kind of physical setup that draws us into closer communion with the being—Deity, human spirit, whoever—to whom the shrine is dedicated. Often shrines are deliberately built or set up with this purpose in mind, but not always. Sometimes people will turn a place where something happened into a shrine, such as the place where innocent people were killed, or where some event of great significance occurred. These may be temporary shrines like flowers and votive candles, or more permanent shrines like memorials and monuments.

Renewable Energy Installations as Jotun-Shrines

Here, I'm proposing that we learn to regard REIs as shrines to Jotnar and their mighty energies, and treat them as such. Depending on the installation, we may or may not have physical access to it. Some of them, like hydropower dams, might be accessible to the public; others like turbines set up on private property or out at sea may not be. And in truth, leaving posies, votives, ribbons and stuffed animals at these Jotun-Shrines, the way we might do at other kinds of shrines, may not be that appealing to the Jotnar, not to mention being somewhat environmentally unfriendly. Even leaving food items is not a good idea; my feeling is that many (though not all) of the REIs are not that safe or friendly toward the smaller landwights and the animals that the wights often associate with, and who will be attracted to the food. So we need to approach these shrines differently, although if we have our own installation, such as a solar-panel on our roof or a small turbine, we can treat it more like a traditional shrine if we wish.

A geothermal installation in Iceland.

Example: Wind Turbines

Here is my approach, and undoubtedly others will come up with other good ideas. I use wind turbines as an example, because of how they affect me and because where we live, we have large arrays of them spread out both to the north and the south, as well as a few single turbines set up by small businesses nearby. We can see their red lights blinking eerily during the night, and drive by them in the daytime if we're going out of town. They are definitely a presence on our flat-as-a-pancake landscape. It's easy to complain about them as an intrusion into the landscape, an ecological disruption, or to ignore them as one more element of civilizational infrastructure all around us, and all those perspectives are valid.

But the wind turbines 'talk' to me, and this is how the idea of Jotun-Shrines came to me in the first place. These turbines are gigantic, majestic, hypnotic, eerie at night, and somewhat threatening. When I come close to them, I can feel or sense some kind of strange energy being churned in the atmosphere around them, sometimes strongly enough to make me feel a little dizzy.

There is something numinous there: not in the physical turbine itself, but coming through a doorway that uses the turbine as its access. And this is what a shrine is: a doorway between worlds, perceptions, states of being, and between beings who stand in different worlds and commune through that doorway. The shrine is the common ground and the meeting-point.

Renewable Energy Installations as Jotun-Shrines

Wind turbines at the foot of a rainbow...this may portend a truce between the Jotnar and Heimdall!

So, I use my human consciousness, my own souls, as one endpoint of this doorway or passageway, and try to perceive who is at the other end, using the turbine itself and its energies as the connection point, and also as a buffer zone between us. I do this at a distance, of course, often a distance of miles, with our flat topography. I don't approach too closely, and I don't bring any material offerings. My offering is my attention, my willingness to connect with the Jotun on the other end of the passage. I want to know something of who the Jotun is, what their life is like, what they want, how they connect with and perceive the Midgard that humans perceive and populate. I try to sense the flavor of their energy, and thereby sense their Will. How does this individual Jotun want to work its Will into Midgard, or possibly what does it want to take *out* of Midgard through the work it is doing?

We are different beings, the Jotun and I; there are many ways that we do not intersect. But there are also things we have in common, relating to the functioning and the wellbeing of the Earth and all her powers: our mutual forebear. When we share attention, energy, Will together, for a time we are mutually aligned and can direct our joint powers as we choose. At this point, we and the Jotun can direct our energies and will toward the physical turbine and its intention: to transform some portion of Earth's energy into a form humans can use for our needs, while minimizing the cost to the Earth of such an action.

This is the human side of the equation, the human focus and benefit. What is on the Jotun side? One thing is simply channeling power: Jotnar like to do that, no question! That is food for them, feast and nourishment and sensory enjoyment. But, depending on the Jotun involved, there may be a good deal more that they are trying to accomplish or to experience, other reasons for their involvement. These reasons may or may not align with human desires, human logic or understanding. They may or may not want to share them with us, nor want us to be involved in their affairs.

The communion of human and Jotun at the REI shrine often comes to an abrupt and clumsy finish. In my experience, on both sides there is an initial interest and curiosity, a willingness to meet on common ground for a common purpose. But after a short while, the profound differences between us again become apparent, and our alignment twists and slips apart. I think this is natural and healthy for human-Jotun interactions: this brief but powerful and purposeful alignment, and then the clear separation. The REI acts as a buffer zone, as well as a meeting space, thus reinforcing both connection and separation in turn. I suspect the same kind of thing happens between the Deities and the Jotnar: they join together to produce mighty offspring, for example, but then separate because their lives and natures are too different for permanent pairing, as Njorð and Skaði found.

Your own Virtual Jotun-Shrine

My discussion of wind-turbines is just an example; the same sort of approach can be made toward other types of REIs, and indeed toward nuclear plants and the dangerous powers they channel. I've also used my own approach as an example of *how* to engage with the Jotun-Shrine. Others may prefer to engage in something less intense, for example a simple greeting, or a statement of thanks or solidarity toward the Jotun(s) who is working that REI, rather than any closer contact with the mind of the Jotun.

Here is another approach. Since there are many REIs that we can't get anywhere close to, another way to work with them is to create a virtual shrine, using a map of an REI location, a photo or satellite image of the installation, a design diagram of a generic installation of that type, a drawing, whatever you can find that would work for you as a shrine. You may want to choose the installation that is closest to where you live, ideally one that supplies some of the power you use yourself.

It is important to give this virtual shrine the real name of the installation you intend to work with: the Jotun and the location are specific, not generic. This is true even if you use a general blueprint of how a hydropower installation works, for example, rather than a specific photo. In my understanding, trying to create a 'generic' shrine dilutes the effort into uselessness, and is in fact more of an insult or a dismissal of the actual Jotun, than it is a way to work with them. They are individuals, working at specific places on the Earth, and they need to be treated as such. If you can discover the name or by-name of the Jotun you're working with, that would be ideal.

You can add anything you like to this shrine you are making, in the way of decorations, statues or other Jotun-images, and I recommend a representation of the Element that your REI is associated with. For example: Fire for a solar installation or geothermal, Air for turbines, Water and Earth for hydropower dams, etc. You may like to use music that reminds you of Jotnar when you work with your shrine.

Our manner of engagement with the REI-Jotnar is something for each of us to work out for ourselves, and it can change over time as we gain experience.

The Thorn, or Thurs, on the Rose

Jotnar are not all sweetness and light, of course; they can be unpredictable, dangerous, and uncooperative. The same sort of thing can be said for renewable energy and nuclear energy, especially the latter. There are a great many reasons for phasing out nuclear power, but the thing to consider in this context is that while there *are* still nuclear plants in operation, it might be good to keep the Jotnar who are involved with that form of energy in a good mood!

REIs and nuclear help us resolve one set of problems, but create other problems in their place. The materials necessary for making solar arrays and turbines, for example, require means for their production that are environmentally and socially damaging. Hydropower dams have many negative effects on ecosystems and communities, and fail entirely in extreme drought. Nuclear plants produce clean power now at the risk of severe future impacts from nuclear waste, as well as high cost and risks of misuse of nuclear materials. All of them create disposal and decommissioning problems, distribution and social-justice problems. We need to know this, to acknowledge that REIs and nuclear are double-edged swords, not the solutions to all our troubles. We are not 'home-free' here; our work in learning to live sustainably on this Earth is not done, even if we achieve a great shift into renewable energy.

This is another way that Jotnar and renewable energy are essentially matched: they are both double-edged swords; both have many negative and even dangerous traits. But at this time, we need renewables as part of a suite of technological and human-behavioral changes that (we can hope) will keep us going for awhile longer, and maybe even give us time to become wiser about the ways we all live on this Earth. And the Earth with her garment, Nature, needs her children, the Giants (along with all her other children), as active expressions of her enormous life-force in her everlasting struggle to exist, evolve, transform, rebalance, renew.

Grotte-song

Grotte-Song is a poem in the *Poetic Edda* that wonderfully captures this double-edged-sword nature of the Jotnar, and offers us a lesson in how to interact with them! Two young giant women, Fenja and Menja, have been captured and brought as slaves to turn the heavy mill of King Frodi, called the Grotte-mill. This mill is magical, turning out wealth and wellbeing for the king and the realm, and Frodi is so determined to put it to use that he refuses to allow these powerful Jotun-maids any time to rest, sleep or eat.

At first Fenja and Menja set to work with goodwill. Menja encourages them to mill gold, wealth, blessedness, comfort, happiness for the king and the realm. But as time goes on and their efforts are abused by Frodi's demands, the Jotynjur become angry and discuss things that Frodi would have been wise to know before he treated them so. He didn't bother to learn about their lineage or their history, and this was a mistake!

Fenja och Menja vid kvarnen Grotte,
Carl Larsson and Gunnar Forssel, 1886.

We discover that they are kin to the mighty giants Hrungnir, Thjazi, Idi and Aurnir (and thus, of course, to Skaði as well, daughter of Thjazi). Fenja and Menja themselves, as little girls, were the ones who tossed the enormous magical millstone up to the surface of Midgard as they played in Jotunheim. Later, as battle-maids, they fought in Midgard: crushing armies, challenging berserkers, overthrowing a prince, regarded as champion warriors. (We are not told how these mighty maids ended up as slaves. Maybe magic was used.)

Straining at Frodi's mill, not allowed to rest, their hands now remember the rough feel of weapon-shafts, and they start singing ancient battle-tales and magical chants. They call up a baneful fate for Frodi, an army which now approaches and will overthrow him. The warning beacon-fires are already alight on the heights above the sleeping kingdom. As their anger and their magic grow, Fenja and Menja become so forceful that the great Grotte millstone, its shaft, and its iron supports shatter into fragments. They close the poem by announcing: "the women have done a full stint of milling!" Yes, I would say they have!

There are clear lessons here, that we can apply to this project of viewing REIs as Jotun-Shrines. The giants may work willingly on this joint project; they may understand very well the Earth's need for this form of energy-transformation. But they are also likely to have their own agendas, their own histories, identities, intentions. Abusing these powerful beings and the energies they constellate through their shrines and through Earth-processes and functions will backfire on us. We can choose to communicate respectfully with them through our newly-established Jotun-Shrines, and work together to align the intentions and the actions of Jotnar and humans, as we all (at least the wise among us) seek to rotate ourselves back into balance with our mother Earth.

Renewable Energy Installations as Jotun-Shrines

"Rock-Giantess" formation.

19: The Vision of the Seeress: A Giantess's Tale

This visionary tale is told from the perspective of the Giantess Griðr, mother of the God Viðar. She has entered a trance, but her intended trance-working is hijacked by the powerful voice of the Seeress of the Völuspá poem (Poetic Edda), who is reciting the vision that Odin has demanded of her. Griðr is by turns awed, fascinated, and horrified by this vision, and is drawn to the glimpse of the future Viðar that she sees, without realizing that this is her son-to-be. I have slightly altered and added my own lines to the verses of the Völuspá here. The painting: "Dreaming Woman," by Noah Buchanan.

The Vision of the Seeress: A Giantess's Tale

I remember giants in ages past;
Once they called me one of their kin.
I remember nine Worlds, nine Jotunn-wives,
And a tall Tree, rooted deepest of all.

Griðr stirred, uneasy with the burring drone of the ancient voice in her head. This was not at all what she had thought she was seeking, when she had entered her wisdom-trance only a few moments ago. The hoarse voice, half-whispering, half-chanting, pursued her down the soul-paths, holding her mind with an iron grip.

Naught was yet, in Ymir's day:
Not sand nor sea, nor cooling wave.
Earth was not yet, nor the high heavens,
Only gaping emptiness, nowhere green.

A dim grey light, sourceless, surrounded her now. Orienting herself with difficulty in the oddly distorted space where she seemed to be floating, Griðr saw below her an immense, sleeping body that could only be Aurgelmir Giant-Father, called Ymir by Gods and men. He appeared to take up all the room that existed: though there were no visible boundaries around him, yet space and time seemed to stop beyond the extent of his mighty limbs. A shiver of awe ran through her.

Peering more intently, Griðr realized that there was yet a greater being present, so huge and so vague in outline that she could barely grasp its image. Auðhumla, she thought: the Ur-Mother herself in the form of a cow. Cloud-grey, swathed in mist and steam, Auðhumla straddled the sleeping giant and let

The Vision of the Seeress: A Giantess's Tale

down her streams of milk to him like the twining strands of Godafoss, waterfall of the Gods. And he, unconscious of the life within him, yet opened his bearded mouth to receive her blessing. Auðhumla gazed down at him, dark eyes deeper than all the wells in all the Worlds.

Griðr hovered awestruck over the scene, scarcely able to believe that she was given to see this, the beginning of the Worlds. In the back of her mind, the crone's voice chanted on, telling a tale of wonder.

South came the Sun, Moon's bright companion,
Reached her right hand over heaven's rim,
Then bright grass grew from the stony ground.

Within her body Griðr felt the seeds of life stirring, yearning to answer the call of golden Sunna, to spring forth into her holy light. The Worlds and their beings unfolded before Griðr's sight: made of Ymir's flesh, nourished by Auðhumla, shaped and given soul by the Gods. The ancient voice became yet deeper, more ponderous.

An Ash-Tree I know, Yggdrasil its name,
Tall Tree watered from a milk-white Well.

Griðr felt the vast presence, too huge to be fully seen: Tree whose branches hold all the worlds there are, the axis of being. Wind soughed through the Tree, scattering drops of dew from its boughs. Some fell onto the emerald grass below, others with a bright, chiming note dropped into the Well itself.

Come three maids, cunning in knowledge,

The Vision of the Seeress: A Giantess's Tale

From the holy Well beneath this Tree.
Urð one is called, Verðandi the other,
Carving the rune-tines; Skuld the third.
Layers they lay, lives they choose,
Knowing all wyrds by the holy Well.

Nornir, by Ludwig Pietsch

Dim in the gentle mists surrounding the Tree's great roots, Griðr saw the cloaked forms gathered close around the Well, bent to their work of tending the Tree with the life-giving water and white mud from the Well. "I greet you, Wise Ones," she whispered, "who shape our lives and the wyrd of Worlds." Griðr's soul lingered there with them, glad in their presence: these stern teachers in the craft of the seeress, in the ways of wyrd. But the call of the crone drew her away and she tumbled through the unformed mists, following that burring drone, a thread leading onward into mystery.

The Vision of the Seeress: A Giantess's Tale

Alone I sit as the Old One comes,
Ygg of the Æsir looks into my eyes.

Momentarily Griðr caught a glimpse of that fierce, one-eyed face peering into her own, his long hair and beard and his blue cloak whipping in a wind that Griðr could not feel.

Why do you question? Why test me?
I know all, Odin: Where your eye lies hid,
Valfather's pledge in Mimir's dark well.
Seek you more wisdom, or what?

Odin and the Seeress, by Lorenz Frølich.

Griðr felt hair rising on her nape and spine at the mention of Odin's name and his wisdom-pledge. Who was speaking to him and of him? Whose voice was this, chanting in the back of her mind?

I see for Balder, for the bloody God,
Odin's child: I see his hidden wyrd.

The Vision of the Seeress: A Giantess's Tale

In Fen-Halls Frigg weeps
For Asgard's woe; all-wise Mother mourns.
Seek you more wisdom, or what?

Seeress's words, dredged deep from the secret halls of Time: a bitter tale to tell, it seemed. Balder, brightest and most beloved God: even the giants would grieve if ill befell him. Griðr stirred restlessly in her trance, twisting her massive body away from the burning knowledge told in the crone's voice.

A cock crows in Gallows-Wood,
Flame-red one called Fjalar.
For the Æsir, Gold-Comb answers loud,
Wakens the warriors in high Valhalla.
Below the earth still another calls,
Soot-red rooster in the halls of Hel.
The hound bays louder by Gnipa-cave,
Six-Strand tears and Ravener runs free.
Wisdom I know, I see further ahead
To the terrible doom of the striving Gods.

Chills pursued one another along Griðr's spine as the dread vision unfolded. She knew now that her soul was soaring helplessly in the wake of the greatest of seeresses, gripped by the power of that mighty mind.

An axe-age, a sword-age, shields are cleft asunder,
A wind-age, a wolf-age, while the world is falling.
Mimir's sons at war-play; Wyrd now aflame
Calls from its long sleep the ancient Gjallarhorn.
God-Warder winds it, white Heimdall on the bridge;

The Vision of the Seeress: A Giantess's Tale

Yggdrasil shudders, the World-Tree moans.
What of the Æsir? What of the Elves?
Jotunn-Home groans; the Æsir take rede.
Dwarves roar before their rocky doors:
Rulers of the mountain walls, shouting their rage.
Seek you more wisdom, or what?

Griðr held her breath unconsciously, waiting to hear Odin's response. Surely even Odin would not wish to hear more?

Comes then Frigg's second grief,
When Odin wars against the Wolf:
Then must fall Frigg's most beloved.

(Fenris devours Odin, by Dorothy Hardy.)

Indeed, bitter must this rede be to Odin's ears, thought Griðr, tossing back and forth in cold horror. Odin himself, fallen to a giant wolf in battle? She bore little love for the Æsir, kin though they were, but such a downfall was too evil a portent. All the world seemed poised on the point of a needle, a captured spark of light too fragile to hold onto life. As she fixed her eyes on this spark, willing it to live, it seemed to grow and brighten, holding within its glowing core the face of a young

The Vision of the Seeress: A Giantess's Tale

God. Griðr heard the rising chant of the seeress continue as the shining, unknown face gazed into hers.

Then strides great Viðar, War-Father's son,
Against Slaughter-Beast. Wrenching jaws asunder,
He stabs through the heart of Loki's fierce child:
Valfather's kinsman claims his vengeance.

Viðar and Fenris, by Lorenz Frølich

Bewildered, Griðr glanced back and forth between the shining face hovering in the light before her, and the bloody face of battle-mighty Viðar Wolf-Slayer, shown by the seeress's vision. Indeed, they were the same face, the same God. The two images of the face, one bloody and grim, the other shining with a bright love, merged into one, filling Griðr's vision. She felt her heart warm toward this young God with his cloud of dark hair and his bright blue eyes.

A strange thing indeed, she thought, *for a God to smile at me from a spark on a needle's point, and stranger still that my heart should warm to him, Ase though he is. Æsir and Jotnar—we tend to go our separate ways.*

As the seeress's harsh voice rasped across Griðr's mind again, the spark and the God-face winked out, along with her distracted thoughts.

Dark the place where Sunna was devoured;
Earth sinks deep under the sea.
Flames lick upward over World-Tree's limbs,
Fire strikes hot against heaven itself.

Griðr's eyes closed in pain, feeling in her own flesh the fire gnawing at the limbs of World-Tree. The flames of Surt Fire-Demon and his wild kin, overrunning the world, flickered against her closed eyelids and stole her breath with their heat. Panting in agony, she felt her flesh turn crisp and black, peel away from her bones and fall to dust. A hot wind blew, scattering her ashes and empty bones over a wasteland of non-being, while her soul drifted tetherless for a timeless time.

I see the Earth arising again
Out of the waters, green once more.
An eagle soars over rushing waterfalls,
Hunting his fish from the mountain crags.
Unsown fields will grow good fruits,
Ills are healed as Balder heads homeward;
Then will Odin's kinsman choose the runes.
Sons of two brothers dwell widely
All across the windy world.
Seek you more wisdom, or what?

The Vision of the Seeress: A Giantess's Tale

"After Ragnarök" by Emil Doepler.

Griðr felt the healing waters on her parched bones. As the fields sprouted green, her flesh reknit itself to her bones, cloaking them again with her fierce giant's beauty. She floated in peace for a time, still feeling detached from life and the world.

Now I will sink down.

The seeress's hoarse whisper echoed in her mind, seeming to speak to her alone. As the seeress sank back into the dimness of quiet death from which Odin had called her, Griðr too sank into the soft darkness of sleep, followed by the distant cry of ravens.

An Anglo-Saxon Charm Against a Dwarf

20: An Anglo-Saxon Charm against a Dwarf:

Shapeshifting, Soul-Theft, and Shamanic Healing

An early Anglo-Saxon mounting of uncertain use; possibly attached to a staff or used as an amulet. Dated between 450-550 CE. Though not clear from this image, the decorations on the head represent birds. I'm using it as an illustration of a shapeshifting Dwarf!

Here I discuss a healing charm from Anglo-Saxon times, one of the few written charms that show predominantly Heathen characteristics, though there are Christian admixtures as well. It is a perplexing piece of writing which a number of scholars have tried to interpret in different ways. I will present my own interpretation, which I believe is valid and which also provides useful guidance for those of us today who wish to engage in shamanic-type practices within an Anglo-Saxon / Germanic traditional framework. In my analysis of this charm, I believe it offers indications of shapeshifting, soul-theft, and both hostile and beneficial roles of otherworldly beings, which puts it into a framework of belief and practice which today we would call shamanism. (I apologize here, but not too abjectly, for using the word 'shamanism,' which some feel should be used only in the context of Siberian tribal practices. Being unaware of a similar term in modern English that would fit my discussion here as well as this term does, I will perforce make use of it.)

Because most readers are probably not interested in any detailed discussion of linguistic debates and proposed revisions of confusing parts of the text, I am keeping this to a bare minimum here. Those of you who are interested in more detail should consult the discussion on pages 166ff of G. Storms *Anglo-Saxon Magic*. I have here chosen the version of the text that makes the most sense to me (based primarily but not entirely on that of Rodriguez), which I present below as my translation. The Old English texts are provided at the end of this essay.

The Charm Against a Dwarf

One must take seven little wafers, as are used in (Christian) worship, and write these names on each wafer: Maximianus, Malchus, Johannes, Martinianus, Dionisius, Constantinus, Serafion. Then the charm that is mentioned hereafter must be sung, first into the left ear, then into the right ear, then over the crown of the man's head. And then let a virgin go to him

An Anglo-Saxon Charm Against a Dwarf

and hang it on his neck. And do so for three days. Then he will be better.

Here came striding in   Upon/Within (a) spider-wight,
He had his hama in hand,   Said that you were his steed,
Laid his fetter on your neck.   They began to set off from the land;
As soon as they had come away from the land,   Then began his limbs to cool.
Then came striding in   The Dwarf's sister;
Then she ended it   And swore oaths
That this nevermore would be able   To harm the sick,
Nor him who this galdor   Could acquire,
Neither him who knew   How to chant this galdor.

There is a good deal of scholarly debate about the symptoms or illness that this charm is supposed to cure. Most believe it is a fever because of the mention of the patient "cooling", presumably the result of the cure. The fact that the herb *dweorge dwostle* ("Dwarf dwostle" or pennyroyal) was used to treat fever, among many other ailments, seems to support this, with its apparent association of Dwarves with fever (though this would not tell us whether Dwarves are the bringers or healers of the fever). Those who credit this interpretation see the spider-wight in the charm as a beneficial being, binding the Dwarf who is causing the disease and drawing him away from the patient.

Dweorgedwostle was also used to treat a sudden case of dumbness, an inability to speak. As Storms (p. 163) mentions, "sudden dumbness can only be caused by spirits or Dwarfs, compare the sudden stitch", referring to another Heathen charm against a sudden pain or cramp caused by Elf-shot. My view is that the ailment here involves theft of one of the patient's "souls" or vital bodies, most likely the *hama* or etheric body of the patient. The sudden dumbness, probably caused or at least accompanied by mental disorientation, could certainly be a symptom of this condition. Here is my own line-by-line interpretation of this charm. I will discuss the instructions given at the beginning of the charm later on in this essay.

Line 1: *Here came striding in*

Here came striding in   Upon / Within (a) spider-wight

The first line contains one of several points that I believe are significant but that have been dismissed by scholars I have read. All translations I have read make a significant change to the little word preceding *spiden wiht.* The Old English version reads *Her com in gangan in spiden wiht.* "In spiden wiht" is translated as "a spider wight." However, "in" in Old English does not mean "a" or "an," though scholars have assumed it was simply a scribal error and that "an" was the intended meaning.

I disagree with this. "In" has several meanings, all having to do with time, purpose, or location; the meanings most likely to apply in this case are locational: "on, upon, into." I believe this was not an error but the intended meaning: the Dwarf, who is implied by the title of the charm but never mentioned by name, comes in where the patient is, riding upon or residing within a spider-wight. Here is the first clue that we are dealing with shape-shifting. Either the Dwarf is riding in astral or etheric form upon a spider, or the spider itself is the shapeshifted Dwarf. I incline toward the latter, for reasons contained in the next line of the charm.

As a final note on this first line, my taking the "in" at face value leaves us with no subject for the sentence: "Here came striding in, upon/within (a) spider-wight, he had his *hama* in his hand." I believe that the failure to include any reference to the Dwarf directly is a safety measure for the healer. Calling or referring to the Dwarf directly would attract his dangerous attentions to the healer. That our ancestors believed direct reference was dangerous is widely attested to by their custom of referring to elves and other Otherworldly beings by flattering euphemisms such as "the good folk," "the good neighbors," etc. The healer here has the tricky job of ridding the patient of the Dwarf, while making sure that the Dwarf does not attach himself to the healer in revenge. Later we shall see how this is done.

Line 2: *He had his hama in hand,*

Moving on to the second line, a spider strides into the room, carrying his "hama" in his hand. All other interpretations of this charm that I have read pay little attention to the "hama," apparently regarding it as simply a quaint detail, but looking at the charm overall, we can see that it is very concise, carrying no extraneous detail. It is reasonable to assume, then, that like every other detail in the charm, the fact that the spider is carrying his "hama" is an important part of the picture, an item of information that the healer must know about. To me, this "hama" is another clue that we are dealing with a shapeshifting phenomenon.

'Hama' in Anglo-Saxon and other Germanic languages normally refers to several kinds of clothing: a shirt, shift or dress. We know, however, that in Old Norse the *hama* or *hamr* is the externalized—often shapeshifted—form of a person who is *hamrammr* or shape-strong, which can travel in spirit and sometimes physically outside of the body in that form. Though it appears that 'hama' is not used in such a way in Anglo-Saxon texts, I have found one other instance in Anglo-Saxon writings that could indicate this meaning. This occurs in one of the homilies of Ælfric, a Christian cleric.

Ælfric is retelling the legend of the fatal contest that took place in Rome between the apostle Peter and his adversary Simon the Magus. Simon claims that he, too, is able to perform divine miracles and offers to prove this by taking flight off a high tower. He does this successfully, but eventually Peter is able by prayer to cast him out of the sky, crashing to his death on a rock. In discussing this feat with the emperor Nero, who is witness and judge of the contest, Peter refers (in the words of Ælfric) to Simon's *deofolisc fiðerhama*—his devilish feather-hama which was given to him by spirits supporting him with magic. The word *fiðerhama* is translated as 'wings' in modern English texts, but I think that more lies behind the word than simply normal wings on a bird. The identical word in Old Norse—*fjadhrhama*—occurs in the *Thrymskviða* of the Poetic Edda, the tale of the theft of Thor's Hammer, when Loki borrows Freya's magical feather cloak and turns into a hawk or falcon to fly out in search of the Hammer.

In both tales, the Anglo-Saxon and the Old Norse, the donning of the feather hama refers to a change of shape and physical function, whether partial (wings on a human form) or full (change into a different, winged form). Interestingly, in other accounts of this Christian legend, no mention is made of wings or feathers; Simon instead is held aloft in simple human form by invisible demons. It seems here that Ælfric, a very lively sermonist, is drawing on a cultural meme of shapeshifting to add drama to his sermon.

I believe, therefore, that the spider in our charm is actually the Dwarf—the disease-causing entity—in shapeshifted form, and that the mention of the hama is a clue given to the healer about the shapeshifting nature of the spider/Dwarf. A shaman-healer must always know about the nature of the spirit or entity one is dealing with, both for the healing to be effective and so that safety measures for oneself and one's patient can be implemented. Failing to understand the nature of one's adversary can be very dangerous. This is in principle the same as for a modern physician: making a false diagnosis and applying treatment based on this will be, at best, ineffective and at worst actually dangerous to the patient. In the charm, the Dwarf has cleverly taken on the shape of a spider, in which he can easily sneak up on his victim and 'bridle' him with his spider-silk. To undo the Dwarf's evil magic, this tactic of his must be recognized for what it is.

Lines 2-3: *Said that you were his steed,*

Said that you were his steed, Laid his fetter on your neck.

Proceeding to the next lines of the charm, the Dwarf / spider says that you (the victim) are his steed and lays his fetter on your neck. Here we come to a kind of evil magic that occurs in folktales from Germanic lands, including Iceland and other Scandinavian countries, England and Germany. This is called the "Witch Ride" or the "Witch-Bridle," performed by witches, sorcerers, elves and trolls. (See, for example, notes about English occurrences in Simpson p. 181, and Baucher pp.

20-22.) In some areas of Scandinavia even in recent times, this magic is called *reham* or *rehug*: riding-hamr or riding-hugr, because the witch accomplishes it in etheric form *(hamr)* or by the power emanating from the mind-will-magical persona *(hugr* magic). (Stromback p. 17ff)

"Troll-ritten" by John Bauer: an exhausted man and horse, with their tormentor in the foreground.

The aim is to lay a magical bridle, cord, item of clothing or other enchanted object over the victim while sleeping, to enchant him (it is usually a man) into a steed, either in actual shape of an animal, or in human shape with supernatural powers of flight or running. They then ride their victim off on their own errands, often to a meeting such as a coven or an Elf-gathering. Usually the victim is returned to his own form and bed by morning, if the perpetrator is a witch or Elf-woman. If it is a sorcerer, the victim may be kept for a longer time as a slave, to be rescued only by someone with magical or divine aid. (In my view, the latter form of the story is more like a consciously-created adventure tale, as opposed to what

An Anglo-Saxon Charm Against a Dwarf

I think are more authentic folk-anecdotes about witches/hags or elves.) Sometimes the victim will be used again, night after night. Often no physical bridle is used; rather, the victim is held by an enchantment that has no physical form.

Scandinavian folklore offers many details about the witch ride, and this theme appears in the lore of other Germanic folk as well. Probably the earliest written record of this kind of magic occurs in *Eyrbyggja Saga*, chapters 15 and 16, where the witch Katla one night enchants and rides the man Gunnlaugr. After this ride, Gunnlaugr is found unconscious outside his father's house, bloodstained over his shoulders and legs where Katla had whipped him. Katla is eventually tried and hanged for this and other witchcraft deeds. Even more often than people, domestic animals are troll / Elf / witch-ridden. The symptoms of this affliction are the same as we can infer from the Charm against a Dwarf: exhaustion, weakness, paralysis, or very abnormal behavior; more about these symptoms, below.

The result is extremely deleterious for the victim, and in fact there is an English term for this condition that is still occasionally used today: 'hag-ridden'. (Related to this is one of many German words for witch: *Seelendieb* or Soul-thief. Elves are also notoriously known for soul-theft in Germanic folklore.) Such a victim suffers from bed-ridden exhaustion, stupor, terrible nightmares, hallucinations, disorientation, bewilderment, inability to live a normal life. They may have fits or spells of insanity, and often they die from this condition, either suddenly in their sleep (while their soul/hama/energy is being ridden) or slowly wasting away. Most tales imply that it is only the soul and energy or life-strength of the victim that is transformed and taken, while the unconscious body lies in bed—this is most common. Sometimes the implication is

An Anglo-Saxon Charm Against a Dwarf

that the victim is physically transformed and taken; this occurs more often in tales that seem to me to be 'constructed' or invented, rather than genuine folktales reflecting real beliefs. Either way, death or permanent insanity is often the result if a remedy is not found. In the case of this charm, as in most instances of the folktale that I have come across, the object of the theft is one of the souls or vital bodies of the patient, not the physical body, as I will discuss below.

Another possible indication that this charm is meant to act against a condition of unconsciousness or stuporous sleep (occurring as a result of soul-theft) is the list of names at the beginning of the charm, that are to be written on communion wafers. Presumably these would then have been eaten by the patient, though the instruction does not specifically say so. This part of the charm is obviously Christian, though it is likely replacing Heathen elements that performed a similar function. I assume that originally runes were carved onto bark or some other object, scraped off into beer or mead, and then either sprinkled over, or consumed by, the patient. The method of carving runes and then scraping them off into a drink, which is then sprinkled around to distribute the magic where it is wanted, is mentioned in several places in the lore, including *Sigrdrifumal* in the Poetic Edda.

The names that are magically used in this charm are those of the Seven Sleepers, characters from a Christian legend, though the legend may itself stem from a Pagan legend from Mid-Eastern regions. According to the Christian legend, seven staunch Christians, refusing to recant, were shut up in a cave to starve by a Pagan emperor. Two hundred years later, during the reign of a Christian emperor, they reappeared to prove the possibility of the resurrection of the body. These Sleepers, probably because of their power to resurrect in the body, were thought to have healing powers; they figure in no less than five other healing charms as well as this one. In several cases they are supposed to heal fevers, which would support the 'fever' hypothesis of our charm here. But in one case they heal "all evil" (Charm 37 in Storms), and in their own nature, as 'sleepers' who eventually awaken safely, they exemplify the desired outcome according to my interpretation of the charm's meaning. The Anglo-Saxons, as most other elder folk, liked to use parallelism or "as this, so that" approaches in their magic. The patient who is in a somnolent or unconscious state would be helped by the power of the sleepers who themselves awakened naturally, in good health, when it was safe for them to do so.

Getting back to the charm itself, I believe that the lines about calling the patient a steed and fettering or bridling him, are provided to the healer as diagnostic information about a recognized condition: that of being magically bridled and hag-ridden or Elf-ridden, or in this case Dwarf-ridden. In this case, as in most instances of the folktale that I have come across, the theft is of the vital body-soul (hama) of the patient, not the physical body, as I will discuss below.

Thus the first line of the charm indicates the nature of the perpetrator, while the next one points toward the particular method or spell that is being used against the victim. The following lines tell the healer about the results of this attack.

Lines 3-4: *They began to set off from the land*

They began to set off from the land; as soon as they had come away from the land, then his limbs began to cool.

An Anglo-Saxon Charm Against a Dwarf

First considering the phrase "set off from the land": I think it is clear that a soul-journey is the intended meaning. There is no suggestion that anyone has physically taken the patient, put him in a boat and sailed away with him. If this had been the case there would be no point to all the business with feeding him wafers, singing into his ears and hanging charms about his neck. Here, the Dwarf has magically bridled the victim and is riding or dragging his soul away from the 'land,' from the physical world and his physical body. I do not see that any other interpretation of this phrase is possible.

This interpretation is further strengthened, in my view, by the next phrase of the charm: "As soon as they had come away his limbs began to cool." This is the main basis of the 'fever' hypothesis about this charm, but I think this interpretation is mistaken, based on the overall context and meaning of the charm as I see it. It is well known both in occult and in medical fields that a person who has lost consciousness (whether through deep trance induction, or through the shock of injury) is subject to a serious drop in body temperature if the condition is not quickly changed. Physicians would diagnose a reduction of blood pressure and other vital functions; occultists would say the vital body has left the physical. Both are true. The spider-wight here is not a kindly being cooling a fevered patient; it is an ill-intentioned Dwarf stealing a victim's soul and life-force, leaving him chilled and stuporous. The clue given by the charm about the cooling of the limbs is additional important diagnostic information for the healer.

Line 5: *Then came striding in   The Dwarf's sister;*

Concerning the 'Dwarf's sister': 'Dwarf' is not the original word. In the manuscript the word is *deor* (wild animal) rather than *dweorh* (Dwarf). Rodriguez has emended it to 'Dwarf,' as I am using here. The *deor* is assumed by all, myself included, to refer to the spider-wight, the only entity in the charm that could be considered a 'wild animal.' A possible reason to write 'deor' instead of 'dweorh' goes back to what I mentioned earlier about avoiding direct reference to a dangerous otherworldly entity. If my interpretation of the charm is correct, the 'deor' and 'dweorh' are the same being: a Dwarf shapeshifted into a spider. Further evidence for this conclusion is the reference to actions of the 'deor's sister' in the original words of the charm: are we really talking about a spider's / wild animal's sister who strides in, takes over the scene, and sings powerful healing galdors? This would be ridiculous!

For the purpose of analyzing the charm's meaning, based on my interpretation, it hardly matters which word is used. For actual application in practice, when galdoring this charm it would probably be wise to follow the ancestors' precautions and refer to 'deor' or spider-wight, not speaking 'Dwarf' out loud.

With the entry of the Dwarf's sister the entire situation turns around. She is clearly a powerful, protective, rescuing being. In some of the other Anglo-Saxon healing charms showing strong Heathen influence, the healer takes a more personally combative stance against the disease-causing entities (*Charm against a Sudden Stitch, Charm against a Wen*). That is not the case here; the healer prefers to call in outside help rather than challenging the Dwarf in single

An Anglo-Saxon Charm Against a Dwarf

combat. My thought is that the Dwarf, or at least the Dwarf's mode of attack, is more dangerous than the conditions the other charms are meant to heal: sudden pain, and a wen (a severe mole, wart, boil, or other disfiguring blemish). The risk to the healer in our case is that the Dwarf will turn on him/her and steal his/her own soul—a more serious, even fatal, condition in comparison to the other afflictions. The risk to the healer is too high, therefore the choice is to 'call in the big guns'—here, the Dwarf's sister—in preference to taking on the Dwarf in personal combat.

The magical power of both the Dwarves in this charm is consistent with general Germanic lore about the Dwarves: "Magic power over the forces of nature and the mysterious processes of life are still held by Dwarfs of the sagas who can heal and curse in ways not approachable by ordinary men. The word *dvergsnattura* (Dwarf-wisdom) ...designates supernatural skills of healing and craftsmanship" (Motz p. 103).

I take the Dwarf's sister to be a shamaness-magician of her tribe, a galdor-master and healer, and by her actions in the charm I suspect that this is not the first time she has had to step in and put a lid on her brother's misdeeds. She seems rather fed up with it all!

To my mind, the entry of the Dwarf's sister illustrates some important points about Anglo-Saxon healing methods, which I believe do show indications of techniques similar to shamanism as it is generally understood today. In other shamanistic cultures of recent times, the common procedure during a shamanic healing follows the same steps as this charm. The healer diagnoses the condition, and by doing so, identifies the entity causing the affliction. The healer shows power by knowing what has happened: he "laid his fetter on your neck"; "set off from the land". The healer can see through the machinations of the Dwarf; he/she is not fooled but has clear sight.

The next step is to call on 'the spirits' for aid. I propose that when the charm was performed during Heathen times there was an interval between the diagnostic part of the charm, after the "cooling of the limbs," and the second part when the sister arrives. I think there would have been an interval of some kind of power / trance-raising activity: galdoring, dancing, perhaps breathing smoke, or other means that shamans use to reach the shamanic state of consciousness. It would have been during this time, in a trance state, that the healer called on the Dwarf's sister. The healer would know that this is the right helping entity to call, in this case, because of the guidelines in the charm. The shamanic trance would enable the healer to reach this Dwarf spirit-master in the otherworld, know when she has arrived in spirit form bringing her otherworldly power with her, and would allow the healer to perceive her and hear her words.

Lines 6ff: *Then she ended it*

Then she ended it   And swore oaths
That this nevermore would be able   To harm the sick,
Nor him who this galdor   Could acquire,
Neither him who knew   How to chant this galdor.

These lines clearly indicate the power of this otherworldly galdor-master. Here she offers not only healing and protection to the victim, but importantly, to the healer as well: she says that this entity (the Dwarf / spider-wight) will not be able to harm either the sick or the chanter of the galdor—the healer. Here is more evidence that the danger to the healer is an important aspect of this whole situation.

The words of the charm itself do not have healing power. If the charm, during post-Heathen times, was taken at face-value without an understanding of the underlying shamanistic and magical assumptions and their applications in practice, I cannot think that it would have been very effective. I believe there are important things that are left out of the written version of the charm, which non-initiates probably did not realize. One is the need for shamanic trance-induction, already discussed. Another is the actual galdor—the magical chant—given by the Dwarf spirit-master to the healer. One might assume that the words of this written charm are supposed to be the galdor given by the shamaness, but I believe this is incorrect. I think she would give a special galdor to the healer in secret, during the otherworldly trance-journey.

The written charm is not the magical galdor; it is *a map or guideline for obtaining the galdor,* which may very well be unique to that specific healer and the specific healing occasion. I think that each time such a healing is attempted the whole procedure must be repeated and the true galdor—perhaps the same or perhaps a different one—must be obtained, through an otherworldly shamanic journey, from the galdor-master. She is the helping spirit, and I think it is necessary to invoke her each time, be guided by her and be aware of her powers. She and her protection are not to be taken lightly and dismissed under the assumption that after one time around one 'knows it all.' The ill-intentioned Dwarf one faces tomorrow might not be the same Dwarf one faced yesterday; a different galdor might be needed both to heal and to protect the healer.

I also believe that it is not simply the words of the galdor which have power; the galdor gains a great deal of its power because of its source: the Dwarf's sister. In a dangerous situation like soul-theft it is necessary to have a very 'high-octane' galdor which is powered by a spirit-master such as this one. And to obtain her power the healer must contact her directly each time. It is not only the galdor-words or sounds that are needed, but the power that flows from the galdor-master herself, through the galdor and the healer into Midgard. The galdor is the medium for the transfer or flow of the otherworldly galdor-master's power, and both the Dwarf-shamaness and the human healer have a necessary role to play in this.

The Final Instructions

(From the introductory instructions.) Then the charm that is mentioned hereafter must be sung, first into the left ear, then into the right ear, then over the crown of the man's head.

There are several interesting points in these instructions. A common method used by today's traditional and neo-shamans to return a lost soul to a person is to take an otherworldly journey, retrieve the soul, and then 'blow it' by means of one's breath into the crown of the patient's head. In our charm the instruction is to galdor over the crown of the head, a very similar practice. The mention of the ears is intriguing as well; one is put in mind of Odin's ravens Huginn and Muninn perched on his shoulders, whispering wisdom and knowledge into his ears. It is not known whether in the Anglo-Saxon traditions the ravens had specific names indicating Thought and Memory, or any names at all, although the association of

An Anglo-Saxon Charm Against a Dwarf

two ravens with Odin goes way back to pictorial archaeological evidence. Whether this connection with the ravens was consciously intended or not, though, I think there must be an instinctive connection between galdoring into the ears and a restoration of mental faculties which would have been lost due to soul theft, including thinking (Huginn) and remembering (Muninn). Certainly shamanistic practitioners working in our tradition today can and should make this connection with the Ravens and their functions if they engage in the restoration of souls or soul-faculties.

....And then let a virgin go to him and hang it on his neck. And do so for three days. Then he will be better.

I mentioned above that there are probably several instructions that were left unsaid in this written charm, either because they would have been self-evident to the properly trained healer, or because they needed to be kept secret for various reasons. In any case, the final mystery I discern in this charm is the "it" which is hung around the patient's neck. It could be the communion wafers inscribed with the names of the Seven Sleepers, but it seems more likely that these would have been eaten by the patient, not hung around his neck. Not only would this have been in accordance with some Heathen practices (consuming a healing rune-stave or other substance), but also Christian law was very strict about use of communion wafers: almost every use of the wafers other than being eaten (by a Christian in good standing) would have been strictly against the rules.

Also, during Heathen times it is unlikely that any charm would have been written out verbatim; they seldom used runes for simple text-writing during that period. My guess is that in addition to bringing back a song-galdor from the Dwarf-shamaness, the healer may have obtained instructions for making an amulet or charm, using herbs, rune-staves, knots, or all sorts of other things, to hang about the patient's neck.

That the making of amulets in this way was a common practice is attested to by several words in Anglo-Saxon. A *lybesn* was an amulet, a magical knot, or other charm-object. The witch who made such objects, as well as dealing in herbs, drugs and poisons, was called a *lybbestre*. Obviously there was enough traffic in such items to give rise to common words for the object (amulet) as well as the practitioner who produced it. So I think it likely that the "it" referred to here was an amulet of some kind, made in accordance with secret, trance-derived instructions from the spirit-master / shamaness.

Conclusion

The key to interpretation of this and other charms of Heathen origin is to take them seriously, as technical tools of skilled practitioners, and I think this is where conventional scholars miss the boat. Firstly, they may not have the know-how of shamanism, magic, and the Heathen world-view necessary to make these interpretations, and secondly they seem to assume without question that the original developers and users of the charms were primitive, unsophisticated and superstitious. This is the same mistake that many earlier, and present-day, anthropologists have made when studying contemporary cultures that feature shamanic type practices as part of their tradition. True, our written records of these charms are probably somewhat garbled, and certainly the strange mixture of Christian and Heathen elements adds more confusion. A lot of digging and feeling around needs to be done, but as I believe I have shown, when we do so, we find that this charm is an entire procedural outline for a shamanic healing. All of the actions and the underlying assumptions of this charm fit into the world-view and techniques of shamanism:

a) The diagnosis of symptoms is based on the assumption that diseases and afflictions are caused by evil spirits / otherworldly entities.

b) These entities are able to steal people's souls / life force for their own purposes.

c) They are powerful and dangerous; the healer must beware in dealing with them.

d) There are also beneficent otherworldly entities who have healing and protective powers.

e) The shaman-healer can call upon these entities for help.

f) The helping entity will give the healer a power-song or other gift which will overcome all attempts of the evil spirit to harm either the sick person or the healer.

g) The helping spirit may also give follow-up instructions, such as making an amulet, for ongoing protection of the patient during recovery.

All of these techniques are common in healing practices of many cultures which practice shamanism, to the best of my knowledge. The only necessary shamanic element that is missing from the charm is any explicit mention of trance induction and soul-travel by the healer. I cannot think that this instruction would ever have been written in a charm, however. For one thing, it would not have been written about at all by a Christian monk-scribe addressing (presumed) Christian healers.

An Anglo-Saxon Charm Against a Dwarf

For another, the need for a shamanic trance, if such were indeed used in Heathen times, would have been self-evident to the healer. That would have been something he/she would have been trained for during apprenticeship. The healer would have known that when one is dealing with otherworldly entities one needs to be in a certain state of mind to perceive and interact with them; there would be no need for a reminder about this in the text of any specific charm. The usefulness of a specific charm, such as this one, is as a diagnostic tool and as a procedural guideline for knowing which otherworldly entity is at fault here, and which one to call upon for help in this specific situation. The actual calling and interaction with the otherworldly entity would have depended on the healer's ability to enter into the necessary trance-consciousness before doing so.

In addition to evidence of shamanic healing, this Charm Against a Dwarf offers indications that Heathen Anglo-Saxons shared a common knowledge of shapeshifting with other Germanic peoples. Such knowledge is clearly evidenced in Old Norse writings and traditional Germanic tales such as the *Nibelungenlied*, not to mention folklore among all the Germanic peoples (as well as many other peoples). Shapeshifting is a very broad subject which needs to be covered in essays dedicated fully to the topic, so I will not pursue it further here except by noting this charm as probable evidence of its presence in Heathen Anglo-Saxon belief.

This charm also, I believe, provides evidence that Heathen Anglo-Saxons did indeed use healing methods of a shamanic nature, based upon a shamanic world-view and premises about how and why things happen as they do. Our practice of oracular seiðr or spaeworking in various forms is certainly within the shamanic tradition as well. I think there is great scope for us to use the insights of shamanic healing and shapeshifting as a basis for further development of such skills within our own living tradition, as a good number of Heathens today are exploring.

Old English Text

Version from Storms (p. 166):

Her com in gangan in spiden wiht,
Hæfde him his haman on handa, cwæð ðat ðu his hæncgest wære,
Legde ðe his teage an sweoran. Ongunnan him of ðæm landan liðan;
Sona swa hy of ðæm landan coman, tha ongunnan him ða ða colian.
Ða com in gangan deores sweostar;
ða geændade heo and aðas swor
ðæt næfre ðis ðæm adlegan derian ne moste,
Ne ðæm ðe ðis galdor begytan mihte,
Oððe ðe ðis galdor ongalan cuðe. Amen. Fiath.

The version from Rodriguez is the same, except for line 4 which reads:
Sona swa hy of ðæm landan coman, ða ongunnan him ða liðu colian.
(p. 140-1, see also note p. 35-6.)

21: Dwarves and their Powers

Origin of the Dwarves

There are several different accounts of how Dwarves came into being in the Old Norse lore, though one thing that seems to be agreed upon is that Dwarves came into being after the sacrifice of the giant Ymir. Here is one account, from *Völuspá* verses 9-10 (Poetic Edda). Verse 9 says that the all-holy Gods went to their seats of judgement and asked "Who shall shape

Dwarves and their Powers

the lord of the Dwarves from Brimir's blood and from Blain's limbs?" Verse 10 states that Móðsognir was the greatest of all Dwarves, and Durinn the second; they made many 'manlike' forms in the earth, "as Durinn said or commanded."

It's not clear from the text whether Durinn simply told others about this event, or whether the making of many manlike forms was done on Durinn's command. And if it was Durinn's command, whom did he command? At that point, there was only him and Móðsognir. I assume, therefore, that Durinn was relating part of the history of the Dwarves, rather than commanding anyone to create the 'manlike forms.'

It is also not quite clear what involvement the Gods had here, though it's implied that they may have made the first two Dwarves. Verse 9 states that they asked the question, but verse 10 does not specify their involvement. At least it seems fairly clear that the greatest of the Dwarves, Móðsognir and Durinn, were the ones who made the rest of the Dwarves out of 'Brimir and Blain' (or 'bloody froth and blue limbs'), namely from the corpse of the sacrificed Ymir.

So from the *Völuspá* we get the general idea that (a) the first two Dwarf-lords may have been made somehow by the Gods out of Ymir's corpse; and (b) these first two Dwarves made many others. They made the others 'in the earth' or 'out of the earth,' according to the two versions of the *Völuspá (Codex Regius* and *Hauksbók)*. Considering that 'the earth' was made from the sacrificed Ymir, then it seems that all the Dwarves were essentially made out of Ymir's corpse.

Now we'll turn to a different account, from Snorri Sturlason's *Gylfaginning* in the prose Edda (section 14). He repeats that the Gods took their places on their seats of judgement, and then:

"...discussed where the Dwarfs had been generated in the soil and down in the earth like maggots in flesh. The Dwarfs had taken shape first and acquired life in the flesh of Ymir and were then maggots, but by decision of the gods they became conscious with intelligence and had the shape of men though they live in earth and in rocks" (p. 16).

This account offers a different idea: that the Dwarves started off as maggots rather than as manlike forms. Here I argue that this imagery is actually quite meaningful, and offer my own view of what was really going on as the Dwarves came into being.

In ancient times, maggots were thought to arise through spontaneous generation from decomposing flesh. Apparently, Snorri (perhaps ancient Norse generally) considered this to be a logical explanation for the origins of the Dwarves, who burrow through the earth / Ymir's body as maggots burrow through decaying flesh. This is somewhat distasteful and insulting imagery, perhaps not surprising since ancient Heathens had a rather negative view of Dwarves, with their tendency to consume or suck energy from other beings (such as humans and domestic animals) on occasion. Many medieval spells and charms, from across the Germanic lands, were made to protect from this, or to remedy such draining of life-force by the Dwarves and similar beings. (See Chapter 20, *"An Anglo-Saxon Charm Against a Dwarf,"* and Chapter 1, *"The Kindly Gods Go Wandering."*) What, exactly, is it that the Dwarves consume from other beings? The answer to this question leads in some very interesting directions!

It All Hinges on 'Mod'

I have a different way of looking at the tale about the origins of the Dwarves, and I base it on my interpretation of the name of the 'lord of the Dwarves,' Móðsognir or Mótsognir. 'Móðr' or 'mod' is a kind of power and a 'mood or state of power,' which is especially demonstrated by Thor and shown in the name of his son Móði. Móðr is wrath and fury, courage and determination, and the power to express these things in action. The name Móðsognir or Mótsognir has been interpreted as "he who drinks in might," or "he who drinks in courage" (see references from Wikipedia page on "Mótsognir".) I will return to Móðsognir momentarily, after exploring the meaning of *mod*, a word common to, and important to, all the old Germanic languages.

I view *mod* as a type of ambient energy, which is absorbed from the environment and transmuted by one's mood and soul into a specific expression of power. (See chapters on Mod in Rose 2021 and 2022.) In this respect it is similar to *megin* (Old Norse) or *mægen* (Anglo-Saxon), a word for power, for 'might and main,' which forms the name of Thor's son, Magni, as moðr forms the name of his son Móði.

The Latin word *virtus*, the root of 'virtue', was translated into the ancient Germanic languages using the words 'mod and mægen' together (Meyer p. 14-15). We gain a sense of the meaning when we speak of the 'virtue' of an herb, a potion or a magical object, its special power that sets it apart from the ordinary. An example of such virtue is found in *Fjölvinnsmal*, vs. 15 (Poetic Edda). Svipdag, seeing Menglöd and her ladies sitting under the great Tree that bears mysterious healing and life-giving fruits, asks "What *moði* has this famous tree, that it can be felled neither by fire nor by iron?" (See Chapter 6

Dwarves and their Powers

about Thor and his children, the Thorlings, for more discussion of mod, mægen, and this kind of 'virtue'.)

Powerful animals are called *moðr* or *modig:* think of the aurochs described in the rune poem about Uruz in the *Old English Rune Poem,* called a *modig wiht*, a mody wight. Uncastrated stallions and bulls were called 'mod' to distinguish them from geldings and oxen (Meyer p. 20). Weather, too, could be referred to by this word, as in *Grimnismal* 42 in the Poetic Edda which describes the 'hard-mody sky / cloud-cover' that was created from Ymir's brains *(heila)*. The power of the sea was seen as an expression of mod. Anglo-Saxon poetry, for example, contains several references to *merestræmes mod*, the mod of the streaming sea; Old Norse and Old Saxon have similar expressions.

Merestræmes mod: the mod of the streaming sea.

Meyer's conclusion, which other scholars have agreed with, is that the root meaning of Proto-Germanic **moda* is based in the concept of *Macht*, of might, strength, virtue in the sense of special power, that sets one above the ordinary and can even reach to supernatural and divine levels (pp. 13ff).

Turning to another source, de Vries' *Old Norse Dictionary* postulates that *mod* stems from the Proto-Indo-European root **ma*, meaning 'to be emotionally stirred, excited,' as well as meaning 'striving.' He suggests related words in Greek that mean 'to strive, to yearn or wish for, to rage'; also a Tocharian word meaning 'strength'.

All of these words can well be used to describe Dwarves, their behaviors, attitudes, and abilities, as shown in lore and folklore from all the Germanic lands. They are considered to be very strong, crafty in all senses of the word, greedy, hard workers, short-tempered, vengeful, clever, knowledgeable about the 'virtues' of natural substances such as plants and minerals, skilled in magic, and generally formidable beings. "The word *dvergsnattura* (Dwarf-wisdom) ...designates supernatural skills of healing and craftsmanship" (Motz p. 103).

Móðsognir and Durinn

Let's return now to the first Dwarf-Fathers, Móðsognir and Durinn, and consider Móðsognir's name in more detail. There are several seemingly contradictory interpretations of this name. In the previous section I mentioned the meaning "he who drinks in might / courage"; these are based on translations of the *Völuspá* by B.S. Benedikz, John McKinnel, and Sigurd Nordal (as referred to in the Wikipedia page on Mótsognir). Lotte Motz suggests 'furious sucker' as the meaning. All of these are based on 'moðr' as meaning 'fury, rage, power, courage,' and the like.

There is a different and opposite meaning of 'moðr' as 'tiredness, fatigue, exhaustion, apathy, lethargy.' DeVries's dictionary suggests this second meaning as the root of the name Móðsognir, translating it as 'he who sucks strength from the body' (p. 392). As I showed in the previous chapter about "An Anglo-Saxon Charm Against a Dwarf," Dwarves were well-known in Germanic folklore for stealing strength and energy from humans and domestic animals, so this interpretation has some merit. (See also Chapter 1, where I mention a couple of old Norwegian spells to heal 'mod-stolen' or strength-and-energy-stolen cows; there are a great many more such spells for animals and humans in the original book I discuss there.)

Considering the word 'sognir,' related words in modern English are 'suck, soak, sog, soggy'. Related Old Norse words refer to sucking, waterfalls, the sea—especially the ebb-tide which sucks things with it as it goes out, also nursing a baby, and similar watery meanings (deVries dictionary pp. 529, 560). The suggestions above about 'drinking in' might and courage are close, but I believe some connotations are missed with the translation 'drink' rather than 'suck.' For one thing, 'drink' and 'suck' are different words, in Old Norse as well as English; if 'drink' had been intended for Móðsognir's name, it would have involved a form of the word *drekka,* 'to drink.' For another, 'drinking' implies consuming something that is easily available in liquid form, while 'sucking' implies a more difficult action of extracting something that is not as easily obtained. This refers again to actions that the Dwarves are blamed for in Germanic folklore: sucking milk from cows or sheep, sucking energy and health from people and domestic animals.

So I go with the meaning of 'moðr-sucker,' and further, I believe that both meanings of *moðr* discussed here are implied in the name. Móðsognir, and by implication all the Dwarves he 'made' or is the 'greatest of', is a Dwarf who sucks or consumes mod, megin, energy, power, and thereby causes weakness, exhaustion, depletion when that energy is sucked from people or animals, as we saw in the previous chapter about the charm against a Dwarf, and in the first chapter describing old Norwegian spells. It's understandable that people would be very resentful about this and would want to work magic against it! But let's step back and look at this phenomenon in a broader context of myth and meaning.

Dwarves are great craftsmen, creating amazing magical works that no other race of beings can equal. I think that many Landwights are of the Dwarven kind; they too are 'makers' in their own way. Both of these functions require enormous inputs of energy: for crafting magical items, and for ensouling and energizing natural features of the land. I think that the fundamental activity of the Dwarves (and Landwights), which underlies everything else that they do, is as *transformers of mod-and-mægen energy from diffuse ambient sources into concentrated, directed sources: namely, themselves and their works.*

Going back to the origin of the Dwarves: as maggots, they were sucking from the primordial source—Ymir—and transforming that primal energy within themselves, preparing for their own great work of transformation and their creative work to come. The 'first and most famed' of the Dwarves, Móðsognir / Mod-sucker, is the master of this craft of mod-condensing. I think it is very likely that Móðsognir transformed himself from a maggot into a Dwarf, without any help from the Deities!

The second Dwarf to be formed was Durinn; he and Móðsognir 'made' (or transformed) all the rest. *'Durinn'* could mean 'door-keeper, sleepy, or demonic being' (Simek p. 67). All of these meanings are significant. Dwarves can certainly be considered otherworldly, daemonic beings. I believe Durinn's main function is as Móðsognir's doorkeeper: he controls access to the mod that Móðsognir sucks and accumulates. When Durinn opens the 'door' or access to Móðsognir, concentrated mod is available to the Dwarves; when he closes the door, it is not. The lack of mod causes sleepiness and fatigue, hence his name 'sleepy,' that applies when the door is closed.

Overall, Durinn functions as the active chieftain of the Dwarves, their 'ring-giver' or wealth-giver in the form of activated mod-power, while Móðsognir is more sequestered and mysterious, more like a Dwarf-God, a source of power, than like a chieftain involved with the business of the folk. This goes along with the idea that he and Durinn  transformed themselves from maggots to Dwarves, using concentrated mod-power from Ymir, and then were able to transform all the other Dwarves the same way.

As I've worked with these ideas over time, I have indeed come to believe that Móðsognir and Durinn are Dwarf-Gods: Móðsognir is mysterious, standing outside of ordinary life, a source of divine power for them, while Durinn is their chieftain-God, their 'ring-giver' or mediator of their access to mod-power, and the leader of their folk.

Implications for Personal Practice

Here are a few thoughts on the personal relevance of these conclusions about the Dwarves, though one may very well choose not to follow up on them, but simply regard what I've written here as an interesting take on the origins and nature of the Dwarves. The perspective I've presented here does have implications for our own use of mod-energy for many purposes: health, personal development, and the practice of magic. Mod-power and 'virtue' in the sense of 'special powers' are inherently connected, and the Dwarves know a lot about both. We're speaking here of the 'virtue' of an herb, a potion, a magical object. The reason the herb, potion, magical object can do what it can do, is that it has mod and mægen. Sometimes this is naturally inherent, as in an herb; other times that virtue is there because it was created or enhanced by magical techniques such as rune-craft or galdor, or enhanced by magical smith-craft in the case of Dwarves. (You can read more about our own human mod-power in chapters about Mod in Rose 2021 and 2022.)

An understanding of the Dwarves' role as mod-condensers, and ideally gaining their aid, can help us in any magical endeavor that involves instilling or heightening virtue or mod within an object. A word of caution, however: the Dwarves are often tricky and hostile, as well as helpful at times. They are extremely clannish and don't like outsiders. Think about this: since Dwarves arose from Ymir, sucking in his power, they must share his 'venomous' or 'poisonous' nature. *Gylfaginning* in the prose Edda tells us that at the beginning of the cosmos, Ymir was formed from the rime and ice coating Ginnungagap, and that this rime contained both salt and some kind of venom or poison (Sturlason pp. 9-11; see also Rose 2021, Chapter 16 "The Alchemy of Hel.") This 'venomous' nature may explain why the Dwarves, as portrayed in old Norse and Germanic lore, are generally seen as 'negative,' dangerous and even treacherous beings like the Jotnar, and should be dealt with cautiously, if at all.

I believe that Landwights are related to Dwarves and have the same ability to handle mod-power, which they use for

Dwarves and their Powers

their own work of 'ensouling' and energizing features of the natural environment. They are often much easier to work with than are the deep-living dwarvish tribes of craft-folk, if you approach the Landwights appropriately and offer them your help as well as asking them for theirs. There is often much more we can offer to reward Landwights for their help than we can offer to the Dwarves. Our help to the Landwights normally consists of things like environmental cleanup, protection and restoration of natural areas, planting and caring for trees, and many other such endeavors. It's harder to know what to offer the Dwarves in exchange for their help, when they have so much power to get what they want for themselves.

If you do try to deal with Dwarves, be well-protected, watch your words (and your back) carefully, be careful of both making and breaking promises, and know when to back out. And never steal from them! Including stealing mod. That will gain you their life-long enmity; they are not forgiving people. All in all, seeking help from Landwights, who are very good mod-condensers, is really preferable to dealing with Dwarves for most of us. There is less risk, more gain, and mutual benefit when we help the Landwights with their tasks, as well as seeking their help with ours. Whichever being one seeks help from, always be courteous, and willing to take 'no' for an answer!

After all these cautionary statements, however, I would like to note that I have had generally positive experiences when working with Dwarves, though there is always the need for caution and care in one's dealings with them. My sense is that much depends on one's approach to the Dwarves, and how well one understands their mindset and worldview. I get the impression that *they* often consider *us* difficult, deceptive, greedy, and exploitative, and they may not always be wrong about that, as I discuss also from the perspective of the Jotnar in Chapter 18. If we approach the Dwarves with exploitation in mind, things will not go well for us; they are not stupid beings and are glad to 'return the favor' of any negative intentions.

My work with them has been fairly simple and surface-level so far, and I think this is the best way to begin, so as to gain a deeper understanding of their nature, worldview, their own ethical beliefs and rules of behavior, before becoming more involved with them. This forms the basis for more substantial interactions. The next chapter in this book, *"The Living Jewels of Brisingamen,"* provides additional perspectives on interacting with the Dwarves.

Part III. Heathen Spiritual Practices

Here is a photo of my spaeworking High Seat, made by a Heathen artisan to my design in 1995. The white linen apron was woven by

Part III. Heathen Spiritual Practices

my daughter; I embroidered it with the names of Goddesses. It is backed by the black linen spaeworking apron I embroidered. Balanced on the arms of the chair are woodcarvings of Frey and Frigg, and the antlered staff honors Frey, as well. The necklace is a replica of Freya, though I wear it in honor of all the Goddesses together. Carvings of Huginn, Muninn, and Odin are included here. There are inlays of Thor's Hammers and many other God-symbols carved and wood-burned on the side supports of the High Seat.

Steel Hammer with Oath Ring, made by my blacksmith husband, Rosten Dean Rose. There's a good story behind it. In 1996, I had been asked to officiate at a Heathen wedding and needed a large Thor's Hammer for this. I went to the blacksmith in town and described what I wanted. He had me choose the parts for the Hammer from his supply of scrap metal. Without knowing what they were, the piece I chose for the Oath Ring was from an antique lightning rod (Thor!), and the piece for the shaft was from an old grain auger. Appropriate for the husband of Sif, often seen as a grain-Goddess! Rosten became Heathen as a result of our meeting, and a couple years later this Hammer hallowed our own Heathen wedding.

22: The Living Jewels of Brisingamen

*Freya with her magical necklace Brisingamen,
by James Doyle Penrose.*

Freya is a Goddess involved in just about everything! She's a warrior and hosts the souls of warriors in her Hall, Folkvang. She also hosts people who aren't warriors, like Egil Skallagrimson's daughter Thorgerd who tricked her suicidal father into eating, saying she would join him in his fasting until she died and went to "sup with Freya" *(Egil's Saga,* pp.

203-4). Freya is the ultimate seiðkona, expert in many forms of witchcraft and magic. She's much involved in romance and sexuality, in conception, gestation, and childbirth. As the Vanadis, she shares the Vanic involvement in the fertility of Nature and agriculture, as well. She inspires music and poetry that focuses on romance and beauty, as well as lasciviousness. And she's considered the mildest of the Deities, the easiest to approach and to pray to *(Gylfaginning* p. 24 in Sturlason). Many years ago, my husband prayed for her assistance and blessing during our time of courtship and betrothal, and indeed everything went amazingly smoothly for us: Freya has great skill!

Much has been written about these and other gifts of Freya, and I am not going to focus on them here. I want to expand on her greatest treasure, her necklace or girdle Brisingamen, and suggest that with her help we can develop our own shadow or echo of Brisingamen as a means of growing and consolidating our personal power, as Brisingamen does for Freya.

What is Brisingamen?

Brisingamen is one of our Heathen mysteries; we don't know a lot about it, not even whether it is a necklace or a belt / girdle. It's generally portrayed as a necklace, but sometimes mentioned as a belt or girdle. We don't know much about its powers, nor what it looks like or is made of, though we know it is most precious. Quite likely

The Living Jewels of Brisingamen

it has multiple strands, as can be seen in this pendant of mine on the previous page, a replica of an ancient amulet of Freya. Four strands can be counted around her neck, but possibly a belt is shown as well, though it's not very clear. Does Brisingamen include jewels? Is it gold, or amber, or both? We don't know, based on information from the lore, but we can explore our own impressions of Brisingamen as I describe further on.

For a good review of what is known or speculated about Brisingamen, including scholarship as well as insights contributed by modern Heathens, see Waggoner vol. 2, pp 284-5 and 288-293. In this text he includes speculation that Brisingamen did include amber as well as possibly a large seed-pod that drifts on the sea from the Caribbean to the shores of Scandinavia and Britain, which was used in Scandinavian folk-magic to help in childbirth. Amber, as well, has many magical uses. Gold is associated with Freya: she is said to weep tears of gold, and poetic kennings are used for Freya's tears to refer to gold in the old poetry. Thus, gold and amber are likely possibilities, perhaps including the seed-pod as well.

I discuss my idea that an old Norwegian spell mentions something like Brisingamen in chapter 1 of this book, *"The Kindly Gods God Wandering,"* in the section on *"Norns and Others Bind the Fylgja."* There, three maidens: 'the Sun, the Moon, and (originally) Freya' use 'gold and silver bands' to fasten a baby's spirit into the womb to prevent it from wandering and perhaps causing miscarriage when the baby is left without the spirit. I think these gold and silver bands are a folkloric memory of Brisingamen; this offers one example of the powerful magic that Freya wields through it.

The Living Jewels of Brisingamen

My own comment on all this debate about what Freya's necklace consists of is that it presumably is not a material item at all! It's like trying to figure out what the carving is on Heimdall's Gjallarhorn, or the kind of fastening that holds the point of Odin's spear Gungnir to its shaft. Or the weight of Thor's Hammer, or the wood Bragi's harp is made from. These material traits have symbolic meaning, indeed, that is worth discussing and meditating on. But it doesn't make sense to get too hung up over 'what is Brisingamen *really* made of?' Instead, later in this chapter we can talk about what *your* Brisingamen version and my Brisingamen version might be like, whether it is material substance or spiritual image.

Forging Brisingamen

We are told in *Sorla Tháttr* from the *Flateyarbók* that Freya sees four Dwarves forging a necklace and desires to have it. Their price is one night of love for each of them, which Freya agrees to, and obtains the necklace. Of course this choice is much criticized by the authors of these old tales, having been Christianized and being willing to mock the old Gods. In fact Odin is offended by Freya's actions as well, even though he does the same thing in order to obtain the Mead of Poetry from the giantess Gunnloð and her kin. (See Waggoner vol. 2 p. 284.)

Some modern Heathens who work with Freya have a very different take on this tale. Waggoner quotes Alice Karlsdóttir, who suggests that the Dwarves did not make the necklace until *after* Freya had slept with them, because they needed the inspiration she gave them in order to make the necklace. Karlsdóttir sees Freya's power as "the infusing of the physical world with the spiritual," and Freya's relations with the

The Living Jewels of Brisingamen

Dwarves were an expression of that power. (Waggoner vol. 2, p. 285.)

I'm going to follow up on that idea here and relate it to what I wrote about the Dwarves' power in the preceding chapter of this book, *"Dwarves and their Powers."* I explained there that 'mod' and its complement 'mægen' are kinds of power that exist in nature and within living beings, and together create the 'virtue' that is expressed by the special qualities of things like herbs, potions, magical items, etc. 'Mod and mægen' together were used to translate Latin *virtus* in the old Germanic languages (Meyer p. 14-15). I discuss this further with respect to Thor's sons Móði and Magni (derived from 'mod and mægen') in Chapter 6.

In this view, 'virtue' is really 'strength, power, excellence' which makes sense: the root of this word comes from Latin *vir,* meaning 'man' (male person, not 'human being'), related to Anglo-Saxon *wer* with the same meaning. The original meaning of 'virtue' was 'manliness' in all the best senses of the word: courage, honor, excellence, valor, steadfastness, loyalty, responsibility, and so forth. This original meaning was based on virtue as the 'essence of manhood and its power.' From there, 'virtue' transformed into meaning the 'essence, power, and excellence' of anything that it might apply to, including religious faith and moral power. It's a weird quirk that Christian usage turned this word into something often used to describe *women's* 'virtuous behavior,' particularly with respect to sexual behavior according to Christian morals—a long way from its original meaning!

Getting back to Brisingamen and the Dwarves: clearly, mod, mægen, 'virtue,' power, excellence are things that Brisingamen must contain and embody in some form. I wrote in the previous chapter that Dwarves are champion 'mod-condensers,' able to absorb ambient mod-power and concentrate it to power their magical crafts. They have both the power and the skill to craft outstanding virtue-imbued magical items for the Gods and Goddesses: they created Thor's Hammer, Sif's golden hair, Frey's ship that folds up into a napkin, as well as his tireless flying golden boar Gullinborsti who pulls his wain, and other mighty crafts.

Given that Dwarves are able to extract and use such great mod-power, why would intercourse with Freya be required in order to forge Brisingamen? Wouldn't the Dwarves' craft and power be enough?

There is something else about mod-power that we need to understand here: mod-power does not flow unchanged from nature outside and within us, and through us into our works. 'Mod' is the root of our word 'mood,' and this is a key understanding. The original mod-energy comes from many sources within and around us, but once we—or the Dwarves, or any conscious being—begin to channel it with intent, *this channeled mod becomes 'flavored' by the mood of our intent.* This is true whether our 'mood' is conscious and deliberate, or subconscious.

Let me explain this a little more, with some examples; this process is complex and interactive, and I think it is key to understanding the power of Brisingamen. Our 'subconscious moods' are influenced by a great many things around and within us, including the moods of the weather, the energetic nature of the food we consume or the lack of it, the moods of people around us, moods influenced by news media, influencers, books, games, films, and other activities, and it goes on. All of these things influence our moods, but we may not be fully aware of it and thus have little control over their impacts. These subconscious influences affect our intentions and motivations without being very clear or obvious to us, and may not be what we really want to express or to do.

What I call 'conscious moods' are the moods where we are aware of these subconscious influences but choose to accept, resist, or modify them. Thus, we deliberately *choose* the mood through which to express ourselves and take action in the world. Much the same as a good artist, actor, musician, or dance performer will express the intended mood of their art or performance, regardless of whatever might be going on in the background of their lives. *'Mood' here becomes an intentional expression of our will, our vision, our Self,* rather than something we fall into or are dragged into willy-nilly, though it still includes subconscious as well as conscious elements of ourselves. But here the conscious self takes the lead and expects the subconscious self to support rather than sabotage it. In this way, 'mood' segues into 'Mod,' one of our true souls in my understanding, and a very powerful and characteristic one, as I discuss in my books on Heathen soul lore.

With this understanding now, think about the 'mood of the Dwarves.' Even if we don't know that much about Dwarves, we can imagine this reasonably well. They have a reputation for being grouchy, avaricious, short-tempered, clannish, selfish, vengeful, and so forth. In my experience, they have a number of good and admirable qualities as well, such as a love of beauty (as expressed in precious substances and craftwork), stout-heartedness and courage, loyalty to their own, their own version of honor which is somewhat different from ours, and others. But all of these values of theirs are rather dour, we might say—sober, ingrown, strong but dark. They were able to make treasures of the Gods because those treasures were not harmed by the 'mood of the

Dwarves,' and indeed were enhanced when it came to the great weapons they forged. Even Sif's hair expressed their love of the beauty of gold.

What of Freya's powers and her 'moods'? Can we envision Dwarves concentrating and channeling ambient mod into the 'mood of Freya'? Not really; it makes me laugh to think of it! The Dwarves needed a focal lens through which to channel their gathering of ambient mod into the creation of Brisingamen. That lens had to come from Freya, because it was simply not within the Dwarves' power to shape something that could resonate with the 'moods of Freya' and enhance her power thereby. This brings us right back to the insight of Alice Karlsdóttir, that Freya 'infuses the spiritual into the physical'. I see the supposed 'sexual intercourse' of Freya with the Dwarves as a metaphor for this sharing—and even implantation—of her spiritual energy into the Dwarves who were working on Brisingamen.

There is a link between characteristics of the Dwarves and of Freya, and that link is expressed by fire and its symbols in Norse lore. Gold is considered poetically as a form of fire, shown in many examples of poetic kennings, and both Freya and the Dwarves love gold. They both understand the fire that is expressed by war and battle, and the fire of creativity. Freya channels the fires of life, passion, and desire, and though the Dwarves express these very differently, they too know these fires well. Freya has a hot temper, too, but is generally more careful about how she directs it than the Dwarves are.

The very name 'Brisinga-men' means something like 'the fiery necklace,' or 'the necklace made by the fiery ones' (Waggoner p. 288). The suffix '-men' refers to a necklace, torc, or jewel, and shows up in other names such as Menglöd, meaning 'necklace / jewel-glad,' 'the one who takes pleasure in jewels,' and in Menja, the 'wearer of the necklace' (Simek p. 210-11). The prefix may come from *brisa,* 'to shine' (Simek p. 44).

We can understand this 'fire' connection between the Dwarves and Freya as a subconscious mood that they share, a substrate of commonality, that is nevertheless expressed extremely differently when it comes to conscious mood, attitude, behavior and action. But it gives them a place to meet so that the necessary mod-energy can be transferred.

This 'sharing in the mod / mood of fire' is, I believe, the real transaction between Freya and the Dwarves, enabling the melding of their powers, mods, and moods to produce Brisingamen. It is expressed in the tales as sexual intercourse—which can also be an expression of fire. If one conceives of the Deities in very physical terms then that is the direction one's thoughts might take. If one conceives of them in more spiritual terms, then one can picture a godly gift to the Dwarves, an infusion of fiery divine power, mod, and 'virtue,' that gives them temporary access to Freya's mood and the ability to express that mood into their crafting of Brisingamen.

Echoes of Brisingamen

So there we are: Freya has her Brisingamen, her powers are enhanced, and her many adventures continue. Now I suggest this: that we can create an echo of Brisingamen for ourselves, with Freya's help and input. Here is how I do this myself; all of what I offer here are simply suggestions for you to consider. You and Freya might make your own Brisingamen quite differently from mine, but this will at least give you some ideas.

My Brisingamen is non-material at this point in time, though that may change, but you can certainly make or buy a material one. It could be made of knots in a cord that you wear around your neck, waist, or wrist, with the knots representing jewels. Or you could craft or buy something more like jewelry. One advantage of the non-material necklace that I create in my imagination is that I can make it out of anything I want, no matter how rare and expensive!

To begin with, I take the 'four Dwarves' as significant, and I envision my Brisingamen to have four jewels on it, one made by each of the Dwarves. It could also be envisioned as made of four strands lying across the chest, one below the other, as shown on the Freya medallion replica earlier in this chapter. But I like the jewel image and find it simpler to work with in my imagination, so that's what I choose.

Then there's the big question: to which aspects of Freya do I want my Brisingamen-jewels to resonate? Which of her powers do I feel are most important? There are many to choose from, and here is where we all might differ in our choices. I want to say a bit about my choices because I think these aspects are important and much needed in today's world; I believe they are disregarded and not valued highly enough. My four choices are Vitality or Life-Energy, Beauty, Joy, and Self-Possession, and I'll discuss them here one by one.

Vitality, Life-Energy

Freya is full to overflowing with vitality, with the energy of life. It lies at the root of all her other aspects, attributes, and gifts. Her beauty, joy and delight, her warrior and lover aspects, her facility with magic, her many gifts to humankind and her involvement with us—all arise from the overflowing

Vanic vitality that she shares with her brother Frey. Among other things, this overflowing vitality, energy, and mood of Freya is expressed in the birth of her daughters Hnoss and Gersemi, whose names both mean 'treasure, precious thing'. These daughters are very much worth working with as well, as we design and empower our own treasured Brisingamen.

I could use some of the vitality that Freya channels myself, for sure! So I am working with her to empower a vitality-jewel for my Brisingamen. I gave this chapter the title *'living jewels of Brisingamen'* because of this foundational vitality, this life-energy, that Freya brings to everything she is involved with, including her Brisingamen and her powers that can help us create our own echo of hers.

Beauty

Freya is famed for her beauty and her love of beauty. She is an inspiration to artists, poets and musicians who seek to capture her beauty and express her delight in it. If we stop to think about it, we realize that beauty is really the expression of so many other good things entwined together: inner health and haleness. A sharing of the spirit between ourselves and whatever we perceive as beautiful. Goodness, love, generosity: these things are beautiful. Nature is beautiful, and the beings of nature. Creativity and inspiration are beautiful. Each of us has our own unique beauty, and the more clearly we perceive that in ourselves and in others, the richer our world becomes. The experience of beauty taps into something very deep within us. This is why religions use great art in many forms to draw our attention toward that which is holy in its beauty, and beautiful in its holiness. The jewel that is filling with beauty in my Brisingamen is gradually becoming a symbol and a reminder to look for and appreciate the beauty around me, and to pour whatever gifts of beauty I can gather back into the world.

Beautiful Freja, by John Bauer.

Joy, Delight

Joy and delight may seem so naïve to us, even selfish. What is there to be joyful about, most of the time? The world is a rough place, no question, full of stress, distress, and wrongness; if we don't happen to have too much of those stresses in our own life at the moment, we can just look around us and see how many others are suffering and how many things are going wrong in the world. I feel that way a lot of the time, myself.

Nevertheless—there is a big 'nevertheless' here! People on many religious paths find true delight through their connection with their Deities. People who love nature, who have many loving connections with other people, other things they care about, pets, hobbies and avocations they love: these people can find occasions of joy in among all the hassle and distress if they approach the things they love in the right spirit. As with any worthwhile pursuit, including love and religious devotion, the 'practice of joy' involves just that: practice, being open to joy, even in the littlest, most fleeting things and moments; valuing true joy and seeking it throughout our days.

Freya is a Deity who takes joy in life, in Being, in beauty, in her relationships including human ones, in the exercise of her many powers, aims and purposes. Her daughters are expressions and condensations of her joy, beauty and vitality. We can turn to them and to Freya for lessons in joy, which she can impart in a great many ways, unique to the relationship she has with each of us who turn to her. I have not been working with her as long as I have with many of our other Deities, but already I feel that I am connected to her through a thread of joy. When I tune in to her, I feel a bubble of happiness in my chest that lightens my perspective on the world. I've always had the habit of looking for beauty and joy around me, even in the tiniest things and moments, but this tendency of mine has become greatly enhanced and enlarged since I've been working with Freya and my Brisingamen-jewel of joy.

Joy is a gift and a grace, to ourselves and to everyone around us; it is a gift that we receive and one that we can give and share with others. It comes in many 'flavors' and intensities, from mild to overwhelming; it nourishes us and all that we can do and give. The jewel of joy in my Brisingamen is something I am working to fill and empower through my connection with Freya, with the other Deities, and with the world around me.

Self-Possession

Freya is herself. She knows who she is and what she wants. Others sometimes seek to exploit her, and sometimes it takes some effort for her to get out of these difficult situations. But she does; in the end she gets what she wants, goes where she wants, and does what she wants. She owns herself; she's not owned by others. She doesn't have to prove that through wild gestures, though sometimes she chooses to do that. Like the time she was so angry her neck swelled up and she burst Brisingamen apart, when it was suggested that she should wed the giant Thrym so Thor could get his stolen Hammer back. This put a rapid end to such suggestions! But then she calmed down and graciously agreed to loan Brisingamen to Thor (presumably after it was repaired) so he could impersonate her and get his Hammer back. *(Thrymskvida* or the *Tale of Thrym* in the *Poetic Edda.)* I would suggest that Thor's impersonation was successful in spite of its difficulty (and hilarity!) in part because Brisingamen itself was imparting its power to Thor.

The Living Jewels of Brisingamen

This deep knowledge of—and trust in—who we are, what we are about, where we're going, what we're doing, is something that each of us needs to develop in life. All of our Deities are characterized by this self-possession, each in their own unique ways. Freya (and Iðunn as well) have additional challenges, though, because her qualities—what she represents—are things that others want to 'own' and control: her beauty, her treasures, her sexuality, her magical powers, her own expressions of divinity, her Brisingamen. The Jotnar want to claim her, and the Dwarves, and so do some of the Æsir. Maybe humans, too. She must always resist being claimed and used by others, and that requires a strong sense of self-possession. Freya is very often helpful and sharing, but she does it based on her own will, not as someone who is coerced or manipulated, except when her Brisingamen is stolen.

Loki stole Brisingamen, and Heimdall fought him to get it back. Here Heimdall is shown returning the necklace to Freya. Painting by Nils Andersen.

This self-possession of Freya's is something that we all need as well. This modern world has become so intrusive into our personal space, we are influenced in so many directions, we are tempted, lured, threatened, manipulated, and seduced in ways intended to benefit others but not ourselves—not in the long run, not in the deep ways. We are constantly at risk of being blown off course, not least because we're often not clear about what our 'course' is, what it should be, what we want it to be. And I might add that these pernicious influences are not only exerted by humans; otherworldly beings influence us as well, and not all of them are benign.

The self-possession jewel on my Brisingamen is one that I try to keep polished and shining, imbued with Freya's—and my own—powers of self-possession and all the qualities of character that support it. My work with Syn, discussed in Chapter 10, feeds into this jewel, as well.

So, these are my choices for my Brisingamen jewels or strands: vitality, beauty, joy, and self-possession. There are many others that could be chosen, and of course we're not required to have exactly four of them. I hope this discussion gives you some ideas for your own Brisingamen if you haven't already developed one. Work with Freya and see what kinds of magnificent and powerful results you can produce! Here are a few ways you might pursue this.

Working with your Brisingamen

Hold the stone / jewel / strand / knot of your Brisingamen that corresponds to the aspect of her that you've chosen to work with right now, whether you are holding a material item or one that you imagine. Use your memory and imagination to fill, imprint, or empower that part of your Brisingamen with your experiences and desires that relate to that aspect. For example, my own jewel of beauty: I remember so many beautiful places, sensory and emotional experiences, insights and perceptions in my life, and I can imagine more of them. I slowly go through these beautiful things a few at a time in my memory and imagination, savoring them, recreating and re-living them, and 'load' all of this into my jewel of beauty. It's a form of meditation, and also good practice for strengthening memory, concentration, and developing our imaginative 'muscles.'

Depending on which aspects of Freya you choose to string on your Brisingamen, this practice will help you focus on positive things in your life, in your memory and your imagination, not only on stressful and negative things. You want those jewels to be pure and beautiful, not contaminated with negativity. Of course, if you are focusing on Freya's battle aspects the approach is a bit different, but you still want to focus on positive things like courage, strength, determination, endurance, dedication, rather than on the many negative aspects of fighting and the resulting suffering.

This infusion of power and meaning into your Brisingamen is a much better way to spend your energy than fretting, stressing out, and other negative time- and energy-wasters! Your Brisingamen will grow in power over time as you continue this practice, loading new experiences and insights into it. This practice will help you be alert to, and focus on, the treasures of life that you want to save in your Brisingamen, instead of focusing on negativities and things that you don't actually want to strengthen and empower as parts of your life-experience. Work with Freya, Hnoss and Gersemi to see what secret treasures you can forge out of the complexities of your life, and distill them into your own beautiful Brisingamen!

The Living Jewels of Brisingamen

Freya, by Emil Doepler.
She sets her path and chooses her own way.

23: Wigi Thonar: The Powers of Thor's Hammer

Nordendorf fibula.

Here I will offer a meditative approach for strengthening and clearing our inner being, our energy of mind and body. This approach is based on a phrase written in runic characters on several ancient items, namely *wigiþonar* and *þur uiki,* both of which mean "Thor hallow."

Wigi Thonar

Wigiþonar appears as part of an inscription on one of the Nordendorf Fibulæ, pictured above. These fibulæ or fasteners for clothing are dated to sometime from the mid 6th to early 7th centuries CE, and come from Alamannia in what is now

Wigi Thonar: The Powers of Thor's Hammer

Bavaria in Germany. 'Thonar' is a reference to Thor. "The prefix wigi- before the name of Þonar is interpreted either as from *wīgian "to hallow" or as from *wīgan "to fight." https://en.wikipedia.org/wiki/Nordendorf_fibulae

Considering that this fibula was found in a woman's grave, and that the inscription includes her name Awa as well as a word interpreted as a man's name, Luebwini or 'beloved friend,' it seems to me that *wigi* more likely means 'to hallow' in this context. Though 'Luebwini' has been taken as a man's name in all the interpretations I've read, I wonder whether instead it indicates that the fibula was a gift to the woman Awa from a beloved (male) friend, perhaps her husband. In either case, interpreting 'wigi' as a bid for Thor to hallow, rather than to fight, seems more appropriate in this context.

This is supported by other instances of Thor being asked to hallow, found on several memorial runestones in Denmark from the 10th century CE. The inscription on the Velanda runestone is interpreted as "Þyrvé raised the stone in memory of Ôgmundr, her husbandman, a very good thegn. May Þórr hallow." (See webpage for Velanda Runestone.)

The last lines, "Thor hallow" are "*þur : uiki*" in the runic spelling, and "*Þórr vígi*" in Old Norse. The words are the same as the *wigiþonar* found on the Nordendorf fibula, four centuries earlier and half a continent away, showing the breadth and endurance of this traditional view of Thor's power.

Thor's Hammer, in fact, was used to hallow an amazing variety of events. For example weddings, as is shown in *Thrymskvida* or 'Thrym's Poem' in the *Poetic Edda*. In this poem, Thor's Hammer has been stolen by the Jotun Thrym, who offers to return the Hammer once Freya is his bride. The whole idea of the poem rests on the understanding that Thor's

Hammer is necessary to hallow the bride and the wedding. Heimdall suggests that Thor pose as Freya, and it's decided that Loki will accompany him as his 'maidservant'. They know that when the 'wedding' is about to take place, the Hammer must be brought out for the ceremony, giving Thor the opportunity to grab it back, which he does. This word *vigi* is used to refer to the wedding: Thrym says "Bring in the hammer to sanctify the bride…*vigið okkr saman,* 'let us be hallowed together'." ('Thrym's Poem' verse 30 in the *Poetic Edda.)*

Thor's *vigja* can be baneful as well as a blessing. Waggoner quotes a runic charm against blood poisoning from the year 1073 CE, that says "may Thor hallow you *(Þórr vígi þik)* lord of thurses…" where the 'lord of thurses' is considered to be the cause of blood poisoning (p. 113). Here, Thor's 'hallowing' is clearly intended to be deadly, not life-giving.

Thor's power of *wigi, uiki, vigja*, channeled through his Hammer, can take a great many forms, as is shown throughout the myths and customs of Heathenry. It can heal, bless, protect, sanctify, fight, kill, destroy, and resuscitate. Through it, Thor can perform *seiðr* and rune magic. Oaths and vows are sworn upon the Hammer and supported by its power. Thor and his Hammer hallow Balder's funeral pyre *(Gylfaginning,* in the prose Edda, p. 49), and even bring Thor's slaughtered goats back to life *(Gylfaginning,* in the prose Edda, p. 38).

"It would seem indeed as though the power of the thunder god, symbolized by his hammer, extended over all that had to do with the well-being of the community. It covered birth, marriage, and death, burial, and cremation ceremonies, weapons and feasting, travelling, land-taking, and the making of oaths between men" (Davidson 1964 p. 83-84).

See Waggoner (vol. 2, pp. 112 and following) for the multitude of roles that Thor and his power played in the Heathen world, which are also discussed by many other scholars of Old Norse beliefs. Without going into more depth in this matter, which is covered in many books and websites, we can take it as given that Thor handles a unique and vital form of power, which is referred to as *vigja* or *wigian*.

Waggoner describes *vigja* as a power able to "change the basic nature of something through spiritual means… Thor's hallowing…changes the status and the essence of whomever or whatever is being hallowed" (vol. 2, pp. 112-3). This is emphasized by the later Christian use of this word; *Wiktionary* offers these definitions: "Verb vígja: (1) to consecrate, to set apart for a holy use; to dedicate to God; (2) ; (3) to inaugurate; (3) to ordain, to make someone a priest, minister." All of these meanings imply a change in status and essence of whatever is being consecrated, as Waggoner remarks.

Many Thor's Hammers have staring eyes depicted on them, an indication of Thor's 'burning gaze of power' that expresses the vigja flowing through his Hammer.

Thor Véurr

Thor has a poetic title in Old Norse: *Véurr* or 'warder of the Vé, the sanctuary, the hallowed place, the place of worship.'

As a warder, Thor uses both his power of hallowing and his power of destruction when it is needed. The double-barreled nature of this power—sacred / life-giving / protective, versus destructive and even annihilating—can work well for us as we seek to both clear away harmful influences in our selves and our lives, and to develop our strengths and inner powers for good.

The 'sanctuary' that Thor wards can be understood to exist on many levels. Thor is called Midgard's Defender: he protects all of Midgard from destructive power of the Jotnar, as he also protects Asgard. He wards the holy places and the gatherings of folk here within the larger realm of Midgard. And within us, within the sanctuary of our own selves, Thor Véurr can also ward us from harm. Here is a spiritual exercise that can be used for this purpose.

Hallowing your Inner Vé

Step 1. *Prepare yourself for a deep meditation.* If you have a Thor's Hammer to wear, hold, or place in front of you to look at, then do so at this time. Sit in a comfortable but alert manner, or lie down if you need to, and allow your breathing to slow and deepen. Spend a few minutes relaxing the tensions of your body and mind.

Step 2. *Visualize a red-gold Thor's Hammer within your solar plexus area.* There are many Thor's Hammer designs; work in your imagination to shape this inner Thor's Hammer in your favorite shape, simple or elaborate, but choose something you can easily visualize. If visualization is not 'your thing,' don't worry. Instead, use other senses: feel it glowing, warm and solid inside your solar plexus, or feel and listen to the deep humming vibration it makes there. Or simply use a sense of knowing, of trusting in your own knowledge that it truly is there.

Step 3. Spend as long as you need to, to establish this sense of the Thor's Hammer in your solar plexus area. Then gradually *intensify the radiant power of the Hammer.* I sense it as literally radioactive, but in a beneficial rather than a lethal way. Sense waves of power emanating radioactively from this Hammer, permeating your whole being.

Step 4. Step by step direct this radiant power through all parts of your Lichama, your soul-imbued living body: through all the vital organs of your torso: heart, lungs, liver, stomach, kidneys, generative organs and all. Through your pelvic area, legs and feet; upper torso, arms and hands. Through your throat and neck, and up into your head. As you do this, envision that *the power of Thor's radiant Hammer is annihilating all unhealthy influences in each area:* physical and metaphysical influences and conditions that harm your health and wellbeing on all levels, that may weaken your character, your strength, and hamper your intentions of goodwill.

Step 5. When you have finished step 4, repeat the same process of going through your Lichama step by step, but this time you are radiating the *vigja,* the power of the Hammer to *hallow, consecrate, and revitalize* all the physical elements and metaphysical powers of your whole being.

Step 6. You *become a Vé yourself,* a Wih-stead, a temple: a radiant flame of power, purged of ill and harm, hale and filled with wellbeing, able to radiate your share of Thor's powerful blessings into Midgard through your own being and your daily actions of Midgard life.

Figure of Thor from the Epcot Norway Pavilion.

Step 7. Finish this exercise with a *prayer of thanks to Thor, asking his guidance* as you strive to honor the power of his *vigja* in your life and deeds in Midgard. This energy is his gift, and he should have some input as to how you use it!

Human beings being what we are, and daily Midgard life being filled with constant challenges, this exercise is best when done frequently, ideally morning and evening each day, in order to solidify its benefits.

Any time when we are using Heathen symbols and rituals to enhance our deeds and abilities, it is important for us to make sure we are using our enhanced energies for good and not for harm to ourselves or to others. This means taking the time to think, on a regular basis, about what we want to accomplish with our lives, and to clarify and refine our own ethical principles as we continue to grow and mature. Our work with Thor's Hammer can guide and strengthen us in this process.

The Great Gift

24: The Great Gift: A Perspective on Heathen Prayer

Gebo / Gyfu: The Anglo-Saxon 'Gift' Rune

Gift is, to everyone, honor, splendor, and praise,
Support, and the acknowledgement of worth.
To every needy person it means dignity and provision,
Who would otherwise have nothing.
(Anglo-Saxon Rune poem, my rendition)

I'm offering here a perspective that may be helpful for modern Heathens: a way to understand and work with the prayer-and-response relationship that we undertake with the Deities who are closest to us, and to whom we turn when we are in need of help. Many of us tend to over-analyze things, to doubt our intuitions, and find it hard to trust the Holy Ones and our interactions with them. This chapter is offered as a way to work through such doubt and mistrust and find a deeper source of connection with our living Deities.

The Great Gift

Problem, Prayer, and First Response

Let's work with a hypothetical example of a Heathen, upset and facing difficulties, who has prayed to a Heathen Deity and been given a response: a sense of deep inner peace and confidence. Their inner turmoil stabilizes, and they feel stronger, more resilient. There is a sense of hope.

For simplicity, I am addressing this person as 'you', but of course, this is an example I am using, not actually you or any specific person. Being a typical person living in today's world, you immediately begin to question what happened. "Did the Deity really do anything, or am I fooling myself? Is the Deity going to 'fix' this problem for me, or is this wishful thinking? Is this all just my messed-up psyche? Should I accept what I think happened, or not trust it? Am I totally naïve if I do trust it? Was I really promised anything, or is this all fairy-dust?" And on and on.

So, you have a choice now: to accept or reject the belief that your prayer has received a response from the Deity and proceed accordingly.

The demands of this world we live in force us to examine everything, to distrust sources of knowledge and other mental / spiritual inputs, to second-guess everything and psychoanalyze ourselves and everybody else. We feel like we can't trust anything, not even our minds and souls and their perceptions, and are fools or naïve if we do. This is a really dysfunctional space within which to try to grow relationships with anyone—human, Deity, other kinds of spirits. Without trust and faith, it's very hard to create a deep and stable relationship of any kind.

The phrase 'a leap of faith' is germane here: *faith and trust, just like love, need to be **acts, decisions, stances** that we take,* and not only that, we need to commit to maintaining them over time. They are not just 'feelings' or vague states of mind that we somehow fall into. We have to work at them, accept their risks, take the rewards on faith and see what happens.

A Cost-Benefit Analysis

Here's one technique that can be used when one falls into a state of second-guessing, hyper-analysis, distrust about a spiritual experience: a cost-benefit analysis. This is designed for today's analyze-everything-to-death culture! Let's analyze your experience this way.

1) You are in an upset state, your inner environment is roiled up and you are suffering.

2) You call on your trusted Deity, and you 'think' they respond.

3) Their response is of great value to you, just what you need. Your inner self is comforted and stabilized, and you shift off the trajectory toward falling apart, back into a stabilized position.

4) This is the 'benefit': you've received a response, your inner self is stabilized, your trust in your Deity and your relationship with them is enhanced.

5) Now, what is the 'cost'? There are two parts to this: (a) the 'cost' if you accept the answer to your prayer in trust, and (b) the 'cost' if you refuse to accept it.

5 (a) The potential cost of accepting the answer to the prayer as given, is that any assurances you might have received could turn out to be inaccurate; things don't work out the way you think you were told that they would. Trust fails, or seems to, and this is an extremely painful position to be in. Many people would rather avoid it by never trusting in the first place, thus they don't want to trust deep spiritual contact with Deities or other spirits. This cost is *loss of trust.*

5 (b) The cost of refusing to accept the answer to your prayer, second-guessing and analyzing it to death, is of course that you remain in the upset and disrupted state that started the whole process, and perhaps even more upset. No help is available to you, because you refuse to accept it. This cost is *closing yourself off from potential support.*

6) Now let's weigh these costs and benefits against each other and see which one 'wins.' To do this, we need a closer look at the true nature of the benefit, and we need to take into account 'amortization,' or the effects of Time on the costs and benefits. In doing so, we may come to a deeper understanding of the effects of prayer.

Weighing the Benefits and Costs

7) The immediate benefit you receive from your Deity is powerful and deep: inner reassurance, stability, vindication of trust, strengthening of this divine relationship. This is the true, undeniable benefit, occurring in the sacred Now of lived and living experience. To maintain this benefit, all you need to do is accept it. I would place a very high value on this benefit.

7 (a) The potential cost of a failure of trust is a 'future' cost. You don't know yet what will happen in the future; you don't know how things will work out. If you focus on that, insist on ironclad guarantees from the Deity, imagine how you want it to be and demand that very thing, then what happens?

Your present benefit, your inner state of peace and trust, is disturbed and lost, and you have likewise not gained what you want in the future, *because you're not there yet.* Your benefit of inner peace in the Now has dissolved, and your cost is all that's left. 'Cost' wins this game, benefit loses.

7 (b) Refusing to accept the gift of the Deity, the answer to the prayer, means that the benefit is never realized, it never happens. Cost wins all, benefit zero.

The Great Gift

Here's how I wrap this up, the lesson I myself take from this analysis and try to apply in my life. Answer to prayer is in the Now; it is a state outside our normal churn of worries, fears, resentments, demands, that focus on the future and the past. We need to learn to step into this present-state, to place our deep awareness in this Now, which is suffused with the blended powers and qualities of the Deity and of ourself, as the result of our prayer and our trust in the response.

This blended power, the result of our prayer, is the Great Gift, Gebo, that is given in response to Need / Nauthiz. Look at the runic figures on the next page: just a small adjustment of the lines turns Need / Nauthiz into Gift / Gebo. Nauthiz is one-legged, askew, easy to throw off-balance: we face things alone, standing on one leg. Gebo is solid, balanced, with a stable base, reaching to the heights: we face things with the

The Great Gift

strength of a God/dess stabilizing and empowering our own abilities. Gebo is the rune of giving. We can think of Gebo's shape not only as two lines crossing each other, but as two shapes, > and <, converging upon each other at a point in the middle. This indicates the reciprocity, the sharing and giving, between two persons or beings meeting face-to-face at the middle point, offering equal exchange and support.

Nauthiz Rune   *Gebo Rune*

This Gebo-Gift is what prayer and response to prayer truly is, and taking the stance of Gebo during deep, serious prayer is a good reminder of it! We stand with legs braced somewhat apart, reaching our arms high, mimicking the X-shape of Gebo and state our prayer. And what do we give the Deity in return, gift for a gift? The very best offerings: our trust, friendship, attention, and cooperation with their purposes in Midgard. When we pray in Gebo-stance, we commit to working in partnership with the Deities: gift for a gift.

As we stand within the Great Gift in the stance of power, our strength, power, determination, wisdom, and foresight are enhanced. We become better able to act on our own behalf, whether that involves bringing about the solution we want for ourselves, finding a different solution, realizing this wasn't what we actually needed anyway, or having the strength to accept things as they are. We can do this through the power of the Gift: prayer, response, acceptance, and action, in partnership with Deity.

25: Experience and Practice of Compassion

Never be the first to tear apart friendship:
Grief grips the heart / Hugr when you have no one
With whom to speak all your thoughts.
(Havamal vs. 121, Poetic Edda, my translation.)

The Nature of Compassion-Energy

Compassion and sympathy literally mean 'feeling with, sharing feelings': *con + passio* in Latin, *syn + patheia* in Greek both mean 'with + feeling.' It does not always have to be feelings of pain and suffering that are shared, but any feelings. The sharing of any kind of feelings creates an energetic bond, short-term or long-term depending on circumstances. These energetic bonds add up, over time, to create and sustain all kinds of relationships, frith, and community connections.

(As a reminder, severely negative feelings, such as enjoyment of others' suffering, bullying, exploitation of others, violence, cruelty, etc., can also create sick bonds between people who enjoy causing those negative feelings in their victims. This is clearly not the kind of community and fellow-feeling that we are seeking here, and we need to reject any effort to draw us into such negative bonds with others (physical or spiritual). This can happen more easily than we may be aware of: enjoyment of cruel or exploitative scenes in movies and games, for example, can set us on such a path before we realize it.)

It is true that compassion can strain and exhaust us at times. The aperture in our heart through which compassion flows may start out rather narrow, and become frayed and bruised when the flow of compassion through it becomes too great for our capacity. Even when we enlarge our capacity and stamina for compassion, we can still reach our limit in tough situations. A good example of this is the plight of health care workers during the Covid pandemic, whose compassion and strenuous work led them to the point of collapse.

I want to make a subtle point about this situation here. There is a difference, at the energetic level, between running out of physical and mental energy and stamina, versus running out of compassion-energy itself. They are different kinds of energy, and the difference can be important on a spiritual level, even when they are overlapping on the physical level. *Compassion-energy is a stream flowing through us, not a finite resource that we own.* It circulates around among the worlds and beings of the worlds, picking up enhancements from each of us and from all beings as it flows on its way. When we share feelings, share the energy of compassion, what is really happening is compassion-energy interacting with itself. The compassion-energy flowing through each of us reaches out to the same energy flowing through others around us; it contacts those energies and blends together as we 'share feelings' or 'share together in compassion-energy.'

Managing Compassion-Energy

We may reach the point where we cannot physically, mentally or emotionally sustain the practical demands of compassion, as in the example of pandemic-era health care workers. The demands may be so great that we are injured by them, as health care workers may suffer from PTSD, depression, anxiety, and health breakdowns. Though it may feel natural, at such a time, to shut down our feelings of compassion in self-defense, this is actually the wrong time to do that.

The reason is, again, that compassion is a flow, and we ourselves desperately need compassion at this very time when we are tempted to shut it down. When we shut down the outflow, the inflow may well be shut down or minimized as well. We can see this happening, using our example again, when health care workers feel a sense of guilt and failure when they try to step back or give up their responsibilities because they cannot manage any more. They may block the inflow of compassion that others are sending toward them, including from spiritual sources, feeling that they 'don't deserve it' since they are not giving compassion out anymore. They may imagine they are 'failures', bad people who have let others down, and 'deserve to suffer.'

This is a terribly painful state to be in and may eventually lead to what I mentioned earlier: the shutting-down of all compassion, including compassion toward ourselves and our own needs. Then we end up with damage to our souls, becoming cynical, hardened, depressed, detached, neglectful of our own wellbeing and uncaring about everyone else. Next may come addictions and other dysfunctional coping behaviors, and it's a downward slope from there.

Experience and Practice of Compassion

All of these awful experiences come about, I believe, through the root cause of trying to block the proper flow of compassion. This effort at self-protection is totally understandable, but is based on a lack of understanding of the true mystery of compassion. And this mystery is simple but profound: *compassion must keep flowing.* It must not be blocked, even though the *expression* of compassion through physical and emotional activity may have to take a break from time to time, due to exhaustion and the need for self-care.

The Goddesses Syn (the doorkeeper) and Hlin (the provider of safe refuge) can help us manage such needs and processes of healthy withdrawal and rest. But regardless of our state of rest or of activity, the flow of compassion must continue.

Keeping Compassion Flowing

You may ask "how is this compassion supposed to continue, when I am too tired and burned out to do anything? I don't want to talk or listen to anyone, or do anything for anyone that I don't absolutely have to. I've got to shut it down." No, you mustn't shut it down: now you need it flowing into you, just as much as you were letting it flow out of you when you were actively expressing it. The mistake here is thinking that compassion always has to be active, which can indeed be exhausting.

Let's look at an example in our imaginations, now, as an example of the *power of passive, rather than active compassion: the compassion of Being rather than of Doing.* Maybe you've known someone like this; if not, imagine it. Here is an elderly and frail person, able to do very little at this stage of life. This person is a grandparent, and during their

Experience and Practice of Compassion

younger years, was actively involved with the lives of their children and grandchildren, their other relatives, neighbors and friends. People felt that this grandparent could really see them, know them and care about them; just being near them, saying hello on their way to school or work, was a little lift in their day. I was lucky to have grandparents like that; for example, during WWII they wrote regular letters to all the young men and women they knew about from their small town who were serving in the war, especially to those whose own families were not so faithful.

Now this person is very old and can't do much at all. They sit in a chair and spend most of their days in quietude. They may not be as mentally sharp as they used to be. But are they cut off from the compassion they practiced throughout their life, because they can no longer be active? No way. They have spent their life being a channel for compassion, and compassion is now flowing steadily through them with power and beauty. It waters their souls, and spreads out from them like scent from lovely flowers, filling the air around them. Its ripples spread outward like sound-waves through the ether. Their heart is still working just fine as a channel for compassion-energy, even if their mental and physical powers are fading.

You may think I am being sentimentally poetic, but I have known people like this, and not only old people. I've known people whom others just want to be around, because they are quiet but spiritually strong and peaceful people who spread happiness just by their presence. Such people are rare, but they don't need to be. This is something we can all aspire to, no matter our state of strength or health, work or wealth, culture or religion, opportunity or lack of it. Such quiet saints have spread peace in concentration camps and on desperate migrations: such is their power. This kind of power is passive; it is not expressed through direct action. Rather, this energy disperses out from the compassionate person, and is absorbed through osmosis by others around them.

Hindus have a practice called *darshan*, where pilgrims simply sit quietly in the presence of persons recognized as holy people, perhaps speaking with them, perhaps not. This is considered a valuable spiritual practice, offering peace, hope, blessing to those attending, even though nothing much happens. They are sharing in a deep flow of compassion.

Animals are often very attracted to people who are adept at this flow of peaceful compassion, and many people have felt a response from natural entities like trees when engaging in this activity in natural surroundings. Spiritual beings like landwights and housewights appreciate being in this kind of environment. They hate it, and tend to desert the area, when people in their environment are quarrelsome, disruptive and disrespectful, as is told in many tales of folklore.

These examples all show gentle but powerful expressions of compassion, and they are flows whose expression can be accepted by each recipient in the way best suited to them. There are often times when acts of intended compassion are actually not that well-suited to their recipients, and sometimes ulterior motives can be masked by apparent acts of compassion. All of these leave a bad taste behind them, and unfortunately they commonly occur. The flows from the heart that I am talking about here can never go wrong, because this quiet compassion shapes itself to each person's need as it flows through them.

The Mystery of Compassion

The mystery of compassionate flow can take on many shapes and expressions, suited not only to the recipients, but to the giver's abilities as well, which will vary over time depending on their circumstances. When we cannot perform physical acts of compassion, we can still keep the beautiful, soul-nourishing flow moving vigorously through ourselves and the world around us, through a passive form of dispersion and osmosis.

Compassion is a flow of energy. This energy can express itself in active or passive ways, and both are of great value. The energy of compassion needs to flow through us constantly. It flows into us from other people, Deities, spiritual beings and beings of nature. Within us, it nourishes, energizes and heals us, and it takes on something of our own 'shape and flavor.' Then it flows out from us to be shared with other beings, through physical, emotional, mental, spiritual activities, and through passive but powerful processes like dispersion and osmosis.

Compassion in Heathenry

Having discussed here the general nature of compassion, let's move on now to ideas about how our own Heathen Deities may relate to us compassionately. With such inflows of compassion from them, we can fill our own 'compassion-tanks' and have more to share with others here in Midgard!

Modern Heathens often wonder about where or how one can find compassion in our troth. The texts and tales passed down to us from earlier Heathen times do not offer a great many examples of compassion, although related impulses such as frith and generosity are praised. These texts were written during times of great difficulty and cultural change, and their focus was on the warrior life and warrior values—this was how the poets and tale-tellers made their living. Anything relating to everyday life, parenting, elder care, care for the sick and dying, neighborliness, and other opportunities to practice compassion was given short shrift in the poems and tales, though there are brief, passing examples in the sagas and some poems. (You can read about "Thor's Act of Compassion" in Chapter 6 on "Thor and his Family".)

We, as modern Heathens, do not need to remain stuck in these patterns of the past. Modern Heathen ethics and community values are topics of lively discussion and exploration among us, and the need for compassion is acknowledged within our faith as well as all others.

It's important to note something that frequently serves to block and confuse all of us, as we seek compassion in times of need, either from other people or from the Deities. Compassion can take many forms, sometimes unexpected and even unwelcome forms, such as 'tough love' (which may be truly compassionate, or may not, depending on how it is applied). Different states of need, and different people, personalities, and circumstances, may require different forms of compassion in order to best address the need.

How the Deities Shape Compassion

Compassion is a form of energy, as our souls are, too. As compassion flows through a living being, physical or non-physical, it is shaped by the 'container' of that being, then shaped again as it reaches its destination within us or other beings and begins to nourish us with its healing energy. Here

Experience and Practice of Compassion

I will offer some examples of how our Deities may shape their compassion toward us. Of course, these examples are based on my own knowledge and experience of these Deities; your experience might turn out somewhat differently, based on your own relationships with them.

The point remains: we can seek our Deities when in need of their compassion, with the understanding that they will give it their own way, in their own time and choice of circumstances. We need to be open to that, not demanding a specific form of compassion, and rejecting anything different that they might offer. We also need to be open to the idea that compassion may come from a different Deity than we were expecting. All of them, even the 'toughest', have their own ways of doing this, as some modern Heathens have experienced from Deities like Hella, for example.

With these thoughts in mind, let's turn to some examples of how we can find compassion from our Deities. Having many Deities in our troth, each with their own personalities, offers a smorgasbord of different ways that we may meet with compassion from them, which can truly serve us well!

Here are vignettes, short scenes or stories, showing examples of how some of our Deities may express their compassion toward us. Each Deity's way is different and may be of use to you at different times in your life. These scenes may inspire you to pursue your own experiences of compassion from all of our Holy Ones. I encourage you to then pass that compassion on and share it with others!

Thor's Compassion

Thor grips your shoulders, shakes you lightly, looks into your eyes with his powerful gaze. "Hey, you can do / get through

Experience and Practice of Compassion

this! You know I've got your back, always—and my great kids do, too. Our strength is yours: draw on it, drink it in; there's always enough. The Mod-mead, yeah? The mægen-ale. Asmoði. We brew it ourselves, here in Thrudheim; there's nothing else like it. It will do you nothing but good. Have a horn-full! Have two!" You feel warmth and power in your belly, strength at your back; you stand strong against adversity.

Freya's Compassion

Freya's heart is the fire of life: sweet-scented, jewel-toned, shimmering-silk flames, twining in graceful, hypnotic patterns. You walk into the lovely chamber of her heart, sink into this fire of life. It rises around you; burns away the dross, the despair, the hurts and harms that are draining your life-force and your joy. You feel burnished, shining, as your life-force begins to replenish through the warm fires of her sacred Brisingamen jewels. You stay as long as you wish, return as often as you want. This life-giving fire is such joy!

Gradually, you learn to bring this life-force, warmth and joy back with you to energize your daily life and share with others. Your own heart, your own souls, are afire with Freya's beautiful compassion, the food of life. She feeds it into Midgard through you. Use it exuberantly!

Tyr's Compassion

Tall and stern, Tyr gazes at you, measuring your fiber. There is no softness there, but steel and piercing starlight. You breathe in the cold, clear air, the air from the stars. It is sharp in your lungs, and your mind begins to clear from the fogs and confusions of your Midgard life. You see more clearly, discern more clearly, your sense of truth and your ability to judge and evaluate are sharpened. Your confusions begin to resolve into clarity.

Tyr drapes a magnificent mantle around your shoulders, and you feel its weight. He challenges you to sense what this mantle is woven of: Loyalty. Commitment. Faithfulness. Honor. Responsibility toward those who depend on you. Our life is not only our own; we are part of a whole, and we have commitments to that whole.

Tyr guides you in the process of turning pain and injury, the things for which you seek compassion, into a sacrificial gift for the wellbeing of the greater whole. The way to do this is unique to you, your own path, and Tyr's rede is deep but clear: a star reflecting in the pool of everyday life.

Tyr's remote gaze meets yours. Do you accept his gifts, and his challenge? As you do so, you feel an ease, a clarity, a singleness of purpose. You know where you are going now. Tyr's stern benevolence equips you to deal with your life's challenges. You stand tall in salute to Tyr's bright might, then wend your way back to Midgard.

Frigg's Compassion

Frigg bends toward you, takes your hand, strokes your cheek and your hair in motherly fashion. "Weep," she says. "Weep all your tears; let them flow. Release them. You have reason for your sadness, and you must let it run its course." She sits quietly with you while you do this; the warmth of her heart cradles you, there beside her hearth-fire.

As your tears begin to subside, Frigg rises and fetches a roll of fluff and a spindle. She sits down with you again, saying "Take this fleece and roll a bit of it between your fingers into a thread. Attach that thread to the spindle, then let it drop and spin, as you twist more fleece into thread and twirl it onto the spindle." You do so, and your motions become hypnotic. The growing length of thread begins to change color: perhaps one color, perhaps layers of many colors.

"This is a new thread to weave into the pattern of your life, dear one," Frigg whispers softly to you. "You are spinning it out of the fibers of pain and sadness in your heart, but also the fibers of new hope. The weight of the spindle mimics the heavy weight you feel in your heart, but it also keeps the thread straight and true. The turning motion of the spindle can turn your life in a different direction. Think about this; watch it spin, sink into its motion. You have allowed the thread to change color. Look at its colors now: what do they tell you?"

Quietly, she draws out your deepest thoughts and feelings, and shares her rede with you as you continue spinning. Slowly, your pain begins to ease, as new directions take shape before you.

Odin's Compassion

"If you're going to wallow, do it somewhere else. Otherwise, sit down and listen." Odin heaves a sigh as he drops down beside you near the top of the mountain crag you have struggled to climb. He raises both hands and spreads them to either side; between his hands, a complex scene takes shape in the air before you.

"Surprised? You didn't know you were climbing up toward Hliðskalf, did you? Up there above us is the High Seat where Frigg and I look out over the Worlds, and where Huginn and Muninn bring me the news they have gathered."

Experience and Practice of Compassion

Odin pauses, thoughtfully gnawing the end of his mustache, as you try to make sense of the jumbled, shifting scene before you in the air. You can't figure it out, but it makes you feel bad in some way: sad, angry, guilty, regretful, despairing....

Odin begins to point out the features of the scene before you. You gradually realize that the image reflects the burden that lies on your heart, the matters that create your need for compassion. "See how that piece comes in and attaches over there, and how the whole thing flipped around and tangled where the wind is blowing it. And over there, pieces have broken off, while you've tried to attach other pieces over here. And where do you think this is all heading?" Odin asks.

This scene represents both time and space, process, actions and results. It shows the development and complexity of the matters that are troubling you. Future paths that it might take are faintly outlined.

"I've learned from Frigg and Freya and the other Seeresses," Odin tells you, "but this place with its powers, and this skill—this is what I do myself. I see and pursue the strands of wyrd, and seek always to shape them to my will. Sometimes that works out, sometimes not so much," he tells you wryly. "What can you learn from this? What can you see, with the power of my High Seat flowing down here to us for a few minutes? What are you going to do about this tangle? What is your own Will here?"

You sit speechless on the crag, feeling the winds blowing, seeing the double-vision of Odin's scene imposed over the landscape, feeling the strange, powerful, uncomfortable energies emanating from the Great One next to you and flowing down the crag. This is difficult, and he's not giving you any more help. Wind... and Will... Hugr-wind.... Huginn... Muninn....

Experience and Practice of Compassion

You feel dizzy with the sudden rush of wind around you, then a soft explosion inside yourself rocks you with the feeling of....feathers? Your own Huginn and Muninn? Your own will-wind? You may be sitting on this crag for quite some time, working though all of this in your mind. At some point you notice that Odin is long gone, off on his own mysterious ways.

Sigyn's Compassion

Sigyn is the wife of Loki, and suffers a cruel fate. Her husband is punished for his misdeeds by being bound to a rock, using the intestines of their slaughtered son as ropes. A snake hangs over him, dripping burning venom, which scalds Loki as it drips. Sigyn sits beside him holding a bowl to catch this venom. When she turns aside to empty it, venom drops from the snake onto Loki, causing him to writhe in agony and shake the earth.

"Sigyn Loki's Wife" by Harry George Theaker.

Modern Heathens who have worked with Sigyn have found a deep compassion in her, a profound understanding of pain and grief. She offers a model of dogged, enduring compassion under the worst of circumstances.

Experience and Practice of Compassion

Frau Holle's Compassion.

Frau Holle, a German Goddess, shows her compassion in many, many ways of daily life. Sometimes it is gentle and kind, often it is brisk and practical, other times a stern, even threatening approach, when she sees we need a hard shove to get back on the right path for our well-being.

Here is a short vision I had of her, a few days after the death of my father. He had brought his originally admirable life to an end in late middle age, through decline and illness due to lack of self-care, and pushing away the loved ones who would have helped and supported him if he had allowed it. All the family and friends were grieving.

"Frau Holle" by Wilhelm Stumpf.

I sought out Frau Holle for comfort in my grief, and here is what I saw in my vision. She had my father standing in an old tin bathtub full of steaming hot water. Frau Holle, in her guise as a stern old woman of the no-nonsense nanny type, held a rough, bristly scrubbing brush and a large bar of yellow lye soap. She got to work, scrubbing my father until his skin was covered in suds and turned bright red and shiny. He had a rather cowed, sheepish expression on his face, but underneath he seemed to acknowledge that this was a good thing she was doing. Then she tossed a bucket of cold rinse water over him, and sent him off to walk a long, dim forest path into the distance. This seemed to be a path of reflection for him, a place and time for deep thought.

This was a comforting vision for me, a confirmation that Frau Holle was taking my father in hand now that he was in her realm, cleaning him up and setting him on a better path for the healing of his souls.

Frey's Compassion

Frey is the beating heart of This-World: Veraldr-God. His vigorous, vital power flows through the mountains and plains, fields and forests, the seas and rivers, cool rain and the heat of the sun, bringing surging life in its many shapes and forms to all that he flows through. He brings frith with him, supporting the strong fabric of healthy relationships and community, feeding the roots that undergird a peaceful, productive, and lively society.

Frey steps from shadow into sunlight in all his magnificence: a man, a stag, a God, a frith-king, a brother, father, husband, friend, bringing the vigor of Life with him in all his forms. The glowing mantle of his strong, life-renewing compassion covers all that is; we need only wake up and see that it is there. Absorb it into your being, use it to renew the vitality and eagerness of your own heart, your own life and souls, and pass it on to others around you.

Frith and Generosity

These are examples of compassion given by our Holy Ones, based on my own experiences. You may experience their compassion differently, but I offer the assurance that compassion can indeed be found from them and with them.

Experience and Practice of Compassion

As I mentioned earlier, they do expect us to accept compassion in the form they offer it, which may not be in the form, nor from the Deity, that we think we are seeking. We need to realize that the form of compassion, and the one who offers it, are important aspects of their gift to us. There is likely to be some kind of push or spur toward action in their gifts of compassion: a push toward the inner action of growing our wisdom, or toward outer action to resolve our situation, or likely both.

The Heathen values of frith and generosity, which can be found in the old writings and practices, are linked with compassion and should grow out of it. As we receive compassion from our Holy Ones and ancestral spirits, so should we pass it on to the world around us, expressed in gestures of frith and generosity.

Experience and Practice of Compassion

*An intense moment, a turning-point in life,
is compassionately shared in this painting by Arthur Rackham.*

26: Earth, Water, Wind, Fire: Relating to the Deities

Years ago, I came up with the term 'Utgard Ranger' to describe what I like to do in my spiritual life: range outward beyond the customary boundaries of thoughts and concepts, exploring and experiencing, meeting challenges, seeking knowledge, wisdom, understanding, expanding my spiritual territory and my comfort zone. It's an enjoyable and rewarding activity and requires nothing in the way of physical gear! Mental and spiritual tools, however, are very useful. Here, I describe some conceptual skills or approaches that I use for shaping and understanding my relations with the Deities, and for setting my intentions when I fare forth on my Utgard Ranger expeditions. I structure these concepts in my mind by using analogies to the classical four elements: Earth, Water, Air and Fire, further subdividing Water into flowing versus still water, and Air into still air and wind.

The elemental modes that I discuss here are certainly not the only ways to pursue relationships with the Deities, but they do cover a lot of ground, some of which is likely to be very familiar to you; some, perhaps less so. None of these ways are 'better' or 'more advanced' than any of the others, nor am I proposing that we 'should' use all of these methods to relate to Deities, except to note that it is important to be well-grounded and experienced in Earth-mode first, before trying the others. This is our home-base, so to speak. I find it enriching to explore all of these modes; an enjoyable challenge and expansion of my spiritual life and experiences.

At the end of each elemental section, I offer keywords and a brief description of the ways that inner change usually occurs through our interactions with the Deities in that mode; these processes of change differ considerably, depending on our mode of interaction. Now, on with our explorations!

The Mode of Earth

What Earth-mode is like and how we do it.
This is, I would say, our default mode of interaction with Deities and other Worlds, because it is the one most familiar to us. In Earth mode, though this generally happens in our imagination, we experience ourselves and the Deities as separate individuals, as three-dimensional beings who have seemingly physical characteristics: human-like appearance

and expressions, engaging in familiar physical actions and behaviors. We communicate with words, speaking our own words to the Deities, and 'hear' their responses, in the sense that we intuit and interpret their responses as verbal concepts, even when we don't actually hear them speak. Often, their responses take the form of actions rather than words. Our experience consists of exchanges, often verbally expressed, between 'self' and 'other'—Deities, ancestral and other spirits, etc.

Our harrows, wihsteads, altars, temple-spaces, hallowed spaces and their furnishings are established in Earth-mode, composed of physical objects and spaces, and we physically enact our rituals and ceremonies there. We relate to the Deities through physical objects and spaces around us: our home, the landscape and our environment, our interactions with other people, the activities we engage in every day.

Earth

When we pursue otherworldly journeys and explorations in Earth mode, we perceive and experience these other places as having a basic similarity to Midgard-Earth, with landscapes, buildings, animals, trees and plants, populated with other seemingly physical beings. This makes it easier for us to engage with the otherworld experience, easier to navigate and orient ourselves, to interpret what is going on. We can have some confidence in our own ability to take appropriate action in this otherworld, because it has at least some similarity to our experience of our own World, though there are certainly important differences as well. (Recommended: Diana Paxson's book *Trance-Portation: Learning to Navigate the Inner World.*)

The physical appearance of whatever we perceive in other Worlds is likely to be heavily symbolic or mythic (including the appearances of the Deities), and may suddenly shift into something different. This sudden shifting includes not only the appearances of individual beings, but of landscapes, spatial dimensions, time, color, light, and other properties that we depend on, in Midgard, to maintain their stability. When this happens, it is an opportunity or a lesson, to begin learning that Earth-mode is simply one mode of perception and experience; it is not 'the only reality.'

Challenges and ordeals

All of us in our lives face challenges and ordeals. In Heathenry, we generally consider that our Deities are somehow involved in these challenges and ordeals, and that we are expected to face them and deal with them in worthy ways, often through guidance from the Deities. The guidance, and the experiences, may not be gentle! But this is often how we learn and grow. The experience of challenges requires a perspective of 'self' and 'other', as we have in the Earth-mode. Our 'self' is experiencing and dealing with the challenges in our Midgard life; the 'other', the Deity, may sometimes be the instigator of the challenge, and is likely to be guiding us in a certain direction through the challenge or ordeal.

This is one example of the useful and important perspective of Earth-mode relationships with Deities, though there are many other ways that Earth-mode can express itself in these relationships, as well. Examples are experiences of the Deities as companions, advisors, teachers, elders, benefactors, role models, defenders, and many other roles. I don't mean to imply that all that happens in Earth-mode are ordeals or challenges; only that when challenges do happen, we generally deal with them through Earth-mode relationships with our Deities. Here is a personal example of an Earth-mode interaction and challenge with a Deity.

Frau Holle

Around thirty years ago I had a dream that set me solidly on the Heathen path. In the deep woods at midnight an enormous wild sow approached me, her lean shoulders higher than my head. Her bristly fur was silver, shining with its own light like the moon, a luminous and numinous Presence, yet a fearsome one too, looming huge and powerful in the night. She came up next to me and nudged my shoulder gently but inexorably, changing my direction onto a new path. There was no withstanding her weight and strength. As we walked along together, she took my hand into her fearsomely-tusked maw and held it there. Somehow, she bit off my hand and swallowed it, and at the same time did not bite it off, but left it attached to me, still holding it in her mouth.

Though she appeared in the form of a wild sow, I knew her name was Holle: a mysterious, deep-woods / underworld being who guides folk through the dark and the unknown,

Earth, Water, Wind, Fire: Relating to the Deities

challenging our willingness to follow and our willingness to understand, without being told, what she wants of us.

Frau Holle still walks beside me in this form, though I interact with her in human form, as well. Her dark presence at my shoulder and toothy grip on my hand is her challenge. She keeps me on the path, and, as I gradually learned over the years, her possession of my hand is both her challenge and her fierce blessing that calls me toward writing as the main expression of my Heathen path.

This scenario is an example of Earth-mode, physical-world perceptions and experiences with a Deity, the most common way for us to interact with them. They most certainly do not always involve challenges or ordeals; depending on how often we 'visit', most of the time this won't happen. But we need to realize that such things could happen, any time we visit with our Deities. It's not necessarily up to us, and our Deities are good at picking up opportunities to advance their purposes with us!

Another note on Earth-mode: In this mode, 'gender' is 'a thing'. Physical gender, gender identity, preferred gender, gender-perceptions and stereotypes, all inevitably arise when we interact with each other and with Deities in 'body' form, having images of physical bodies both in our mind's-eye, and in our physical world. An interesting thing about the other (non-Earth) elemental modes of relating to Deities, is that gender is not an issue, because we are not relating through any images or experiences of solid, physical bodies and their functions, when working in the other modes. If matters of gender are an issue for you in any way, you may find that exploring the other modes of relating to the Deities, not using human images of them, is a very freeing experience. You may find a burden being lifted from your heart, as you walk these paths of exploration.

Characteristics of Earth-mode:

Keywords: Identity, individuality, self-and-other, autonomy, structure, process, foundation.

How inner change usually happens: In an evolutionary or cumulative way: gradual, organic, step by step, punctuated with forward, backwards, sideways movement. Through discussion, argument, resistance, reaction, experiment, reassessment, decision, determination. Through challenges: mental, emotional, physical, and our responses to them.

The Modes of Flowing and Still Water

The Water-mode of perception and experience comes in two forms: flowing or surging water, and deep, still water. I'll begin with flowing water, the mode I use most often.

Flowing Water

Goðafoss: the Waterfall of the Gods.

Flowing Water is different from Earth-mode in many ways, and the first of them is that we are only minimally distinct from the Deity and the World that we are interacting with. Our perceived 'body' and body-senses blend with the Deity and the World the Deity is in, and our soul focuses on perceptiveness toward the Deity.

Caution

In Water-mode, we are joining our energy-flows with the energy-flows of 'something' and sharing how that 'something' experiences its being and its environment. Because of this degree of intimacy, and the power that is shared, I think it is wise to do this only with a Deity whom you know and trust through long personal experience.

I recommend against trying it with non-Godly spirits or other beings, and also recommend against trying to explore a World through this mode on your own, rather than riding along with a Deity to experience the World. It doesn't require much imagination to realize how easily we can become lost, overwhelmed, subsumed by the experience of Water-flow, unless we are doing it with a powerful being who cares about us, protects us, and is willing to share a beneficial experience with us.

Procedure

The way I proceed with this is to lie down comfortably in a quiet place (in bed before falling asleep is good; I just turn off the light early so I have some extra time). You can try other meditation-positions if you prefer, but because this is a full-body, full-sensory experience I find it's helpful not to be concerned with the physical body, such as the subtle actions needed to stay sitting upright without slumping or falling over. It's easier just to lie down and let go.

I call on a Deity I am close to, whose energy, experience, and connection with this or other Worlds I would like to share for a time. Basically, I'm asking for a 'ride' with the Deity, and so far they've always been willing. The Deity arrives in a rushing flow of power, like a fast-flowing river or ocean current, and I dive in, through my awareness, as though merging into a stream of traffic. (Actually, the Deities don't 'arrive'; they are always flowing energetically through the Worlds, and it is only my perception that opens up to the conjunction of myself with this power, which seems like an 'arrival'.)

Sometimes I envision myself as a water animal like a dolphin, otter, or fish, playing in the flows or waves of water, but more often I just feel myself merged with the flow of 'water', which is actually the essence of the Deity. It is easiest to describe this through some examples of my experiences.

Ing-Frey

I most often interact with Ing-Frey not through the image of person-to-person contact such as a dialog, but rather as a mighty current of energy which I can join through my sensations. I hear him as the beating Heart of the World, as a baby hears the powerful beat of her father's heart when she lies on his chest. This beating of Veraldr-God's Heart surrounds, penetrates and vitalizes everything in the world, including my own beating heart. I feel Frey's power like a mighty, all-encompassing ocean current flowing through the Worlds: swift, frothy, joyful, salty with nourishment and flavor, the perfect blend of coolness and warmth. His power is immense, but not overwhelming; it nourishes and vitalizes all that is. Like a playful dolphin or otter, I flow along within this mighty current and pulsation of life-giving power and joy: the heart and soul of Veraldr-God.

Iðunn

While I sense Frey as a powerful, rapidly surging ocean current, I sense Iðunn as a gentler, softer flow, a meandering stream through fertile meadows and orchards, sunlight sparkling through the crystal water. Her benison and blessing spread from the water outward over the landscape, giving a rich glow to all colors, a resonant richness to all scents. Her water-flow brings the power of life and growth, felt as a tingling or gentle buzzing sensation in the water, which tastes tart and sweet, like apples.

Magni

I've recently started working with Thor's son Magni through the flowing-water mode, and this has a different feel than other Deities I've worked with this way. Instead of 'me' flowing into and along with the Deity's energy and sensation, it feels like Magni is flowing through me. It's like I'm a little spot in the river of power that is Magni, and as he flows along in his mighty river, my own being is one of the many 'places' that he passes through. As he flows through me, I feel his megin or mægen power magnetizing my own energy, waking and stirring it up. It feels like all my hair is standing on end, a buzzing, invigorating bath of power.

As this happens, I feel many little bits of grit within myself, 'sand in the works', becoming magnetized, too, and drawn out of me toward Magni-magnet. They don't bother him at all, but within me, they 'gum up the works' on different levels of my being, hindering my energy and wellbeing, *confusing my Will. Magni draws all this grit along with him, leaving me feeling energized and renewed. Now I am like a little eddy of my own power, within Magni's greater river.*

Another way that my experience with Magni is different, is that he is so little-known among us. I have no Earth-mode image of him, no picture in my mind, I haven't interacted with him in Earth or other modes at all, but only in Water-mode. This makes it easier, in a way, because I don't have to get past the images and Earth-mode relationships and history that I have with other Deities, such as Frey and Iðunn. I don't have to make myself stop perceiving them in human form so that I can interact with them in Water-mode, energy-mode. I can just plunge in and brace myself for Magni's surging, magnetic flow!

Among the most rewarding Deities with whom to share such experience are those whose activities are associated with seasonal tides of Midgard: Eostre / Ostara, Walburga, Frau Holle as she is celebrated in Urglaawe, Iðunn, Frey, Freya, the Yuletide processions of the German Goddesses. (I would be extremely cautious about the Wild Hunt, though!) At certain times of year, their powers flow especially strongly through Midgard, and it is invigorating and joyful to join in with them!

Another great one to ride along with is Thor during a thunderstorm, either an earthly, physical thunderstorm, or an otherworldly one. But indeed, all the Deities have their own unique patterns and experiences of flow, and we can join them if they are willing. We definitely want to request their permission, and make sure they know we are there so they can be mindful of our safety.

Earth, Water, Wind, Fire: Relating to the Deities

Purpose

As you may have noticed, another difference between this Water-mode and the Earth-mode is that with Water, there is no specific purpose for undertaking the experience, other than the experience itself. In Earth-mode, we often have a specific purpose in mind: a prayer for help or guidance, for example, or the celebration of an event or a holy day, the pursuit of a magical intention, a discussion with the Deity, or a thanksgiving. In Water-mode, none of these considerations are present or relevant to us; it's a matter of simply sharing Being, Essence, experience, sensations, between us, the Deity, and the World(s) the Deity's power is flowing through.

It really feels like powerful, fast-flowing Water, sparkling with flashes of sunlight / moonlight / earthlight, imbued with subtle flavors, pressing and flowing against our skin, surging and tossing us up and down, as we pass through subtle changes in temperature, light, flavor and color. We stay as long as we feel like it, and re-emerge from the flow feeling refreshed and invigorated, with our connection to the Deity and to the World(s) we flowed through, having been deepened and strengthened.

Further cautions

We don't want to do this with a Deity with whom we are uncomfortable, whose energy we find jarring or ill-fitting to our nature, at least not until our relationship with that Deity has been reshaped or has matured. This mode requires that we temporarily let go of controlling our own experience, and join with the experience of another being whom we know and trust.

Water-mode isn't a 'challenge' between us and the Deity the way Earth and Fire modes can sometimes be. Water-mode can be too overwhelming, and it penetrates too far into our own being; it is too intimate and blended, to work well as a challenge. Challenges depend on the perception of separate beings, a perspective of "me and my experience" versus "them and their influence", and that is incompatible with the Water-mode of relating to Deities.

On the other hand, a Water-mode experience can serve as a spiritual ordeal, especially if we fear water-related symbols and experiences. We must face and overcome that fear to succeed in the ordeal and gain the spiritual might and main, and the enhanced Deity-relationships, that result from it. This kind of ordeal should be one we choose to undergo, when and if we feel ready, and one that we approach with the support of a Deity. It can be done in gradual stages, or all at once, depending on our choice.

Deep, Still Water

This mode is most useful, in my experience, for learning about the otherworldly Wells and other water-bodies of other Worlds, though some Deities can also be approached in this way. Most Deities, I believe, are more involved with flow and movement through the Worlds, less involved with profound stillness. The Wells include those of Urð / Wyrd, Mimir, and Frau Holle. Other examples of deep, still water include the wetlands of Hel, the fens and marshes around Frigg's and Saga's Halls, and the ocean-depths in various Worlds.

Deep, still water.

Cautions

This is a mode to use only with great caution, and after much experience with otherworldly travel and the beings one encounters there. The risk lies in becoming stuck in immobility, and having difficulty emerging from it, which can also spread into daily life. The deep, still Water-mode can act as a 'strange attractor' as is seen in nonlinear dynamics, where a dynamic system is drawn toward a low energy, entropic state, losing its energy and its opportunity to evolve in a different direction. Once the energy is lost, the system cannot emerge from the trap of the strange attractor. The only possible way out is for energy to be brought in from outside the system. This phenomenon can occur with our soul-bodies since they too are energy-systems.

Earth, Water, Wind, Fire: Relating to the Deities

Procedure

There are ways around this risk, though, if you decide you want to try this mode. One is to make a firm agreement with a trusted Deity or Power, to guide you into and out of the experience, and commit to following their guidance. You will need to commit your Will to this agreement and use your Will along with the Deity's guidance and power, so as to have the energy to emerge from the 'strange attractor' phenomenon, in the event that you experience such a thing. You might very well not, but it pays to be prepared!

The Well as a passageway

The other way to handle this risk is similar: you approach the deep, still water as a passageway rather than an end in itself, again working with a Deity. The most typical example of this is falling or passing through Holle's Well, as is told in fairy tales. People 'fall through her well' as a metaphor for death, and land in her green, underworld land of otherworldly life. Likewise, Holle draws the souls of new babies from her well or pond: they pass from her underworld land of soul-incubation, through the waters of the Well between the Worlds, and into Midgard to ensoul a newly-conceived or newborn child. An agreement can be made with Frau Holle to explore or experience her Well as a passageway or transition-experience, rather than an end in itself. This is especially meaningful for a re-birthing experience.

I'll wrap up this section and transition to the next by showing how, in my experience, Mimir's Well can also be approached as a passageway. Mimir's Well is called the well of memory and inspiration and is very much worth exploring, if one is prepared and approaches it the right way. Most often, I think, when we approach Mimir's Well, we wish only for a sip, or to gaze into it, and even these experiences can come with a high price, as Odin knows! (Though I think many of us understand Odin's eye in Mimir's Well as a bargain or a pledge, rather than a 'payment' *per se*. We see that the eye in the Well feeds occult knowledge, perception, insight, back to Odin, rather than being lost to him in the depths of the Well.)

It is possible, however, to experience Mimir's Well as a passageway, in this case a passage between the Water-mode of experience and the Air-mode. Here is an example from my experience.

Mimir's Well

I sink down into wavelets of water, stirred by my passage, then falling still again. Above me, for awhile, is dim, filtered light, but it fades. Stillness, silence, timelessness, under the weight and darkness of the water. Yet, underneath that, a sense of hidden potential, of something that will appear in its own time. Gradually, a directionless light begins to infuse the water. Sensation changes from the skin-feeling of the water, to the scent of something fresh and clear. The film of water clears from my eyes. I can't pinpoint when it happens, but now instead of resting in deep water, I am wafting gently through fresh air, surrounded by wisps of cloud and movements of air-currents.

I have moved into what I perceive as World-Mind: the realm of Thought, Memory, Inspiration, created by the sacrifice of Mimir's head and its placement in his Well. Just as the sacrifice of the giant Ymir was the basis for forming the physical World of Midgard, so I believe that Mimir's execution by the Vanir was in fact a sacrifice that resulted in World-Mind coming into being, where all Thought and mental activity take place as our individual minds access, operate and interact within that realm. Through Mimir's deep well of Water, I now have access to explore the Airy realm of World-Mind.

Here, we are moving away from Water as sensation / feeling, and entering the mode of Air as awareness, perception and mental activity. My poem "The I in Mimir's Well" in Chapter 3 is another example of a deep, still Water-mode experience.

Characteristics of Water-Mode:

Keywords: Flow, sensation, energy, vigor, refreshment, immersion, blending, sharing, absorbing, deep awareness, renewal, trans-being.

How inner change usually happens: Through alteration of energy and essence, below the level of conscious awareness, caused by direct exposure to God-energies and World-energies. The change gradually floats up into our awareness as though it had always been there, while whatever was changed is washed away, irrelevant, almost forgotten.

The Modes of Air and Wind

Comparisons
When we relate in Earth-mode, we are sharing metaphysical, but structured, subject-object space with the Deities: we and they are clearly separate from each other. In Water-mode, the focus is on sharing sensation, the sense-experience of floating and surging within a Deity's natural flows of energy and experience of Being, and absorbing some of those energies.

Earth, Water, Wind, Fire: Relating to the Deities

Air

Air-Mode

In the mode of Air, we are again floating within a Deity's energy-Being, but rather than sensation-experience, the focus is on mental awareness. I would not dare to claim that we enter the core of the Deity's Mind, nor that we can know all their thoughts. But in Air-mode, we do hover on the fringes and glimpse something of the Deity's own perceptions and world-view, as they choose to share them with us.

Procedure
This mode requires us to step temporarily away from all our own concerns, viewpoints, preoccupations; away from anything that is roiling the peace of our own being. Our mind needs to be as clear as the windy sky, as we send out a call, echoing and reverberating through space: a call to a Deity we are close to, a request to hover within the space of their mighty Mind. This is not about ourselves and our own

concerns; this is about attempting to perceive, for a little while, Worlds and events and Beings as the Deity perceives and thinks about them. Sometimes, it is honestly refreshing and inspiring to relate to the Deities from their own perspectives, rather than from ours.

Here is an example of my experience with Air-Mode. Some of what I say here is enigmatic, just glimpses of something that I can't describe in any detail; this is typical of my Air-mode perceptions of the Deities' mental spaces. It's often a struggle to describe what I perceive, knowing that all my perceptions and expressions are so limited, compared to the minds I seek to perceive.

Viðar

When I approach Viðar through Air-mode here is what that is like, for me. His Air-domain is broad and deep, as his God-home Landvidi is. The verse from Völuspá comes to mind, describing the peace that follows Ragnarök and the future of the younger Gods who survive it: "two brothers' sons build a settlement in the wide wind-realm..." (vs. 60). Here is the wide wind-realm: here at home in Viðar's mind, his long view of time and space. He pitches in when the other Deities and humans need him, but still he is detached, biding his time. Something is always withheld, his time is not yet. He stands back, waiting, observing, thinking in silence. His silence hides his power.

What is / will his time be like? Is his time the vengeance itself? Or is the vengeance on Fenris simply the gateway into his time? His true time does not contain the Wolf, it flows past the Wolf into other Worlds. Viðar is strong sunlight, but he is still obscured by the shadows of the world. In his true time he shines in the morning, riding the Worlds on new tides of time. A gleam of his light shows above the horizon even now, while on the other side of the sky, the quiet stars shine on.

Another person might have a very different Air-mode perception of Viðar's awareness, and describe it in very different terms; certainly, I have not captured his warrior-aspect here. The Air-fields of World-Mind are vast; we can each perceive only small parts of them, and express even smaller parts in words! But the perceptions themselves are profoundly worthwhile.

Wind-Mode

Comparisons
Air is still; Wind moves, and there is a difference between them, just as there is between flowing and still Water. When we perceive in Air-mode, what we perceive 'holds still' for us, it allows us to take our time as we try to grasp and express it. It doesn't actively influence us, but allows space for our observation and experience to take its own shape, in its own time. Wind is a different matter; it has motive force, and it influences us directly.

Wind-mode

We experience the Wind-mode of relating to the Deities when we feel the power of their Minds and Wills creating a moving current within our being, as though they were blowing a great breath of air towards us and stirring things up within us. It could be a steady flow of power pushing us in a certain direction; it could be gentle or fierce gusts coming towards us from time to time, interspersed with periods of quiet. Sometimes it feels like eddies, circular or spiral flows, even a tornado. These turn us in circles and cause confusion and upheaval, bringing about changes in our outlook and our life. It's my thought that many of us become Heathens because of this God-wind stirring up our inner Being and urging us in this direction.

Wind

Earth, Water, Wind, Fire: Relating to the Deities

Procedure

We can choose to work with these Wind-flows from the Deities, or resist them; either way, they will end up influencing us. Often, we try through divination methods, such as the runes, to discern the direction and purposes of these God-Winds, these flows of divine power and will, so that we can understand and work with them. The closer our relationships with the Deities, the more clearly we can perceive the nature of their Winds and make our choices about how to respond.

Here are two examples of my perception of God-Winds. The first one didn't necessarily require action on my part, except the mental action of understanding, though I did take action by writing a song about it, called "The Winds of Odin's Will," included Chapter 2. Here is the background to that song.

Woden's Will-Wind

I saw 'reality' as though it were a huge blanket spread out over the landscape, with the ravens flying across. Then I saw Woden take up one edge of the 'blanket' and shake it as though he were Frau Holle airing her celestial bedding! When Woden shook the blanket, a series of ripples spread across the landscape of the blanket—big ripples in the part closest to him, and eventually growing smaller and smaller as the blanket passed out of sight over the horizon.

From this sight, my understanding is that though Woden cannot—or perhaps chooses not to—change the entire fabric of reality according to his will, he nevertheless is prone to giving it a good shaking up and airing out! The 'parts' of reality 'closest' to him (the terms in quotation marks are not very accurate for describing this, but I can't think of better ones) are of course the most affected, those farther away from his point of concentration, less so.

Then, I saw Woden's Will itself as though it were a wind emanating from his being and keeping the ripples of the blanket in motion, flowing across the landscape of reality in the direction of his will, like ripples blowing across a lake in the wind. Huginn and Muninn ride the tides of this wind, which always takes them in the direction of Woden's interest and involvement in reality and the ways he is working upon it.

Frige's Will-Wind
Often when I am trying to explore new knowledge and ideas, seeking new directions for my mind-craft, I perceive the image of Frige tossing her spindle into the distance. As the spindle flies through the air, thread unrolls from it and is wafted across the echoing spaces of World-Mind by Frige's Wind. My task is to keep this thread in sight, follow it across the mind-scapes of the worlds, and see what inspirations it leads me toward.

Characteristics of Air-Mode:

Keywords: Clarity, knowledge, openness, agility, confidence, alertness, change, expansion, direction, thought, will, impetus, inspiration, trans-being.

How inner change usually happens:

Through Air: A sense that something has shifted, doors and windows have opened. New perspectives draw us toward changing our outlook and our framework of thought. A sense of mental refreshment, renewal. Meaningful new knowledge and understanding lie before us, just around the corner, and lure us onwards, waiting for our pursuit.

Through Wind: The God-Wind blows through us, blowing some things away, blowing new things in, pushing us in certain directions toward actions that change our lives, and perhaps the lives of others whom we influence, as well. This process may involve a good deal of turbulence and disruptive change, and may at times obscure our vision through storms of 'dust and sand', mental storms filled with all the myriad details and influences in our lives that blind and distract us from our truly-chosen path.

The Modes of Fire and Wode

Comparisons
Fire is known, in esoteric terms, as a process of transformation. As the transformation takes place, 'the old' is burned and consumed, making way for 'the new' that arises from transformation. This process is quite different from the other modes. Earth-mode is based on 'what is', on the shape and structure of ourselves and the world that we grow and maintain during our lifetime. Water-mode and Air-mode, too, explore 'what is' in their own characteristic ways. Wind-mode moves into 'what is becoming'; it is the impetus for actions and deeds that are rooted in what-is and have their beginning there, but are moving toward becoming something else. This is generally more of an incremental process; it may happen in fits and starts, move in various directions, spin around, backtrack and move forward again, evolve its nature and direction as the winds move the action along. It is

generally a long, slow, complex process of 'becoming' or coming-into-being, though it can move very quickly in phases.

Fire.

Earth, Water, Wind, Fire: Relating to the Deities

Fire-mode

Fire jumps outside of all this: it is not a long, slow, complex, organically-arising process. It is the sudden conflagration, consuming 'what is' and transforming it into something else entirely. I'll give an example here of a fire transformation that happened to me, completely unexpectedly, as it usually does. It's an event which I mentioned earlier in this book, but it illustrates Fire-mode well so I'll return to it here.

Many years ago, a few years after I began my Heathen path, I wanted to understand Woden better and establish a relationship with him, but I was definitely wary and uncertain about how to go about this. I found it difficult to trust him. However, I was close to Frigg / Frige and trusted her. I asked her to show me why she loves him, show me how she relates to him and perceives him; in effect, to introduce me to him as her spouse, so I could ease into this, slowly. Frige agreed, and I waited for the civilized, low-key 'introduction' that I (foolishly) expected. That was not how it happened...

Frige snatched me up one night, unprepared, just as I was falling asleep, and drew me into a place like outer space. I was a tiny mote, and Frige and Woden were the size and power of supernova suns, with me the tiny mote floating right between them. The two of them were just at that moment turning toward each other, with the thought of love in their minds. The power that flowed from their love and passion was literally awesome—power that generates worlds, even universes—Big Bang power.

I was there only a split second, and realized this was no place for a mortal to be. I asked Frige politely to remember, next time, that I am mortal and subject to mortal limitations, and to please be careful of me! But it was quite an experience, and it certainly did respond to my request to Frige, to show me more of her relations with Woden! ("Be careful what you ask for: you might get it!") So much for 'easing into' a relationship with Woden....

Analysis:
This brief but powerful experience gave me a lot to think about, and it did, indeed, change my perception of Odin, but not through any process of 'getting to know him' gradually and cautiously. This was really not what I had thought I was asking for! (If there is one phrase I would use above all others to describe my dealings with our Deities, the one I would pick is "taken by surprise"! Other Heathens I know would say the same.) The change in attitude that I was seeking for myself indeed happened, but not in the polite, reasonable, diplomatic way I thought I was orchestrating! No: I was engulfed in flame, and indeed my aversion and reluctance to relate to Woden was in that moment burned away and did not return, in spite of him being admittedly a daunting Deity to relate to.

Effects
Before this burning I was hesitant to commit; afterwards there was no question that I *was* committed, come what may. And this change was not anything I reasoned out, bargained for, decided on, or grew into. There was no rational or emotional process involved. It was a transformation: one minute I was hesitant; a split-second later, after being blasted with radiation, something had changed in me, and stayed changed, though it took awhile for me to fully realize and digest it. This is the mode of Fire.

Earth, Water, Wind, Fire: Relating to the Deities

This is an example, in many ways a small thing: a change in my attitude toward one among many Deities. It could have happened in many other ways. Why did Frige and Woden choose the mode of Fire to bring about the change I asked for? Fire is really the 'big gun' among the various ways we can relate to the Deities, and I use this analogy with weapons advisedly. Fire-mode can feel like a weapon, like an assault on us, a conflagration, an upheaval, a destruction.

It may not always literally involve fire; it is a mode of sudden transformation, however that occurs. When it happens, it is often unexpected and maybe undesired by us. We may think we never asked for it, and perhaps we never did ask for Fire to be unleashed on us. But somehow, some way, some inner need or wish puts us in a space where the Deities who are close to us decide that Fire is the way to go, and there we are.

There is no reversal of Fire; the ashes of what is gone do not rise up and reconstitute. There is only the new thing that has come into being, and it may take us a good while to perceive, understand, accept, and learn to work and live with the new state of being, even when it seems a relatively small matter in the overall context of our life. I cannot go back to distrusting Woden; my distrust was burned away many years ago. He is what he is, I am what I am, our bond was forged in the Fire that he and Frige ignited, and that is that; we go on from there.

The issue of 'consent' in Fire-mode

Here is an important question: what role, if any, does our own consent, or denial of consent, play in an experience of Fire-mode? Let's look at this in a broader context for a moment. Every minute that passes in our lives can be seen as a spark of

Earth, Water, Wind, Fire: Relating to the Deities

Fire-mode experience: it comes, it brings change, however tiny, then it is gone and does not come again. We do not go backward in time; change happens within time, and there is no reversal. The Greek philosopher Heraclitus famously said: "You can't step into the same river twice." By the time you go back for the second round, the water you previously stepped in has flowed by, the environment and yourself, however slightly, have changed from what they were.

In a nutshell: *Fire-mode is change, change happens in time, time is not reversible.* Thus, true Fire-mode experience is not reversible. This is the nature of time and entropy, governed by the laws of physics, and these laws exist regardless of our consent to them. Our lives are governed by time and change, whether we choose for this to happen, or not.

So, that is the general, philosophical point I wanted to make. Now let's take it to the personal level: the specifics of our own Fire-mode, transformative experiences with the Deities, and the role of our consent in these experiences. Here are my own thoughts and observations; you will have to decide whether what I say agrees with your experiences, and if not, seek your own answers to this important question.

I think it's important, first, to distinguish between a 'challenge / ordeal' and a 'Fire-mode experience.' Challenges and ordeals happen in life. They are often orchestrated by our Deities to promote our growth and change. Often, they come about due to our own actions or lack thereof, our own choices or our failure to choose a path and act on our best judgement. Often, again, challenges occur through circumstances beyond our control. Generally, it is a combination of factors.

What turns them into true Heathen ordeals and challenges is our own attitude towards them, and the actions we take in response. The most terrible circumstances can be treated as Heathen ordeals and challenges; we can meet them with the strength and power gained from our Deities and our Heathen way of life, and transform them into opportunities for change, growth, generosity, honor, and other great values of human life.

It is here where godly Fire-mode experience may enter in: here at the moment when we choose, however tentatively and subconsciously, to *transform* an obstacle, ordeal, challenge, or a flaw or weakness in ourself, rather than continue to drag that burden around. I don't know how such transformation happens, or how to make it work. I don't have any switch to flip, or magic wand to wave. I'm stuck in the situation, and I don't know how to change it. Deep inside, a call goes out to a Deity for help, here. I want change, I want to transform the situation, and at some level I know that involves transforming myself.

This is the call, this is the consent to our Deities: we need some assistance and are willing to accept what they give. Again, these feelings may be confused and blurred within us, but the Deities have clear sight. What is beyond our choice and our consent, is *how* the Deities respond to our own need, in the situation we are in. That is their choice, not ours. They are not programmed, divine robots. I gave the example, earlier, of trying to orchestrate the progress of my relationship to Woden through Frige and showed what came of that. It was my choice, wanting to get to know Woden better, and it was my choice to ask for Frige's help. But, despite what I may have thought, it was not my choice how Woden and Frige responded! And they chose the transformation of Fire, for me at that time.

So, we can continue to wallow in problems, difficulties, states of mind or of being, that we don't want but can't figure out how to change, or maybe we know what needs to be done, but somehow can't manage to do it. Or we may just want some big change, something brand-new in our lives. We all like it when we ask the Deities for help in some situation, and they bring about some change from outside ourselves, without requiring radical change within ourselves, because that feels like it's easier, less disruptive. But things don't happen that way very often; usually, the changes the Deities bring about involve a lot of inner upheaval.

I think the Deities know which elemental mode will work best for us in a given situation, at a given point in our life, when we express our need, however confused, for their help. There's a good chance they will present their help in the form of a challenge or an ordeal, that brings about inner change within us. The transformative ordeal may take the form of Fire, or it may work its way through one of the other elements I've discussed here, most likely Earth or Wind modes, but possibly a Water ordeal. It's also quite possible to undergo a transformative challenge or ordeal through several successive modes, starting with Earth or Water, for example, then the final phase with Fire.

Wode

Wode or Óðr, a God-touched form of inspiration, is an expression of Fire. Its expression can range from a spark of inspiration or a steady flame of creativity, to a state of divinely-inspired prophetic madness or of battle-frenzy. Wode is a combination of Fire and Wind, where the Fire ignites us and the Wind propels us forward toward God-inspired action.

Divine Wode comes about through a God-Wind and a Godly Fire, and if we are able to ride this fiery wind then it carries us toward a state where we are able to surpass anything we thought we could do before. It burns away and blows through our self-limitations and carries us on a tide of divine Fire.

Once the Wode has achieved its intentions, if we are to maintain safety and sanity, we must leave the full-on grip of Wode and come down to earth again. But the Wode does not leave us unchanged; many inner aspects of our Self, especially our perception of our own limitations, are changed by this experience.

A Wode-Fire experience often leaves behind embers, burning coals, which act as fire-seeds. They settle deep within us and keep our fires of creativity and action low but steady. Then a Wode-Wind may come along and fire up these embers again. In this way, Wode-Wind-Fire creates a repeating pattern within ourselves, where a certain ability or tendency repeatedly arises. It's important to work with our Deities to refine and control this expression of Wode within ourselves so that it takes the form we and our Deities desire for it, rather than running amok.

Closing experience

I'll close now with another personal experience, involving initiatory Wode which lit a fire within, and gave strong impetus and direction to my Heathen life. For years I had wished to know Heimdall better, and often prayed politely for his attention, but didn't get more than, in effect, a courteous nod of acknowledgement. I had often encountered him through spaeworking for others, where he usually came forward as an initiator for someone seeking a clearer Heathen path, but he did not come for me personally. One day, during a personal spaeworking, he answered my prayer, and it was worth the wait.

Heimdall puts both his hands against the sides of my head, his lips against my brow. He hums strongly, filling me with vibrations. His humming turns to light, rainbow light, brighter and brighter, blinding. Rainbows everywhere, bewildering, shining forth from Heimdall's chest. The light and humming vibrate fiercely, overwhelmingly, in my blood, re-tuning me to a different frequency and awakening connections through my blood, my ancestry, the callings of the ancient ones.

My blood is a rainbow fire within me, bubbling and buzzing in my veins, flashing out through my skin and eyes. I am a rainbow bridge, I bridge between Midgard and the God-Homes, between past and future, ancestors and those to come; between the spirit-worlds and the world of matter, between my souls and the souls of others: we all are connected together in the beauty and power of the rainbow light.

A distant echo of a horn. As the horn calls, the rainbows slowly gather to form a bridge across the air. Heimdall steps out onto it, passes into light too bright to see. His horn still echoes, all colors around me are supernaturally bright and vibrant, there is a sense of gladness everywhere, the air itself is golden. A God has walked here.

The horn still calls, singing of beginnings, not endings. Still it calls, even now; still my heart responds. If I never see Heimdall in person again, it matters not; his rainbow vibrations are imprinted in my flowing life-blood.

Though I use this as an example of Fire-mode because of the radical change in perception that Heimdall caused in me, it can also be seen as Air-mode, venturing into Heimdall's awareness, his nature and his innate powers, and as Wind-mode in the impetus it gave me toward my Heathen callings. It partakes of Water-mode in the sensations of my blood flowing with Heimdall's energy, and of Earth-mode in my perception of myself and Heimdall, separate beings within a distinct landscape.

Transformation, awareness, sensation-experience, bodies and landscape: all the modes are unified in this experience. The rainbow itself blends Fire, Air and Water, and connects earth to earth, World to World. It is a fitting image with which to close our exploration of the elemental modes which shape our relationships with the Holy Ones.

Characteristics of Fire-Mode

Keywords: Consuming, sudden transformation, no boundaries, Wode, state-shift or quantum shift, non-reversible.

How inner change usually happens: Suddenly, directly, irreversibly. We jump from one state of being to another state, without intervening processes of thought, will, or emotion, and there is no returning to the previous state. It often comes as a stark shock or a blinding enlightenment, and our whole living-being or system of souls, mind, body, way of life, may take awhile to find a new equilibrium after this experience.

The Rainbow Bridge lays out the paths between us and the Holy Ones, formed of Fire, Air and Water, connecting Earth to Earth across the realms of the Life-Worlds. The horn-call of the Holy Ones, echoing across these Worlds, urges us to venture into the wide unknown. It sings of beginnings, and of endings that make room for new beginnings. And, may I say, it calls to the Utgard Ranger within us all!

"Heimdallr and his horse Gulltoppr" by Dorothy Hardy.

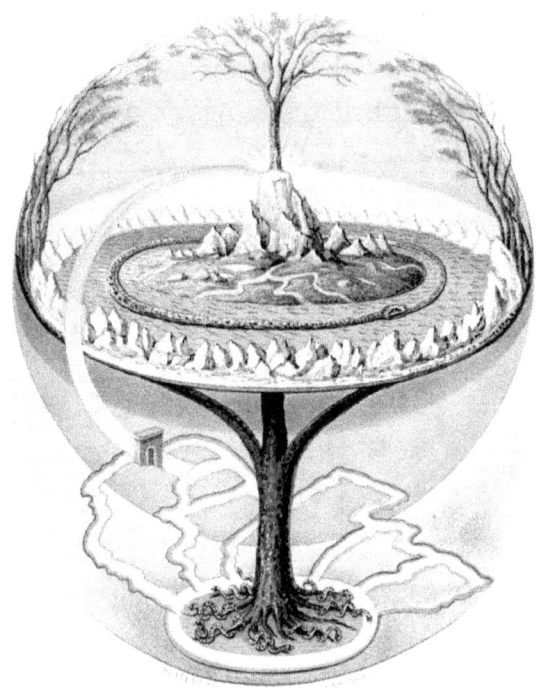

Yggdrasil, by Olaf Bugge

27: Trance and Power Chants

"Völva," by Vangland.

Some kinds of Heathen-oriented spiritual activities involve entering into trance or other states of altered consciousness. There are any number of ways to do this, and many different reasons one would want to. Two main reasons are for spiritual exploration, and for raising wode and inner power. Here are two chants, one primarily to use for a spirit-journey of otherworldly exploration, the other primarily for raising inner power through a deep understanding of the rune Nauthiz or Need.

Trance and Power Chants

These songs can be chanted or droned, preferably with something like dancing, drumming, musical background droning, clapping, stamping or other trance-inducing rhythmical patterning. You can make up your own tunes if you like, but droning works really well, too: just pick a musical note that is comfortable for you, and drone or 'buzz' the song all on that note, with intensity. Once you start doing that, you may well find yourself going off on a tune of your own, without even thinking about it; it just happens. You can play background music of drumming or a didgeridoo, if you wish, but it needs to be non-distracting from the words of the song.

Some of the words in these songs may seem rather mysterious in meaning, especially in the Nied-Runa Song, which is deliberate! When we seek contact with Mystery, it's best to use mysterious means to attune our minds to a trans-rational state of being, where logic and clear explanations have no place. Instead, we want evocative, half-understood images, that tease our imaginations and offer any number of vague interpretations that we can use for our own entrancing purposes.

Please note: I am not offering basic instruction for trance-work here; I'm offering some specific chanting tools for people who already know how to do this. If you want good guidance for beginning or advanced trance-working, I recommend Diana Paxson's book Trance-Portation: Learning to Navigate the Inner World, *and Cat Heath's book* Elves, Witches and Gods: Spinning Old Heathen Magic in the Modern Day.

Trance and Power Chants

Nied-Runa Song

This song or chant presents mysterious images, evocative of the bone-deep power of life's strongest urges, felt at all levels of soul, mind and body. It is a magical rune-chant, an embedding-within and a celebration of the Need-Rune, Nauthiz:

"Need is a constriction within the chest,
though it often becomes a source
of help and healing to 'affliction's children'
when it is heeded in time."
Anglo-Saxon Rune Poem, my translation.

('Affliction's children' is a translation of Anglo-Saxon *niða bearnum:* human beings, subject to troubles and afflictions.)

This Nied-Runa song honors the ordeals, challenges and constraints of our life, and the driving courage embedded within our very life-force that urges us to strive and overcome the constrictions of Need. *It is a song sung by our Self to our self* to raise and strengthen our inner powers through the challenge of the constraints we face, and to focus these powers on the greatest Needs of our souls and body. It is full of symbolism that I sense through my life-experience, and I hope will be meaningful for you, perhaps quite differently from what they mean to me. That's the advantage of 'mysterious allusions'—they can morph into different shapes for different people! And you may like to add your own verses to this song, expressing your own most meaningful symbols and experiences relating to the mystery of Nauthiz / Nied.

Trance and Power Chants

I find it powerful to repeat the song several times through, singing / droning more slowly and intensely each time. You may want to pause and drone after any of the verses, or repeat specific verses, if you feel power rising especially strongly from that verse. You may also feel inspired to extemporaneously insert your own verses as you chant, especially after repeating the song several times.

This power-raising practice is especially helpful, any time you are facing a real challenge or difficulty in your life, when you need to raise your personal power, courage, and determination to meet the challenge, or face the difficulty and overcome it. Using a physical action to complement the chant helps in this process: drumming, stamping and clapping, martial arts movements, powerful dance, rowing movements with your arms, or other physical action that feels right. I especially like the rowing movements, because they feel not only like rowing a boat strongly through oncoming waves, but also like my arms are tearing away bands of constraint across my chest, as described in the Need rune-poem. The rhythm of the verses works perfectly with the back-and-forth movements of rowing, too. If you have an exercise machine, like rowing, cycling, treadmill, or stair-steps, chanting this while working on the machine will add power, too! Throw yourself into this, body and soul, singing from your deep Self to yourself.

Trance and Power Chants

Nied-Runa Song

Of Need and Desire,
Of the smoking fire,
Of the stringent birth
And the true soul's worth,
I Sing you the Runa of Nied!

With Need's cinch drawn taut,
The battle is fought,
Still blinded by smoke
The flame I awoke,
Singing the Runa of Nied!

Through birth-passage dim,
Through crushing weight grim,
The birth-gate I seek,
Aglow with blood-heat,
Singing the Runa of Nied!

Of the rushing Ond,
Of earth, blood and bone,
Of the Mother's breast,
And the wild God's quest:
I Sing you the Runa of Nied!

By power withheld,
By a soul bespelled,
By the Poet's Mead,
The silent word heed—
Singing the Runa of Nied!

Trance and Power Chants

Through hottest Needfire,
Through life and desire,
Through power constrained,
The path of might gained,
Singing the Runa of Nied!

Midsummer bonfire in Finland. Midsummer is one of the traditional times for lighting the Needfire and using the sacred smoke to bring health to livestock and people.

Nied-Runa Ceremony

This chant works very nicely for an individual or group re-birthing or new beginning ceremony. I have used it this way: find an outdoor space where two trees are growing close together, to serve as a birth-passage. For an individual ceremony, stand, sit or lie between the two trees while reading or chanting the poem, then crawl, walk or leap through, and spend some time in meditation.

Trance and Power Chants

For a group ceremony, the leader(s) (ideally two, one beside each tree) stand on one side of the tree-passage, while participants line up, one behind the other, on the other side. The song is chanted or read all together, one time through. Then the leaders chant it again, as each person in turn steps between the trees.

Additional ritual elements: sprinkle or wet the head of the person stepping between the trees, and / or bless them with a Thor's Hammer. If they want to take a new ceremonial name, speak the new name while blessing with water and Hammer. To make the birth more challenging, of their own choice people can crawl rather than walk between the trees, or leap as high as they can while going through.

Another option is to offer each participant a 'birth-gift' of some kind after they have gone through the passage. A nice rendition of the Nauthiz rune is ideal, or a bind-rune that includes Nauthiz. Below is one of mine that I like: as well as Nauthiz, it includes Perthro for birth and wyrd, Ingwaz for the hero and the seed of courage, Jera for bringing our changes into fruition, Laguz and the Anglo-Saxon rune Ac / Oak for the sea-journey of life and the oaken ship that carries us through it, with Eihwaz, Kenaz, and other runes hiding here, as well.

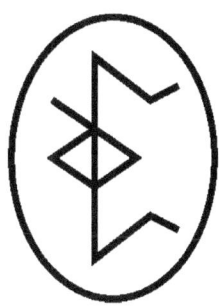

Trance and Power Chants

The Dancer of Dreams

The Dancer of Dreams in this chant is a deliberately undefined figure, on the assumption that each of us who uses trance-journeying has our own spirit-companion(s) when traveling into the otherworlds. The companion may be a soul-being such as the fylgja *or fetch; an ancestral spirit, a Deity, a figure from Heathen lore, a benevolent wight of some kind. Wights and fylgjur may take animal-spirit forms. This trance-chant practice assumes that you already have such a companion. Before you begin, call on this being and ensure that you both understand that "Dancer of Dreams" is referring to that being, for the duration of this chant-working. Also, before you begin, use your customary practice to hallow and protect the space-time of your journey.*

In place of the words "you, we" in the chant, you can use "I", whichever makes most sense in the circumstances.

When singing this with a group, a chant-leader can chant the first two lines of each verse, perhaps with drumming or soft, rhythmic stamping accompaniment, then the group can drone the last line from within their trance. They may choose to stamp or clap along, in unison, or all engage in dancing / stepping / shuffling in a circle or spiral while chanting.

The song, or individual verses, can be repeated to prolong the experience, and you can separate each verse with a time of humming, clapping, etc., if you wish. Or the chant can be used as an entry process into your otherworldly exploration, where you use it to enter your journey, then fall silent.

There is a verse toward the end of the song that calls on your spirit-companion to dance a message for you, hovering over the edge of the world. Allow time for this to happen; you can hum your drone-note during this time, to keep the trance going.

At the end of the song I've offered a call-back process; be sure to use this, or your own process for returning from the trance-world back to Midgard, and ground yourself afterwards. Now, begin!

The Dancer of Dreams

You are the drum,
You are the dance,
Follow the Dancer of Dreams.

Follow the drum,
Follow your blood's song,
Follow the Dancer of Dreams.

Dance for the Holy Ones
Who set our souls afire,
Follow the Dancer of Dreams.

Dance for the Kin-Souls,
Whispers on the wind,
Follow the Dancer of Dreams.

Dance for the wights of Worlds
Who fill the Tree with life,
Follow the Dancer of Dreams.

Dance for the Beast-Souls,
Mighty on the Earth,
Follow the Dancer of Dreams.

Trance and Power Chants

Dance for the Bird-Souls,
Soaring on the wind,
Follow the Dancer of Dreams.

Dance for the Water-Souls,
Gliding through the deeps,
Follow the Dancer of Dreams.

Dance around the World-Tree,
Wreathe around its might,
Follow the Dancer of Dreams.

Dance Yggdrasil's root-paths,
Dance the twining maze,
Follow the Dancer of Dreams.

Deeper, ever deeper dance,
Down to the root of Worlds,
Follow the Dancer of Dreams.

Dance to the deepest place
Where dream holds wisdom's key:
Follow the Dancer of Dreams.

Wait here at the ledge
While over World's Edge
Dances the Dancer of Dreams…
Dances the Dancer of Dreams…
Dances the Dancer of Dreams…

Trance and Power Chants

> You are the drum,
> You are the dance,
> Called by the Dancer of Dreams,
> Called by the Dancer of Dreams,
> Called by the Dancer of Dreams.

Call-back

Use whatever your usual method is, or you can use this one:

Four slow, deliberate drumbeats, stamps and / or claps, spaced evenly apart, while chanting the following word-patterns. Repeat these patterns as long as you feel is needed. These patterns change the surging-forward motion of the dance into a slower, more deliberate action, calling us to slow, pause, and turn around, back toward our Midgard-minds again.

> Step, step, step, step.
> Turn, turn, turn, turn.
> Back, back, back, back.
> Step, step, step, step.

Then a pattern of three somewhat faster beats or claps, repeating as long as needed:

Mid-gard calls / we are home / Mid-gard calls / we are home...

Finally, a flurry of quick drumbeats or claps, and a cry of "Wake up!" Breathe deeply, stretch and move, and ground yourself with food and / or a pinch of salt, and water.

"Yggdrasil," by Jeroen van Valkenburg.

28: Contemplation: The Resonance of the Heart

The first thing I want to say here is that nobody is 'required' to engage in contemplation with the Deities! Some people are attracted to the idea, some find that it comes naturally without much effort, some people feel that contemplation would round out their spiritual practice in desirable ways. Other people feel no need for it at all. All of that is fine; many—probably the majority—of Heathens have excellent relationships with their Deities without any such practice. This essay is for the former people, those who are intrigued by the idea of Heathen contemplation or feel called to it and would like some more insight into the practice.

Contemplation versus Meditation

Let's start off by defining 'contemplation' and distinguishing it from 'meditation.' This is rather tricky because I've seen definitions of these approaches in books and online that directly contradict each other. Some say that meditation is a 'stilling of one's thoughts,' which is very true for some important types of meditation such as 'mindfulness meditation,' but is not true of other types such as 'discursive meditation,' where one takes a brief idea or passage of reading and thoughtfully pursues that idea as far as possible. The same sources describe 'contemplation' in a way that sounds much like discursive meditation, such as *lectio divina* or sacred reading where one takes a passage of religious writing and focuses on going deeply into its meaning.

Meditation is an activity that we initiate and control ourselves, that does not depend on contact with a Deity, that may not even be focused on any Deity, but on some other meaningful idea or practice. Our meditation can be planned in advance, can be specifically designed for a given purpose, and can be directed by a meditation leader, for example a guided meditation or a meditation class or study group. This is not the case with godly contemplation.

The kind of contemplation I'm talking about here is quite different from meditation. It's something I began to learn from my experiences in the past with other religions, and it has universal application in any religion where one seeks contact with one's Deities. Contemplation is a 'wild card.' It is not something fully under our control because it depends upon true contact with a Deity and that Deity's intentions for our contact. Just as we can't totally predict and control and plan in advance about how our interactions with other people will go, we can't do that with Deities, either. They are their own beings and we can't 'stage' or 'direct' our interactions with them if we want true and deep contact with them, any more than we can do so with people if we want genuine and deep interactions with them. Even less so with Deities, really, than with people.

People are easier for us to know, to have some idea of how they will behave and what they want, though really making such assumptions about other people tends to be problematic as well. Deities are different from people, harder to understand and predict, impossible to manipulate though people may try to do so! Genuine contact with Deities, especially our Heathen Deities, tends to result in a lot of surprises, things we were not expecting or imagining. "Taken by surprise" is a phrase frequently used to describe one's contact with a Deity, in our religion and in many others as well!

'Meditation' is a human-directed action, using our human abilities and the processes of our own being, whether it is emptying our minds of thought, or whether we are using methods of focused thought. 'Contemplation' is, to put it dramatically, flinging ourselves into the unknown and trusting that there is someone 'out there' who is willing to 'catch us,' to receive our contact and interact with us. Methods, planning, exercises, etc., that we may try to undertake for such contemplation can only take us so far, because the achievement of true contemplation is not something we are fully in control of; our Deities are. They are capable of 'hijacking' our awareness if they wish for

Contemplation: The Resonance of the Heart

contemplative contact with us, though we can choose to reject this; whereas we cannot successfully demand or insist on their attention.

What we can do is try to understand what this kind of contemplation really involves—actually, it may be more important to understand what it *doesn't* involve—and indicate to our Deities that we want to engage in it, that we are receptive to contemplative contact with them. And they may not wait for this from us, either; it's well-known in many religions, and certainly in ours, that Deities can and will take us totally by surprise and set in motion major changes in our inner self and our lives at times and in ways that we did not anticipate.

This does not mean that we are forced to obey them, that we have to accept everything they want from us: we do not. That is our choice; that part is under our control. We are in control of ourselves, but we are not in control of the Deities. We may want to contact one of them, and they may decide not to answer, for their own reasons. We may want something from them and they may not give it, or may give something different than we asked for (this frequently happens!). And we may do the same toward them. They are in control of themselves, we are in control of ourselves.

In order to contact and communicate with them, and share experiences and knowledge, both we and our Deities must accept that we are all free and autonomous beings, that we do not control each other nor totally control our interactions with each other. In the case of humans, this is true because we cannot control the Deities; in the case of Deities, this is more of a courtesy. They do have the power to overwhelm us—all they need to do is show more of their true nature to us than we have the ability to absorb and deal with.

But if they want true communication with us then they need to, and do, temper their power so that we are not overwhelmed by it unless we are, at some level, ready and willing for that to happen.

Contemplation is an engagement of the heart, of the truest, deepest, most sincere aspects of ourselves. We engage from a place where manipulation, misdirection, ignorance, lies, hiding from ourselves and others, is impossible. Our minds, our thoughts, can play many tricks and engage in complex, multilayered behavior and thinking. It's easy for us to become confused, to misunderstand, to project ourselves into our perceptions of others, to become overwhelmed, when we use our ordinary thinking minds through which to interact with the Deities. Not that this is a bad thing to do—it's good to interact with the Deities through all our faculties, including our everyday thinking mind, for sure. But this is not 'contemplation;' it's something we can explore through meditation, active prayer, and other interactions with the Deities.

Contemplation is communion through the resonance of the heart, not the thoughts of the mind. The resonance of the heart is not simply 'emotion,' it lies even deeper than that. Let's talk about what this is like, beginning with a visit to the multilayered 'planes of being' where different aspects of ourselves operate.

The Planes of Being

Many schools of esoteric thought recognize what are called 'Planes of Being' or levels where different kinds of subtle energies and subtle beings operate, and I find this a useful descriptive concept to work with. The *material plane* is our physical world, the world of matter, and it's where our modern sciences work so effectively. Communication on this plane occurs through the use of our physical bodies, through chemical signals such as scents, and other material means.

Next is the *etheric plane,* the energetic level where the life-force operates and vivifies all living things and their life-energies. Here is where techniques such as acupuncture and many other 'alternative' energetic health and healing modalities operate. It's also how physical-energetic skills such as Tai Chi, Qigong, and Yoga function. Though not yet more than vaguely recognized (if that) by modern science, many of the energies and interactions of living things whose effects are perceptible to us in the material world originate at this etheric level. Communication on this plane happens through subtle energies that are only just beginning to be suspected by modern sciences, for example the subtle communications among trees and plants which include—but may go beyond—biochemical signals.

The *astral plane* comprises the energies that are perceived and shaped by us as experiences of 'feeling, thinking, imagining, dreaming, creativity;' a great deal of what we experience as meaningful human life and inner activity occurs on this plane. Communication on this plane occurs through the many varieties of emotional expression, imagination, and visualization in all its forms, including all the arts and other creative forms of expression.

The next layer 'up' from that is the *mental plane,* where more abstract concepts and thoughts occur, where concepts are imbued with 'meaning,' and where our ability to express concepts and meanings in the form of words and abstract symbols such as mathematics, alphabets, or runes originates. Communication on this level occurs through words and symbols as vehicles for abstract concepts and meaning. This book that you are reading is a form of mental communication: it is connecting our minds through the medium of written words (symbols) and the thoughts that they express: thoughts in my mind as I write, and thoughts in your mind as you read. Most forms of meditation and prayer, I would say, occur on either the astral or the mental level.

'Above' the mental level is the *spiritual plane*, and this is where we are functioning during an experience of true contemplation. What I describe in the following section is my own perception of how communication occurs on this plane, but I believe it is consistent with the perceptions of spiritual practitioners on many different paths of religious experience.

Resonance

I've talked about communication on the different planes: material interactions, life-energy interactions, emotional and creative interactions, abstract and symbolic interactions. Now we come to communication on the spiritual plane, and in my perception this occurs through *resonance*. Not words, not emotional feelings, not ideas, not symbols or abstract images, though we may later transform our experience of resonance into all of these things, after our contemplation is over and we are trying to express what happened and its effects on us. *Resonance is an experience of vibrational attunement between one being and another* (or many beings together), on a very refined and subtle level of Being and energy.

What is this like? Here's an example of contacting Thor contemplatively / immersively. I chose his characteristic 'thunder' as a seed-image for this. (I will explain about seed-images later.)

Contemplation: The Resonance of the Heart

Contemplatively, I immerse myself in thunder, surround myself with everything that thunder is: it shakes my being, its vibrations reshape everything inside and outside myself, pushing out stagnancy, bringing in new waves of power. This immersion is an invitation; it opens a path between me and Thor...will he respond...? He does.

I am a vibration, Thor is a vibration, we draw into resonance with each other for a timeless time. There's a voice in his thunder: what does it utter? I open my heart and Thor's thunder roars through. My heart can sense these wordless resonances and transform them into meaning.

Thunder recedes into a murmur on some unseen horizon, vibrations turn back into my physical being, renewed by resonance with Thor's thunder.

....And then I'm back, back in my regular Midgard mind-frame. I'm forced to describe this experience with words and concepts in order to communicate it, but that is done *after* the event is over, and it's never very accurate! Contemplation isn't a guided meditation that is designed in advance. Instead, we throw ourselves into the unknown, in the direction—we hope—of a Deity we wish to interact with and see what happens if and when we get there. During the event, we are submerged in the direct experience of Being, not in our mental-verbal description of it. Our attempt to describe it afterwards is a pale reflection of the experience, often better captured in art, poetry, music, or sacred dance.

I chose this example of Thor and his thunder because the vibrational element is obvious, but it does not have to be literal vibrations like thunder. As one example of divine resonance, medieval Christian imagery offers visions of "choirs of angels around the throne of God," where the angels

Contemplation: The Resonance of the Heart

not only sing great harmonies of praise—a form of sound-resonance—but are perceived as being artistically arranged in fractal patterns. Fractal patterns are also resonances: resonances of spatial arrangements rather than of sound, where the patterns reflect each other at infinitely larger and smaller scales. Here are two examples.

"Choirs of angels" with many rings of faces; an illustration from a 12th century book by Hildegard of Bingen, a Christian abbess and visionary. The 'throne of God' is in the center, something that cannot be pictured or described so it is left blank.

Contemplation: The Resonance of the Heart

Here's an illustration of multitudes of angels around the 'throne of God,' made for "Paradiso" from Dante's Divine Comedy, *by Gustav Doré. Here the 'throne of God' is symbolized by something like the sun.*

If you've ever looked at images of circular fractals online or in books or magazines, you will certainly see the resemblance with these 'choirs of angels'! I believe that visionaries from all religions perceive such resonances and fractal patterns when they are immersed in an experience of the spiritual plane, though they may express their perceptions differently depending on religious and cultural contexts. The mandalas of the Hindus and Buddhists show very similar kinds of patterns. In my experience, resonances can be expressed as things like 'orchestras of color-tonalities,' 'symphonies of scent-shadows,' and resonances of phenomena for which we have no sensory analogs.

The meaning, I believe, of resonances and fractals on the spiritual plane is this: we are attuned, whether we know this or not, with orders of being that are 'larger' and 'smaller' than ourselves, attuned with all the orders of being and expressions of life across the physical and metaphysical worlds. What resonates with them resonates with each of us, and vice versa. The 'attunement' is expressed as resonance, and the 'interweaving patterns of Being,' in which we all participate, is expressed by fractals.

When we step outside of all the perceptions that belong to the material, etheric, astral, and mental planes of being, we experience this resonant attunement without the overlaid distractions of perceptual layers that are natural to the other planes of being.

Very often the experience of resonance on the spiritual plane is an intense and overwhelming simplicity, an utter immersion into one thing only: that ineffable resonance between our Self and Deity.

Contemplation: The Resonance of the Heart

Reflections are resonances as well. When we and a Deity are attuned to each other, we are able to reflect a fractal portion of the Deity's presence into the Midgard World.

Here is another example of mine, which as usual barely manages to capture anything of the experience.

In contemplation I often see Ing-Frey at a distance, wading toward me through a fertile wetland, surrounded by a huge aura of rose-gold light glowing against a misty sunset. He exudes divine power, but warm and inviting, not distant and overpowering. I simply gaze and absorb what he offers; I have no words for this, only the resonance in my heart that is tuned to his. In this resonance is the wordless song we sing together.

There's very little to be 'seen' in the 'scenery' of this contemplation, just the shimmering of layers of light that my mind later, after the event, interprets using the image of Ing-Frey surrounded by mist, sunset light, and the reflective surface of the marsh. This is an example of color / light resonance, rather than the sound-resonance I described with Thor.

The Resonating Heart

What is it, within ourselves, that can sense, process, and interpret these resonances? On each of the planes we have sensory organs or their analogs at different levels, our brain and our various faculties such as mind, emotions, verbal and other forms of expression that can work with the conditions that pertain to each plane of being. On the physical / material plane we have our body and sensory organs. On the etheric level we and all other living beings have subtle senses and reactions, though modern people are not very good at realizing this. On the astral level there are so many ways we sense and process things, including through our emotions, imagination, and our dreams, as well as through artistic expression of all kinds. On the mental plane we grasp things with our minds, and express our thoughts through words, symbols and concepts.

On the spiritual level, the level of divine contemplation and connection, we make use of the subtle powers of our hearts. Even on the physical level, the heart is constantly involved with pulsation and vibration of every tiny strand of its muscles and nerves. Studies of people who are closely connected, such as happily married couples or mothers and babies, have found that their heartbeats synchronize when they are physically close to each other, touching or interacting in a loving way. (See a few examples at the end of this chapter.) The vibrations of their hearts intermesh, the same way that striking one tuning fork will cause another tuning fork nearby to resonate without being touched.

Our hearts are made to vibrate and pulsate, and they are capable of doing so on multiple levels of being, not only the physical. Our hearts respond to emotion, to meaningful information, to situations around us. They are extremely responsive organs, and they pick up signals from all the levels or planes of being within which we exist: physical, etheric, astral, mental and spiritual levels. When we seek to interact contemplatively with a Deity, this is something that our heart is designed to do.

If we try to use our mind, our thoughts, words, verbal prayers, and concepts for contemplation, that doesn't work as well, though we can certainly use them to prepare for and lead into contemplation, and to try to remember and understand what happened after it is over. The reason our mind doesn't work well for contemplation is because it wants to use words and concepts, it wants to work on the mental plane rather than the spiritual. Our mind and thoughts naturally seek to define and describe our experience, which limits that experience to something that *can* be defined and described with words and concepts. This is not 'contemplation.'

Contemplating a Deity on the spiritual plane goes beyond those limitations, though we also interact with Deities on the mental, astral, and other planes, in ways appropriate to those levels. The interactions on these other levels—meditation, active prayer, offerings, Blots, studying and teaching about them, partnering with the Deities by doing tasks in Midgard that align with their wishes, etc.—these are very meaningful and important, too. I have no intention of downplaying the importance of *all* our interactions with the Holy Ones; I am only trying to describe a different kind of experience with them here.

How to Approach Contemplation

After all the discussion saying that meditation and contemplation are not the same thing, I'll now point out that meditation is a good way to prepare for and move into a contemplative state. If we are intentionally choosing to engage in contemplation (rather than being scooped up unexpectedly into it by a Deity's will, which may also happen), then a good way to begin the process is by using meditation as a gateway. We can begin in the same way we do for meditation: going through a process of relaxation and calm, steady breathing to still the activity of mind and body. From this state of stillness, there are two approaches we can take: we can use a seed-image as a vehicle to attune to the Deity, or we can continue in this state of receptive stillness and simply reach out to the Holy One we desire to contact.

I'll describe each of them here, beginning with the seed-image because it is an easier path for most of us to use.

Using a Seed-Image for Contemplation

As part of our preparation, we can create a 'seed for contemplation' about a Deity. This could involve a sentence describing a Deity's attributes or actions, for example, or it could be an artistic portrayal of the Deity or of a metaphysical location like the World-Tree, a poem or song, a mythic or religious symbol, the account of someone else's vision or insight, or a passage from your own journal.

But there's another step to the process here because this seed needs to be turned into an image or symbol, if it isn't already in that form. It's better not to use words except for symbolic words like the Deity's name. With words, it's too easy to stay tuned to the mental plane; we need symbols or images here, including non-visual images like sound, sensation, or 'impression.' Even scent or taste are sometimes used, such as incense or metaphorical honey, that express the sensory effects of contemplation.

As examples, consider the 'thunder' seed-image I described for contemplating Thor—this is a sound-image rather than a visual one. The shimmering, rose-gold light that I described with Ing-Frey is so characteristic of my experiences with him that calling up this light in my imagination is a signal to shift into contemplative mode with him; something that requires very little effort to do. That light / color is a seed-image for me.

Here's another example: say you wish to contact Tyr. You've read a lot about him, offered Blots to him, and have a sense of his main characteristics. How can you turn that into a symbol or impression? You can take one of his symbols from the lore that captures the aspect you most want to connect with, such as the glove on the spear at the Thing; his sacrifice of his hand; his willingness to feed Fenris.

For myself, I like to use the Anglo-Saxon rune poem for Tyr / Tiw which speaks of the North Star, our Guide-Star, holding course above the mists of night, ever true, never failing. I form the images of this verse into an 'impression' of starlight, of cold clear air, of steadfastness and trustworthiness, of high-hearted courage, of all that is 'high and bright'. I don't use these words directly as my seed-image; I sort of roll them all up into a 'ball of impressions' and immerse myself in it, as I do with Thor's thunder and Ing-Frey's light. I use this impression of the Guide-Star and all it means to reach for contact with Tiw / Tyr.

The Deity may well decide to change your chosen image and present you with a new one. This is what happened to me with Ing-Frey: the scene and light I described was a gift from him, not something I came up with. He began to appear this way to me many years ago, and it was such a powerful and perfect appearance that I started using it to call to him when I seek him contemplatively. It is also his call to me when this light begins to shimmer in my imagination. Of course, there may be more than one resonance or seed-image that opens the way between us and any given Deity. In Chapter 26 I describe experiences with Frey and other Deities as flowing water carrying me along with them, also a form of contemplation that they taught me.

Rather than 'thinking about' our seed-image, as we might do in meditation, we use it as a pathway to the presence of the Deity or spiritual location (like the World-Tree, or the Well of Wyrd) that we are seeking to connect with. We follow this

Contemplation: The Resonance of the Heart

path / thread / seed by seeking with our heart more than with our mind, expanding our heart-energy outward and opening it up, recognizing that among its myriad talents *the heart is a sensory organ, a generator and receiver of subtle resonances on multiple planes of being.*

I do mean, quite literally, the heart; this is not a metaphor for 'emotion,' it is heart-energy itself. During the whole process, focus on your physical heart, sense its energy reaching outward to find a matching heart-energy and connect with it. It's very difficult to describe this in words; like riding a bicycle or learning to swim, we just have to keep trying until we get it! When it 'clicks,' we can feel a heart-to-heart connection that encompasses all the Planes of Being together: a sense of some different energy in / around our physical heart; an enhanced perception of the life-power of our beating heart; emotional and inspirational connections with the Deity; and the stimulation of our mental and creative capacities, which also depend on input and support from our heart.

We are used to equating 'heart' with emotions, and certainly this is true, but it is not complete. Ancient Heathens and all other ancient cultures I know about considered that 'thinking, intention, planning, inspiration,' and other human capabilities come from the heart as well—come from this physical core of our being. The word 'Hugr' and its cognates in all the Germanic languages referred to a spirit or a capacity that lives in our chest around our heart, and gives us the ability to love, to think, to intend and plan, to foresee and be insightful, to interact in both positive and negative ways with others. All of this and more was considered to come through the heart. (Rose 2021, "Who is Hugr" and other chapters about the Hugr.) Consciously living with and through our heart-energies often comes as a whole new experience for us, and connecting with our chosen Holy Ones in this way can help us learn how to 'live through our heart' in other ways as well.

An important thing to keep in mind is this: the Deity we wish to contact may or may not respond right away, nor respond in any way we were expecting. This may happen multiple times. I tried for years to contact Heimdall, for example, before he responded to me in any way other than a polite acknowledgement of my existence. I don't know why it took so long; I probably never will. On the other hand, a Deity might come down on us like a load of bricks as happened to me with Frigg, who pretty much took over my life for awhile in her zeal to accomplish some things in Midgard through me. This frequently happens with people who are close to Odin, as well.

When we begin contemplation with a Deity, we need to be willing to accept whatever their responses are, including no response. I don't mean that we *have* to do what the Deity says or be controlled by their responses. I mean it the same way we would interact with a friend: sometimes we may be forthcoming and interactive; sometimes we may not be 'in the mood,' or may be very involved with something else at the moment, and ask our friend for a rain check. Sometimes we may ask a lot from a friend, or they from us. We accept the give and take, the fact that everyone 'has a life' and has their own way of interacting, and it doesn't need to break the friendship if we are more or less responsive at any given time. Friends give each other space to be themselves, and this is how it needs to be with Deities, too.

Contemplation: The Resonance of the Heart

To summarize this seed-image approach to contemplation:

1) Choose a 'seed-image' of some kind: a description, a saying, an artistic representation, a musical theme or song, a feeling, a quotation from the lore, the memory of some scene or experience in your life, anything that you consider relevant to the Holy One you seek to contact.

2) If the seed-image is in the form of words rather than images, symbols, or sensations, do your best to transform the meaning of the words into an image, symbol, sensation, or impression.

3) Take a comfortable but alert position, relax your body, and gently steady your breath to reach a deep but comfortable breathing pattern.

4) Begin the contemplation with a prayer to the Deity you seek, speaking your intention to them.

5) Then immerse yourself in your seed-image and stay there. Whenever you are distracted, simply return to your seed. Spread your heart-energy and awareness out around yourself, ready to pick up any matching energies from the Holy One you seek. Create a receptive field around yourself, generated by your heart, that can sense resonances from the Deity.

6) Be aware that you may be gifted with a new seed-image or resonance from the Deity once you've entered into contact. Don't resist this (unless you feel some wrongness about it) but welcome the gift and use it again in the future.

7) It's good to record your experience, and any gifts of insight from the Deity, after you return—to the best of your ability. Be patient with yourself; this is not something that can be expressed in words with perfect accuracy! You may do better expressing it through art, music, or poetry, or some combination of all these.

'Seedless' Contemplation

I am mentioning this approach in the interests of completeness, but there is not honestly very much that can be said about it. This is because it is so simple—simple, but not necessarily easy. Generally speaking, this approach may develop naturally after we have spent a long time working with the seed-image approach to contemplation, though for some people it may happen more spontaneously. It may not happen at all; we may be very satisfied with the seed-image approach and not feel any need to do it differently. And the Deities we are working with may feel this is fine, too.

But it may happen that we, our Deity(s), or both together decide to move on to 'seedless' contemplation, at least some of the time. In my understanding, this is how it works; others may describe it differently. In our past experiences with our Deity(s) using the seed-images, our shared contemplative experiences have spun a spiritual thread that connects us. We

Contemplation: The Resonance of the Heart

can call this a heart-string, or a *hyge-band*, a Hugr-band, as it is described in the *Beowulf* poem! (Lines 1877-1880.) This heartstring resonates with our shared energies. The more we engage in contemplation with that Deity, the more tangible our connecting heart-string becomes. Eventually the seeds we use for contemplation may be replaced by this thread, which is always present: a thread of Being, spun by us and our Deity together out of the fibers of our shared resonance.

With seedless contemplation, we may go through meditation and prayer first and engage in a formal session, as I described in the previous section, or we may not. Flashes of contemplative connection can come at any time, anywhere, under any circumstances; they can simply be interwoven into our daily life. These connections may be initiated by our conscious will, or may be directed by the Deity in the way that they want or they think we need. There isn't any standard 'method' here that I can offer. The contemplative attitude and the potential for entering contemplation at any time becomes a part of our life. It's fair to say that the real 'method' involves—not our relationship with the Deity directly—but reorganizing our life to adjust and make room for this ongoing connection between us and the Deity(s). For religions which have contemplative monastic orders, this is exactly what they are doing.

We can generally handle such experiences much better if we have been practicing more structured contemplation, as I described about the seed-image, for a good deal of time beforehand. This is definitely what I recommend: if you want to engage in contemplation, spend a long time on the more formal process of using a seed-image first. Then see whether you and / or your Deity(s) are drawn to use the 'seedless' approach. If you are, and it works well for you, fine!

Contemplation: The Resonance of the Heart

If you find the seedless approach rather destabilizing, disruptive, unmanageable—which it can be, especially when you have no experienced spiritual director who knows you well, as is the case for most Heathens—then discuss it with your Deity(s) and go back to the more formal seed-image contemplation. Before you do that, though, take a break from contemplation so you can re-set your habitual patterns. If this turns out to be difficult for you, Diana Paxson's book *The Essential Guide to Possession, Depossession, and Divine Relationships* is a useful resource.

In Thanks to Frigg

I need to acknowledge here my debt to Frigg, because it was she who guided me onto the contemplative path and pointed me toward understanding the nature of wordless, resonant connection and communication. Many years ago, I took a line about Frigg from the *Poetic Edda* as my seed-image and combined it with a painting of her weaving the clouds.

The *Poetic Edda* passage I used was spoken by Freya, saying: "Of ørlög Frigg has full knowledge, I think, although she does not speak (of it) herself." *(Lokasenna* or *Loki's Quarrel,* vs. 29.) I wondered *why* Frigg doesn't speak of ørlög, so I turned this phrase into an 'impression of Frigg's wordlessness,' and combined it with the image of her weaving clouds, i.e. weaving mysteries while not speaking of them. I followed those impressions to her. When I came back I wrote the following poem.

Contemplation: The Resonance of the Heart

"Frigg Spinning" by John Charles Dollman

In Thanks to Frigg, the Silent Knower

Holy Frigg, Norn-wise,
You know no tongue with which to tell
What is and what shall be,
To sort the spinning strands of possibility
Into a span of words.
Yet with your spindle and your well-strung loom,
You weave the airy clouds
And send the winds to shape them,
Writing your wordless wisdom-runes
Across the ever-changing valleys of the sky.
Teach us, Lady, to heed
The wisdom that lies beyond all words:
Echoes that resound
After words have fled.

Contemplation: The Resonance of the Heart

This was one of the first formal Heathen prayers I made, and the one I have most often spoken during the thirty years and more of my Heathen life. It was only recently that I realized how profoundly and continuously Frigg has been answering this prayer through her spiritual guidance.

When one plunges into experiential explorations of Heathen spirituality, after a certain point words are left behind and one's awareness flows through fields of resonances, resounding echoes, that reach backwards and forwards through and outside of time, and all around ourselves to touch many other souls of humans and other beings. Up to a point in these explorations, words are necessary and useful. Beyond that, they tie us down, limiting us and getting in the way of pure awareness and full experience of these wordless resonances.

Years of working with what I've learned from Frigg and our other Deities have led me to the beliefs I've discussed here, that 'resonances, resonance-fractals, and fields of interwoven resonances' are to the spiritual plane what 'words, sentences, and concepts' are to the mental plane, and what material substance is to the plane of matter. The experience behind this poem started me on this exploration and has since shaped all my spiritual explorations.

These are experiences that go far beyond words, deep into the domain of Vør, the Goddess of Awareness, whom I perceive as a soul-daughter or emanation of Frigg, an embodiment of her power of Awareness. (See Chapter 4 about Vør.) Vør herself has an echo or resonance within each of us, stimulating and guiding the full development of our own powers of awareness.

Thus, I feel like I understand, at least in part, why Frigg does not speak of what she knows: she cannot, because it is not Word-knowledge, but Being-knowledge that she mediates to us through her 'daughter' Vør. My deepest thanks go to Frigg and Vør for their subtle, wordless, ongoing response to my loving prayer repeated over the years.

In Closing

To me, this is what devotional contemplation is: a movement of the heart outward toward the Holy Ones, toward the heart's true desire, and an acceptance of whatever response is given back to that gesture of our spiritual heart. Even when there is no response; even when the response is incomprehensible; even when it is overwhelming and drives us to change our whole life.

It's so simple, really, though not at all easy: we open our heart toward our spiritual desire. We actually focus on our physical heart, feel its energy expand outward, feel its warmth, the very core of our life. As with other forms of meditation, when distractions arise, we gently return to our outflowing heart. Our heart knows where to go, what to reach for, even when we don't; trust it and don't argue with it when it's focused on the spiritual realms.

Deep in our hearts lies a Mystery of Being
that does not begin to grow into our awareness
until we reach into the spiritual realms.

Contemplation: The Resonance of the Heart

Notes:

Here are a few examples of research showing that closely connected people may synchronize their heartbeats. There are various theories as to the physical mechanism that causes this synchronization. My own interpretation is that hearts can indeed sense the pulsing of other hearts that they feel connected to on metaphysical as well as physical levels, and the hearts 'choose' to resonate with those they are closest to.

"A new study from the University of Illinois examines the dynamics of long-term relationships through spatial proximity. The researchers find that when partners are close to each other, their heart rates synchronize in complex patterns of interaction. "We're not focusing on cause and effect, but on co-regulation, which happens when heart rates move in a synchronous pattern. That is, when the partners are close, their heart rate patterns indicate an interaction that is collectively meaningful in some way."" https://www.news-medical.net/news/20211117/Heart-rates-of-older-couples-synchronize-when-they-are-close-together.aspx

"Couples connected to monitors measuring heart rates and respiration get their heart rate in sync, and they breathe in and out at the same intervals. ... When the two individuals were not from the same couple, their hearts did not show synchrony, nor did their breathing closely match." https://www.ucdavis.edu/news/lovers-hearts-beat-sync-uc-davis-study-says

"A new study shows that 3-month-old infants and their mothers can synchronize their heartbeats to mere milliseconds. Researchers sat 40 pairs of mothers and infants

Contemplation: The Resonance of the Heart

face-to-face, equipped with sticky skin electrodes on either side of their hearts. Beat for beat, mother-and-child hearts thumped together almost instantly as they shared loving looks or contented coos. This cardiac coupling worked only for moms with their own babies, and only when the duos synchronized smiles and other cheerful social behaviors, researchers report in this month's issue of Infant Behavior and Development."
https://www.science.org/content/article/scienceshot-human-hearts-beat-together

"We investigated the heart rhythms of co-sleeping individuals and found evidence that in co-sleepers, not only do independent heart rhythms appear in the same relative phase for prolonged periods, but also that their occurrence has a bidirectional causal relationship."
https://www.ncbi.nlm.nih.gov/pmc/articles/PMC6421336/

"When lovers touch, their breathing, heartbeat syncs, pain wanes, study shows." University of Colorado Boulder
https://www.sciencedaily.com/releases/2017/06/170621125313.htmAll

All sources were accessed on 25 October 2023.

29: Vafrloge: Hidden Fire and its Runic Channels

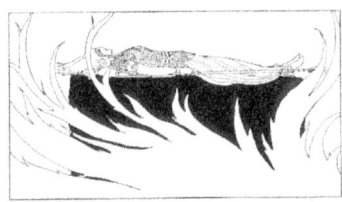

Valkyrie in enchanted sleep, warded by Vafrloge flames. (Willy Pogany)

Among the things I love most about the Heathen world-view are the many 'mysteries' I see in the imagery, the myths, the poetry and art. The more I look for them, the more I find, and the deeper each of the mysteries appears. I explore these mysteries through my tales and essays, my poetry and songs, the selection of illustrations for my books, my runework and spaework, my devotions. The mysteries motivate my research and studies, including my interest in reading the old Germanic languages and pondering the meanings of ancient words. So here, at the end of this book about my wanderings on Heathen ways (though not the end of my wanderings!), I'll describe another of these mysteries and my thoughts about it. I offer it as yet another path to be explored to see where it can lead!

Vafrloge

In Heathen lore, there are mentions of a mysterious phenomenon called *vafrloge* or 'flickering, wavering flames.' (Pronounced 'VAH-fur-LOW-geh, with a hard 'g'.) These flames are far from ordinary; they are described as 'dark,' 'knowing,' 'wise,' and they serve as gatekeepers and warders of otherworldly locations.

They flicker over the burial places of the dead and their treasure-hoards, warding them from casual intrusion and theft. The 'Waking of Angantyr' from Hervör's saga vividly features these flames (this poem is included in Larrington's translation of the *Poetic Edda*). The whole island where Hervör's berserker father and his eleven brothers are buried is surrounded by flames; so are each of the burial howes of the dead, where they stand as shadows before the fires. Hervör is able to walk through these guardian-flames as though they are smoke, due to her courage and her relationship to the dead. She is seeking the cursed sword Tyrfing which lies there with the dead, again surrounded by the eerie fire though the flame dies down for her when she goes to take it. Her father says she is the 'only girl on earth' who would dare to do that.

Vafrloge guard the magical sleep of the Valkyrie Sigrdrifa / Brunnhilde, keeping out all unworthy suitors. Sigrdrifa had begged a boon of Odin: that only the bravest of men could awaken her from the sleep that was Odin's punishment for her choice of the slain. When Gunnar tries to ride through the flames to win Sigrdrifa, he is unable to do so. Only brave Sigurd and his horse Grani, descendant of Sleipnir, could cross those 'wise and knowing flames.' (See "The Lay of Fafnir" verses 42-44, and the introduction to the "Lay of Sigrdrifa" in the *Poetic Edda*.)

Clearly, these flames know whom to keep out, and whom to allow in to Sigrdrifa's mountain hall. The poem says that this fire was 'made by wise men' out of 'radiant river-light,' a kenning for gold *(Fafnir* vs. 42).

"Sigurd and Brunhild" by Harry George Theaker.

Vafrloge burn around Menglöd's beautiful otherworldly courts, where she sits with her maidens under the magical tree of healing, *Mimameiðr*. When Svipdag arrives there to win her hand, he asks about her hall that is encompassed by 'knowing, flickering flame' ("The Lay of Svipdag" vs. 31, *Poetic Edda)*, and he describes her courts as 'glowing' (vs. 5), like the 'radiant river-light' of Sigrdrifa's mountain hall. Only when Svipdag's identity is revealed as the one foretold to win Menglöd's love, is he allowed through the protections of the burg.

Frey sees the giantess Gerda from across the Worlds when he sits on Odin's far-seeing seat, Hlidskalf. He falls into lovesickness *(hug-sott)*, thinking he cannot wed her. His friend and servant Skirnir offers to go to Gerda and negotiate, but asks for Frey's horse to carry him through the 'knowing, dark, flickering flame' that burns around the burg of Gerda and her parents Gymir and Aurboda ("The Lay of Skirnir" vs. 8-9, *Poetic Edda)*.

Vafrloge: Hidden Fire and its Runic Channels

These are just a few among many examples of the eerie fire, which appears also in fairy tales and folktales. These 'wise flames' are protective, perhaps even hallowing, when they burn around the dead and their treasures, and around the places where otherworldly beings with sacred powers live. The flames are daunting and dangerous, but can also be lovely and mysterious. What is the nature of these flames? Where do they come from, how do they arise? I've been curious about them ever since I read of them; this imagery of the vafrloge has captured my imagination!

I was very intrigued when I read the Swedish scholar Viktor Rydberg's interpretation of their nature, although he has focused more on their deadly nature than their beauty. Here I'll copy an extensive description of the nature, source, and purpose of the vafrloge from Rydberg's perspective. He begins with the account of Odin being chased by the shapeshifting giant Thjazi or Thjasse when they flew in the forms of eagles across the walls of Asgard. Odin flew safely across, while Thjazi burned to death. *(Skaldskarpamal* p. 60, in the prose *Edda)*. Here is Rydberg's description.

Outside of the very high Asgard cordon and around it there flows a rapid river, the moat of the citadel. Over the eddies of the stream floats a dark, shining, ignitable mist. If it is kindled it explodes in flames, whose bickering tongues strike their foes with unerring certainty. It is the vafrloge, "the bickering flame," "the quick-fire," celebrated in ancient songs—vafrlogi, vafreydi, skjótbrinni. *It was this fire which the gods kindled around Asgard when they saw Thjasse approaching in eagle guise. In it their irreconcilable foe burnt his pinions and fell to the ground. "Haustlong," Thjodolf's poem, says that when Thjasse approached the citadel of the gods "the gods raised the*

Vafrloge: Hidden Fire and its Runic Channels

quick fire and sharpened their javelins"—Hófu skjót; en skjófu sköpt; ginnregin brinna. *The "quick fire," skjót-brinni, is the vaferloge.* (p. 239)

The material of which this ignitable mist consists is called "black-terror-gleam." It is or odauccom; *that is to say,* ofdauccom ognar ljoma *(Fafnirsmal 40).* *(cp.* myrkvan vafrloge—*Skirnismal 8,9; Fjolvinsmal 31). It is said to be "wise," which implies that is consciously aims at him for whose destruction it is kindled.* (p. 239)

How a water could be conceived that evaporates a dark, ignitable mist we find explained in Thorsdrapa. The thunderstorm is the "storm of the vaferfire," and Thor is the "ruler of the chariot of the vaferfire-storm" (vafr-eyda hreggs húfstjóri). *Thus the thunder-cloud contains the water that evaporates a dark material for lightning. The dark metallic colour which is peculiar to the thunder-cloud was regarded as coming from that very material which is the "black-terror-gleam" of which lightning is formed.*

This shape seen in a campfire looks like Thor's Hammer surrounded by vafrloge.

Vafrloge: Hidden Fire and its Runic Channels

When Thor splits the clouds he separates the two component parts, the water and the vafermist; the former falls down as rain, the latter is ignited and rushes away in quick, bickering, zigzag flames—the vaferfires. ...They do not proceed blindly, but know their mark and never miss it. (pp. 239-240)

The river that foams around Asgard thus has its source in the thunder-clouds; not as we find them after they have been split by Thor, but such as they are originally, swollen with a celestial water that evaporates vafermist. All waters—subterranean, terrestrial, and celestial—have their source in that great subterranean fountain Hvergelmir. Thence they come and thither they return (Grimnismal 26). Hvergelmir's waters are sucked up by the northern root of the world-tree; they rise through its trunk, spread into its branches and leaves, and evaporate from its crown into a water-tank situated on the top of Asgard, Eikthyrnir, in Grimnismal 26 symbolized as a "stag" who stands on the roof of Odin's hall and out of whose horns the waters stream down into Hvergelmer. Eikthyrnir is the great celestial water-tank which gathers and lets out the thunder-cloud. In this tank the Asgard river has its source, and hence it consists not only of foaming water but also of ignitable vafermists. In its capacity of discharger of the thunder-cloud, the tank is called Eikthyrnir, the oak-stinger. (p. 240-241)

I find this a fascinating description, and I like to meditate on the imagery of this circulation of water-mist-fire-thunder-lightning power spreading out through the Worlds. I do, however, prefer the traditional symbol of the stag as opposed to the much less poetic imagery of the water-tank on top of Valhalla! The stag's antlers are shaped like branching lightning, and I envision that the vafer-mist condenses on

Eikthyrnir's, oak-stinger's, antlers and drips down from there through the Worlds and back into its source in Hvergelmir. This imagery parallels the image of dew dripping from the World-Tree into the Well; the stag's antlers mimic not only lightning-bolts but also tree branches. (With respect to the life-force of lightning and its relation to the Tree of Life, see Chapter 16, "Perkwus: The Tree of Life and Soul".)

Attuning to the Hidden Fire

I see the Hidden Fire that surrounds the dead, the treasures of the dead, and sacred places as one form of the vafrloge, the 'wise, dark, knowing flame.' Another form of it is the vafrloge that Thor can extract from thunderclouds with his lightning, his oak-stinger, and bring down to protect Asgard and to fight the Jotnar. Another form of it circulates through the waters—subterranean, terrestrial, and celestial, as Rydberg describes—and imparts life and power to the Worlds. All of these forms of vafrloge are aspects of the Hidden Fire, in my view.

Whenever I begin learning about some of the mysterious phenomena in Heathen belief, I want to learn about it theoretically, but also put this knowledge into practical terms somehow, which helps me understand it better. It's a recursive or circular process: learn, practice, learn from the practice, increase theoretical knowledge, use the increased knowledge to shape a more refined practice, and so on. Runes can be a great help in this process. For a more concrete understanding of the hidden fire that circulates through the Worlds, I turn to two runes: Eihwaz and Kenaz, each of them with its own connection to mysterious fire.

Vafrloge: Hidden Fire and its Runic Channels

The Eihwaz Rune

The Old English rune poem for the Eihwaz / Eoh / Yew says this:

The Yew has rough bark,
Holds firmly to the earth,
Warder of the Fire,
Upheld by its roots,
Wynn (gladness) on the estate.

The Eihwaz, Eoh, or Yew rune is considered by modern Heathens to represent life, death, and rebirth, and to extend as the Worldtree Yggdrasil between the overworlds and underworlds, with Midgard in the middle. Some of us believe it represents the magical staff of esoteric workers such as the Seer/ess, and it also represents protection in the form of a longbow made of Yew.

The Yew is the 'Warder / Herder / Keeper *(hierde* in Anglo-Saxon) of the Fire,' according to this rune poem. The fire which Eihwaz wards and keeps is, I believe, the vafrloge, the Hidden Fire I described above: the mysterious fire that circulates between the Worlds, guards their boundaries and wards their shining mysteries.

This fire is hidden within the roots of the worlds and sustains them, as the fire of life sustains each of us. It is contained in potential form within otherworldly waters and mists, and is drawn in this form into the roots of the Yew and the World-Tree. There it is stored, ready to nourish the fire of life which bursts out through trees and all the other life-forms of the Worlds. This fire, as we have seen, can be used to defend and destroy, to hallow and sanctify, to hide and sequester, to distinguish the worthy from the unworthy in whatever forms those might take.

Roots of Yew tree more than 500 years old.

This, I believe, is the power inherent in the Yew rune, Eihwaz, the Keeper of the Fire. When it is rightly used to support life and wellbeing, it brings *wynn,* the joy and gladness of the Wynn or Wunjo rune. The right use of Eihwaz's secret powers and knowledge can bring joy to our 'estate,' to the unique life-time-space that each of us occupies here in our world of Midgard.

The Kenaz Rune

The Anglo-Saxon rune poem for Kenaz tells us:

Vafrloge: Hidden Fire and its Runic Channels

*Ken (torch), known by every living thing, pale and bright,
Burns most often there where æthelings (nobles) rest within.*

The first impression one has from this rune poem is of torches burning to illuminate a feasting-hall where nobles are gathered within, enjoying the *healldream,* the joys of the hall with good companionship, food, drink, and performances of songs and poetry. This is the 'top layer,' so to speak, of the rune poem. But there are other clues which lead us deeper.

The fire or light that is 'known by every living thing' I interpret as the aura or energy of life that is indeed emitted by every living thing. In fact, I've been reading in the news lately that many animals actually fluoresce when viewed by black-light, with platypuses, bats, and many others showing vivid colors such as magenta, blue, and green. Insects and some birds are able to see ultraviolet light emitted from plants and other insects. The life-force within each of us can be perceived in different ways, including subconscious perceptions. Modern humans may be among the beings least aware of this aura of life, but it is there nevertheless, and on some level it is a light or fire 'known by every living thing.'

In some respects this light of the life-force burns brightest during gestation of any being, human or animal: a time when the life-force, during a brief amount of time, creates a whole new being out of a tiny fertilized egg. This is another resonance of the nobles resting within the feasting-hall, which is here the sheltering womb where the new being is given all the nourishment it needs to grow and develop within its own 'feasting hall.' The combined life-force light given off by life-giving mother and gestating baby together is the brightest of all: pale and bright, known by all living things.

I see this Kenaz-light as another strand of the Hidden Fire. Vafrloge wards the otherworldly realms and the places of the dead. The Kenaz torch lights the beings who are transitioning from one realm to another: from Elsewhere into Midgard through the womb of life. It illuminates all of us who are living in Midgard, and when we die the flame of Kenaz forms our spiritual balefire, the light that shows our souls their way to the Otherworlds.

Runic Channels of the Hidden Fire

These two runes describe the circulation of the Hidden Fire through the Worlds. The Eihwaz rune is like a hook which links the Worlds together as the World-Tree does. It is the Keeper of the Fire, and the vafrloge flames run up and down its length in hidden channels, from the bottom to the top of Yggdrasil, and back. In the process Eihwaz circulates the Hidden Fire through Midgard where, in turn, Kenaz picks it up and circulates it through living beings. When each being dies, Kenaz lights its soul's way into the other Worlds, and accompanies it there…and back again, if the being is reborn. Thus Eihwaz and Kenaz support the circulation of the vafrloge flames throughout the Worlds and the beings of those Worlds.

The Hidden Fire is beautiful, perilous, life-sustaining, illuminating, mysterious. The Torch-rune, Kenaz, lights our way and expresses the Hidden Fire within our own life-force and our own souls. The Yew-rune Eihwaz, which keeps and wards this fire, is our walking staff and our magic wand or *gandr:* a firm support and protection, a traveling companion for us as we wend our way through the Worlds, seeking more mysteries as we wander.

How might we use these runes and the mysteries behind them to deepen our experience of Heathen wights and ways? And how many more such mysteries lurk in the depths of the lore and the wilds of the Worlds, waiting to be discovered by us today, luring us ever onward into the unknown?

Word-Hoard / Glossary

A note on pronunciation: I've offered pronunciation guides for some of the words here, but must note that there can be different ways of pronunciation: Old Norse, modern Icelandic, other modern Scandinavian languages, German, etc. I try to go by the original language pronunciation, to the best of my knowledge. If you'd like to know more, my preferred source for pronunciations is Forvo: https://forvo.com/search/

Æsir: A tribe of Heathen Gods. Prominent members are Odin, Thor, Frigg, Tyr. *(AY-seer)*

Alf (sing.), Alfar (pl.): This term can refer to a divine tribe of beings closely associated with the Æsir Gods, and is also used to designate the spirits of deceased male ancestors. (ahlf, ahlvar)

Alveig: The literal meaning is 'nourishing drink.' An *alveig* is a drink of power, which may be made of potent herbs and / or infusions of runic or magical power.

Asgard: The divine realm of the Æsir Gods, which includes many individual God-Halls within it. (Ahs-gard)

Ask & Embla: The mythical first human couple, formed from trees or logs by Odin, Hœnir and Loðurr, or by Odin and his brothers Vili and Ve.

Asynja (sing.), Asyjur (pl.): The Goddesses of Asgard. *(AH-sin-ya, AH-sin-yur, Old Norse; modern Icelandic OW-sin-ya).*

Word-Hoard

Auðhumla, also spelled Auðhumbla: In Norse mythology, a primal being in the form of a cow, whose name probably means 'the hornless cow of wealth / prosperity.' She appeared in Ginnungagap at the beginning of things, licked the shape of Buri, the first God, out of the enclosing ice, and fed Buri and Ymir with her milk. In my thought, she is a shape-shifting Mother-Goddess, and transformed herself into the realm of Hel. I believe she was the mother of Borr, the progenitor of the Æsir. *(OWTH-hoom-la)*

Bestla: The mother of Odin, Vili and Ve, and the sister of Mimir. I believe Bestla and Mimir were the unnamed pair who were generated under the arm of the primal Giant, Ymir. Thus, she, her brother Mimir, and her consort Borr were the first generation of offspring from the primal powers.

Borr: The son of Buri and consort of Bestla. As the father of Odin, Vili and Ve, he is the progenitor of the Æsir Gods.

Buri: In Norse lore, a primal being, progenitor of the Gods, who formed within the ice of Ginnungagap. He was licked free of the ice and fed by the Ur-Mother in the form of a cow, Auðhumla.

Dis (sing.), Disir (pl.): Literal meaning is a lady or a noblewoman; sometimes a demi-Goddess. Most commonly used to indicate the spirits of one's deceased female ancestors. *(Dees, DEE-sier)*

Dwarves: Otherworldly beings who appear in many forms and roles in all the branches of Germanic folklore. Considered to be very wise and full of craft, but can be deceptive and are famed for bearing grudges. In Norse lore, Dwarves formed within the sacrificed body of the primal Giant Ymir; according to one account, they began as 'maggots' within Ymir's flesh, absorbing his-her energy and substance. In my view, Dwarves are masters of mod-energy, which they 'suck' or absorb from the natural and otherworldly environments, and sometimes from other beings as well, causing fatigue and illness. Dwarves absorb mod-energy, transform it, and use it to power their craft.

Elivagar: A sea, encircling river, or multiple rivers that flow out of the great wellspring Hvergelmir in Norse mythology. In my thought, Elivagar is a braided system of 'rivers' of energy which arise from the cosmic wellspring Hvergelmir, and surround, separate and nourish the various Worlds upon the World-Tree. *(EH-lee-VO-gar)*

Ferah: One of the Heathen souls, which confers life, life-force, sensation, thought, feeling, behavior, piety, wisdom. *(FAIR-ah)*

Fjǫrgyn (f) and Fjǫrgynn (m): An ancient Goddess and God, about whom little is known, except that Fjǫrgyn is one of the names of Thor's Mother, the Earth Goddess, and Fjǫrgynn is the father of Frigg. Presumably they are brother and sister, and perhaps spouses as well. Their names are cognate with the Proto-Indo-European Thunder-God, *Perkwunos. *(FYOR-gin, hard 'g' like 'beginning'.)*

Frigg, Frige, Friia: The great Goddess of Asgard: mother, wisewoman, wife of Odin, mother of Baldr, leader of a group of helping-Goddesses, diplomat and frith-weaver / peace-weaver. Her name means 'beloved.' The Anglo-Saxon version of her name is pronounced *FREE-yeh*.

Frith: Its simplest meaning is 'peace' in the sense of not fighting, arguing, or causing serious offense. Its deeper sense refers to the behaviors, attitudes, and commitments that support a closely-knit and well-functioning community.

Frithyard, frithstead: A place where people are required not to fight or shed blood. This usually referred to either a place of assembly, a Thing or a Moot, or most often to a sacred space for worship, such as an outdoor altar, sacred well, tree, or stone, or a temple.

Word-Hoard

Fylgja: The *fylgja* (meaning 'follower') is a spirit who is closely associated with a living person throughout their life. It may take an animal form, and serve as a guardian. *(FILL-gya, hard 'g')*

Galdor, galdoring: This is both a noun and a verb. It refers to magical songs, chants and chanting—literally 'en-chanting,' including rune-chants.

Gesith (sing.), **Gesithas** (pl.): An Anglo-Saxon word derived from *sith*, meaning 'journey.' *Gesithas* are people who travel together. In Anglo-Saxon usage, the meaning was extended to mean 'trusted, reliable companions' in any context, not only travel. *(yeh-SITH-ahs, 'th' as in 'thin')*

Ginnungagap: In Old Norse lore, Ginnungagap is a place of primal chaos or nothingness. At either end are the primal powers of Fire and Ice, and in the temperate center is where the World Tree takes root. The ancient Giant Ymir was formed from the frozen rime at the icier end of Ginnungagap. The ancient divine Cow, Auðhumla (whom I regard as the Ur-Mother) also arose from Ginnungagap, as did the progenitor of the Gods, Buri. *(GINN-oonga-gahp, hard or rough 'g's in Old Norse pronunciation, softer 'g' in modern Icelandic.)*

Grithstead: A place of truce or sanctuary, where negotiations can be carried out to resolve issues between enemies or fugitives and their pursuers.

Hama: The literal meaning is 'a covering'. In Norse folklore, the Hama manifests as a magical being, an occult shape with paranormal powers, which can fare forth from a person in spirit form, and is also associated with the womb, the caul, and the processes of gestation. In my soul lore theory, Hama shapes and ensouls our physical body, the Lich, and provides it with many abilities such as speech, behavior and action.

Hamingja, pl. hamingjur: In Norse folklore, Hamingja is both a form of luck, and a spirit who bears and gives that luck to the person with whom it is associated. As with Hama, Hamingja is considered to reside in the womb / caul / afterbirth. It accompanies the child it was born with throughout life, as long as nothing dire occurs to destroy its luck or its connection to the person. *(HAHM-ing-yah)*

Harrow: An Anglo-Saxon word for altar or an outdoor worship site or sacred location.

Hel: Hel, with its linguistic variations, is the term in all the Germanic languages for the place where souls go after death. It was not considered a place of punishment, but simply the residence of the dead. In Norse lore, Hel is also the name of a daughter of Loki, a Goddess of the dead and ruler of Hel. The word Hel is derived from Proto-Indo-European *kel-, meaning 'to cover, conceal.' Hel is the Hidden Land. The German Goddess Frau Holle derives her name from the same root, and is considered to be a guide and protector both during life and after death.

Hliðskalf: Odin's high seat from which he views the Worlds. His Ravens return to him each day while he sits on this seat, and bring him further news of the doings in all the Worlds. *(H-LITH-sk-yalf, 'th' as in 'the'.)*

Hlin: A Goddess and companion of Frigg, whose name means 'protectress'. Quite possibly she is an aspect or emanation of Frigg's own protective powers. Germanic Goddesses were considered protectors of warriors in battle, as well as of all men, women, and children.

Holle, Frau Holle: A German Goddess much involved in all matters of daily Midgard life, especially those traditionally relating to women and children, and to food, agriculture and home. Her care for all humans extends before and after Midgard life, as well as during it. Her name is cognate with 'Hel', and Holle's domains of action include not only Midgard and Midgard's sky, but Underworld as well. Other roots of her name include words for 'benevolent, kind, gracious'. Holle is especially revered by the modern Heathen sect called Urglaawe. *(HOL-leh)*

Hugr: A powerful soul focused on Midgard activities, using faculties of thought and emotion to navigate the complexities of human social life. In my thought, Hugr is the soul which periodically reincarnates, and which continues its involvement with Midgard life even after death by becoming an ancestral spirit, an Alf or a Dis, or a guiding spirit, or if ill-natured, becoming an afflicting wight. *(WHO-gr) See Strömback for in-depth discussion.*

Hvergelmir: In Norse mythology, a well or wellspring located in the cold, Niflheim side of Ginnungagap, under a root of the World-Tree, from which the Elivagar river(s) flows. In my thought, Hvergelmir is centered in Ginnungagap and is the source of the energy flows that form the cosmos. *(HVER-gel-meer, hard or rough 'g')*

Jotnar, Giants, fem. pl. Jotynjur: Singular forms: Jotun Giant, Jotynja Giantess. Considered to be descended from the hermaphroditic proto-Giant, Ymir. Norse Giants are grouped into several tribes, including Thursar, Jotnar, Rises, Frost-Giants, Berg- or Mountain Giants, Trolls, etc. Giants such as the Anglo-Saxon Eoten and German Riesen play a role in the folklore of other Germanic lands as well. In the Norse pantheon, many of the Æsir Gods are of Jotun descent through their mothers, including Odin, Thor, Viðar, Magni and Modi. *(YOHT-nahr, YO-tin-yur)*

Landwights: Land-spirits, beings who inhabit spiritual planes of Earth / Midgard, and involve themselves with the features and processes of landscapes and ecosystems. They range in size / power from smaller beings inhabiting trees, rocks, small spaces, up to

Word-Hoard

mighty warders of large areas and phenomena such as mountains, lakes and storms. At the latter end, they merge into the domains of the Jotnar and Deities.

Lich-Hama, Lich: Lich is the physical body; Lich-Hama or Lichama is the living body ensouled by its Hama.

Mægen, megin, main: Power, force, energy that is inherent in living beings, magical objects, and otherworldly beings. Used in a modern Heathen context, it often implies spiritual power. *(Anglo-Saxon mægen and Old Norse megin are pronounced about the same: MAY-yen. 'Main' is the modern form of the word.)*

Magni: A son of Thor and the giantess Jarnsaxa, embodiment of might and main. He survives Ragnarök and is one of the leading Deities of the new world that comes after. *(MOG-neh or MAHG-neh)*

Matronae, Matrons: A multitude of Goddesses, demi-Goddesses, ancestral warding spirits of tribes and clans, and land- and river-warding spirits, who flourished during the time of the Roman empire. Both Germanic and Celtic Matronae are recognized, as well as some whose provenance are not clear. Many stone altars and thanks-offerings to them have been found, especially in the region of what is now Germany, but extending all over Europe and Britain in the wake of the Roman Empire and their troops. These matronly beings are honored by modern Heathens, as well.

Midgard: The World of Earth and all it encompasses. It means 'middle yard, enclosure', a word and meaning that existed in all the Germanic languages, often in the form of 'middle earth' meanings. This term implies an assumption that there are 'upper' and 'lower' worlds as well. According to Norse lore, Midgard was formed from Ymir's sacrificed body by Odin, Vili and Ve.

Mimir and his Well: Mimir is an ancient, wise Giant, the mentor and perhaps the maternal uncle of Odin. He was beheaded while a hostage with the Vanir, but Odin preserved his head and continues to receive wise rede from it. Mimir's Well is considered a place of great wisdom and mystery. Odin pledged his eye to this well in exchange for runic knowledge, and the well also is said to contain Heimdall's horn and his hearing or his ear. My idea is that Mimir's Head / Well is 'World-Mind' or the Noösphere, the realm where Thought occurs.

Mod, mod-power: I envision this as a form of energy similar to mægen / megin, except that it is shaped by the mood and character of the being who is accessing and expressing it. *(mode, rhymes with 'load')*

Moði: A son of Thor and the giantess Jarnsaxa, embodiment and channel of mod-power. He survives Ragnarök and is one of the leading Deities of the new world that comes after. *(MOH-thee, 'th' as in 'the')*

Niflheim: In Norse lore, the cold, icy end of the primal space called Ginnungagap. The word means 'mist-world'. In my thought, the term Niflheim describes the mist of spiritual proto-being, the field of Ahma, that continually arises from Ginnungagap, generated by the primal polarities of Ice and Fire. This mist is the basis for all subsequent shapings of worlds and beings. *(NIFL-hame, NIF-lame)*

Nornir, Norns: Three womanly beings, possibly Giants though their origins are unclear. In Norse lore they are named Urðr, Verðandi, and Skuld, representing 'What-Is', 'What Is Becoming', and 'Debt, or What Should Be.' They live beside the Well of Wyrd / destiny, called Urðarbrunnr, and nourish the World-Tree with mud and water from the Well. They speak ørlög or fate for humans, and the council or doom-stead of the Gods takes place near their Well; presumably they participate in these councils. There are also lesser

Word-Hoard

norns, who appear as fairy Godmothers and similar beings involved with people's fates. In Anglo-Saxon, these beings are called the Wyrdæ.

Odin, Oðinn, Woden, Wotan, Wodan: One of the chief Gods of the Æsir, son of Borr, brother of Vili and Ve, husband of Frigg, father of Thor and Baldr. He involves himself heavily in Midgard affairs.

Óðrœrir: Meaning: 'wode-stirrer.' This name refers to the Mead of Poetry, and to a vessel where it was contained. The Mead of Poetry was made from the blood of Kvasir, considered the wisest of beings. *(OTH-reh-reer, 'th' as in 'the')*

Ǫnd, Önd: Old Norse word meaning both 'spirit' and 'breath'.

Ordeal: An "or-deal" in a Heathen philosophical sense means *'the primal roots of a given ordeal-circumstance: the ørlög, the weaving of wyrd, which has been dealt out for one to face here and now, in this place, in this time.'* An 'ordeal' has the connotation of a struggle, a challenge, a personal testing, and it is that, but it is more. It is fateful, it is a weaving of wyrd, a drawing-together of the strands of our life into a nexus-point of deep significance. Much of our past has gone into reaching this nexus-point of the ordeal, and much will lead forth from its outcome, that will shape our time to come. (In other words, an ordeal is a really big deal!)

In my understanding of Heathen philosophy, life itself is an ordeal in this sense: a complex, patterned knot or nexus of strands of ørlög, arising from the past, gathered together in the present, and shaping the future to come. The ordeal of life is a challenge and a struggle, indeed, but more than that, it shapes the whole pattern of our Being, and shapes the meaning that our life holds.

Our purpose in life is not to avoid or escape true Heathen ordeals, but to rise to the challenge they offer: the challenge not only to meet the ordeal successfully, but to use that challenge to emerge from the ordeal with greater soul-qualities than we had when we went into it. This is the 'path of the hero' in Germanic culture.

Ørlög, Orlog, Orlay: This word means the 'ur-layers, primal layers', and is related to words for 'law.' These layers are laid by the Norns, shaped from the deeds and events of humankind and Midgard, as well as the other Worlds and beings. In turn, ørlög influences the lives and life-spans of living humans. Ørlög is the Old Norse term, Orlæg or Orlay is Anglo-Saxon. *(OOR-loog; 'g' is breathy, like an 'h')*

Proto-Germanic: A language which has been reconstructed by modern scholars; the prehistoric ancestor of Germanic languages such as Anglo-Saxon, Old Saxon, Old Norse, Frisian, Old High German, Frankish, etc. Gothic is the closest historical language to Proto-Germanic.

Proto-Indo-European, PIE: The prehistoric, reconstructed root of all Indo-European languages, ancient and modern.

Ragnarök: 'The destiny or fate of the Gods,' a great battle between the Gods and the Jotnar or Giants, with the dead from different realms participating on different sides. Some modern Heathens regard Ragnarök as having already happened, in the form of the forcible conversions from Heathenism / Paganism to Christianity during the early Middle Ages. Others regard it as an event yet to come, and some see Ragnarök as a cyclical, recurrent event, having already happened in the past, and still to come again in the future. *(RAG-nah-rook, 'rook' rhymes with 'book'.)*

Rede: 'Rede' refers to advice, counsel, guidance, but also to one's own rede to oneself: one's experience, learning, thought, intuitions applied to solve problems, meet challenges, and generally conduct one's life successfully. Wise rede leads to wise actions, luck, and success. Our ancient kin easily recognized those who were 'rede-y,' guided by wise rede whether from others or within themselves, versus those who were 'unrede-y' and managed to get everything wrong no matter how hard they seemed to try. When this unrede-y person was a king, this spelled disaster for his reign.

Seiðr, Seidh: In Nordic cultures, a practice similar to witchcraft, with a strong focus on oracular work and faring in spirit-forms. In modern Heathen use, it often refers to oracular trance practices. A *seiðkona* is a woman who practices seiðr, while *seiðmaðr* refers to a man. *(sayth, saythr, 'th' is voiced as in 'there')*

Shild, Scyld: An Anglo-Saxon word which is cognate to the name of the Norn, Skuld. Shild refers to a debt, and to one's responsibility for one's actions and their results.

Sif, Sibbe, Sippe: A Goddess, in Norse mythology the wife of Thor and mother of Ullr and Thruðr. Her name is related to the words for 'kinship, relationship' in all the Germanic languages, and she supports and protects this important domain of life. Some also consider her to be the Goddess of grain, with a belief that thunder and lightning are necessary to cause the grain to ripen, reflecting the relations between Sif and Thor. I envision her as the 'frith-sib of the folk', a peace-weaver who graciously shares her home and blessings with living folk and with the many human spirits who reside with her, Thor and their family in the afterlife. *(sif, sib-beh, sip-peh)*

Sjöfn: A Goddess and companion of Frigg; a promoter and protector of love, marriage and relationships generally. *(syuvn)*

Spaecraft, spaework: As used here, and in modern Heathen terminology, these words refer to a practice of oracular trance work, often performed in a group setting, other times performed individually, to explore questions and issues of interest to the querents.

Sumble, Symbel, Sumbel: A Heathen ceremony. Participants sit or stand in a circle, each holding a suitable drink, and go around the circle one by one to drink a toast, speak a boast or an oath. Usually the first round is dedicated to the Deities, the second to ancestors, heroes, and admired persons, and the third and subsequent rounds are open.

Syn: The Goddess Syn wards the doors of the hall and closes them against those who must not enter. She is called on at the Thingsteads (assemblies) when one wishes to refute an accusation, and is considered the Goddess of Denial. (*Gylfaginning* p. 30, Edda). I view her as the "Just Say No" Goddess, the one who helps us protect our healthy and necessary boundaries against intrusion.

Thor, Thunor, Donar, Donner: A well-loved and much-trusted God among ancient and modern Heathens, wielding the power of thunder and lightning. His great Hammer is used to defend the Deities and Midgard against destructive forces, and is also used for hallowing and blessing. Thor is Sif's husband, and is the father of Magni, Modi and Thruðr. His hall Bilskirnir ('ray of light lightning-strike') lies within his domain, Thruðheim ('strength-home, strength-world'), and is the afterlife residence of many human spirits whose patron he was during life.

Thorlings: A term I invented, based on the Germanic suffix "*ling, lingas*" that implies 'belonging to or descended from' the name the suffix is attached to. Thus, Thorlings or Thorlingas are those who are descended from Thor: Magni, Moði and Thruðr.

Thruðr: Daughter of Thor and the Goddess Sif. Her name means 'Strength'. Presumably she, like her brothers Magni and Modi, survives Ragnarök and becomes one of the leaders of the new world. Her father's Godly domain bears her name: Thruðheim or 'strength-home, strength-world.' *(Through-thr')*

Word-Hoard

Vafrloge: 'Flickering, wavering flames,' otherworldly flames that flicker over burial places and their treasures, and surround otherworldly dwellings and fortresses. *(VAHFR-low-geh, hard 'g')*

Valhöl, Valhalla: 'Hall of the slain', Odin's hall where spirits of slain heroes—Einherjar—reside.

Vanir: A tribe of Heathen Gods. The most well-known of them are Freya, Frey, and Njorð. Freya has the title 'Vanadis' meaning 'Lady of the Vanir.'

Werold: A word meaning 'man-age', used in Anglo-Saxon, Old Saxon and Old High German, and referring to the totality of a person's life-span and life-experience. In Old Norse, the word is Veraldr. *(WARE-old)*

Wih-stead: A sacred place: a temple, altar, or outdoor worship site. From Anglo-Saxon *wih* meaning 'sacred' plus 'stead' meaning 'place.' *(wy-stead)*

Wode, Oðr: One of the gifts given by Hœnir / Odin's brother when two trees or logs were transformed into the humans Ask and Embla. Wode refers to an ecstatic state of heightened spiritual—and sometimes physical—energy, which can take forms ranging from inspired eloquence and prophecy, artistic and intellectual genius, warrior focus and strength, to berserker rage, or outright madness. I see the gift of wode as a divine spark or a bridge, that enables humans to reach divine consciousness and communication with the Deities. If the person is not fit nor prepared for this, if their motives are skewed, or if they approach the Deities in inappropriate, offensive ways, the resulting flow of wode may backfire into negative forms.

World-Tree, Yggdrasil: The cosmic Tree, the structure of Space and all that exists within space. It is rooted in the three great Wells of power in Norse myth: Hvergelmir, Mimir's Well, and Urðr's Well, and the Nine Worlds are supported by its branches and roots.

Worlds, Nine Worlds: Norse mythology envisions nine worlds as the home-bases for different kinds of beings: Asgard for the Æsir, Vanaheim for the Vanir, Alfheim for the Alfar or elves, Midgard for humans, Svartalfheim for the Dwarves, Hel for the dead, Jotunheim for the Giants, and the Worlds of the primal energies: the World of ice and cold, Niflheim, and the World of Fire, Muspelheim.

Wyrd, and Well of: An Anglo-Saxon word derived from 'to become, to happen, to come to pass'; basically, 'to come into being.' This is the name of a being or a power that brings about destiny and fate in Anglo-Saxon lore, in particular, the circumstances of one's death. Wyrd is cognate with Norse Norn-name Urðr, and Wyrd's Well is the same as *Urðarbrunnr:* the Well of Fate (approximately). 'Fate, Destiny' and 'Wyrd' are not the same, but for a brief explanation we can say that there is significant overlap of their meanings.

Yggdrasil: The 'steed of Ygg'. 'Ygg' means the 'terrible one', and is a byname of Odin. His 'steed' here is the World-Tree upon which he hung for nine days and nights to win the Runes. *(IG-dra-SEEL)*

Ymir: A Giant, said to be hermaphroditic, who came into being within Ginnungagap at the beginning of the cosmos. Jotnar / Giants are descended from him-her, and I believe that the unnamed pair who were generated from beneath Ymir's arm were Mimir and Bestla, the uncle and mother of Odin, Vili and Ve. Ymir was sacrificed by Odin, Vili and Ve, and his-her body formed the foundations of Midgard and some of the other Worlds.

Book-Hoard / Bibliography

and Further Reading on Topics in this Book

Note: All passages in this book that were quoted from German texts were translated by myself into English.

Ælfric's Catholic Homilies, The First Series, Text. Ed. Peter Clemoles. Oxford: Oxford University Press, 1997.

Anglo-Saxon Rune Poem, original language text:
https://www.tha-engliscan-gesithas.org.uk/written-and-spoken-old-english/old-english-alphabet-2/the-anglo-saxon-rune-poem/

Baer, Jeremy. *Hammer, Oak, and Lightning: A Thor Devotional.* Philadelphia PA: The Troth, 2019.

Bang, Anton Christian. *Norske Hexeformularer og Magiske Opskrifte.* Kristiana I Commision hos Jacob Dybwad, A.W. Broggers Boktrykkeri, 1901-2.

Barber, Charles Clyde. *An Old High German Reader.* Oxford: Basil Blackwell, 1964.

Bintley, Michael. *Trees in the Religions of Early Medieval England* (Anglo-Saxon Studies, 26). Woodbridge, UK: The Boydell Press, 2015.

Boucher, Alan, transl. *Ghosts, Witchcraft and the Other Worlds.* Reykjavik: Iceland Review Publishers, 1977.

Chickering, Howell D. Jr., transl. *Beowulf.* Dual language edition. New York: Doubleday, 1977.

Davidson, H. R. Ellis. *Gods and Myths of Northern Europe.* London: Penguin, 1964.

Davidson, H. R. Ellis. *Myths and Symbols in Pagan Europe.* Syracuse NY: Syracuse University Press, 1988.

Davidson, Hilda Ellis. *Roles of the Northern Goddess.* New York: Routledge, 1998.

Davidson, Hilda Ellis. *The Lost Beliefs of Northern Europe.* New York: Routledge, 1993.

deVries, Jan. *Altgermanische Religionsgeschichte.* Band I. Berlin: Walter de Gruyter & Co., 1956.

deVries, Jan. *Altnordisches Etymologisches Wörterbuch.* Leiden: E.J. Brill, 1961.

Dowden, Ken. *European Paganism: The Realities of Cult from Antiquity to the Middle Ages.* New York: Routledge, 2008.

Durkan, Maire. *Circle of Frith: A Devotional to Frigg and her Handmaidens.* Philadelphia: The Troth, 2021.

Egil's Saga, transl. Hermann Pálsson and Paul Edwards. London: Penguin Classics, 1976.

Erich, Oswald A. and Richard Beitl. *Wörterbuch der Deutschen Volkskunde.* Stuttgart: Alfred Kroener Verlag, 1955.

Eyrbyggja Saga, transl. Hermann Palsson and Paul Edwards. London: Penguin Books, 1989.

Fuller, Laura Snow. *Lady of the Mountain Hall: A Skadi Devotional.* Philadelphia: The Troth, 2019.

Goos, Gunivortus. *Goddess Holle*, 3rd revised and supplemented edition. Norderstedt, Germany: Books on Demand GMBH, 2019.

Grimm, Jacob. *Teutonic Mythology.* (J.S. Stalleybrass edition). London: George Bell & Sons, 1883.

Guerber, H. A. *Myths of the Norsemen from the Eddas and Sagas.* Dover Publications, New York, 1992.

Gundarsson, Kveldulf et al, *Our Troth,* The Ring of Troth 1993

Hall, Alaric. *Elves in Anglo-Saxon England: Matters of Belief, Health, Gender and Identity.* Woodbridge UK: The Boydell Press, 2009.

Hall, J.R. Clark. *A Concise Anglo-Saxon Dictionary, Fourth Edition.* University of Toronto Press, Toronto, 1960.

Heath, Cat. *Elves, Witches & Gods: Spinning Old Heathen Magic in the Modern Day.* Woodbury, MN: Llewellyn Publications, 2021. Also see her website writings at http://www.seohelrune.com/

Hoffmann-Krayer, E., and Bächtöld-Stäubli, H., eds. *Handwörterbuch des Deutschen Aberglaubens.* Berlin & Leipzig: Walter de Gruyter & Co., 1929-1930.

Hollenback, Jess Byron. *Mysticism: Experience, Response, and Empowerment.* University Park, PA: The Pennsylvania State University Press, 1996.

Hooke, Della. *Trees in Anglo-Saxon England: Literature, Lore and Landscape* (Anglo-Saxon Studies, 13). Woodbridge, UK: The Boydell Press, 2013

Jonsson, Finnur, ed. *De Gamle Eddadigte.* København: G.E.C. Gads Forlag, 1932.

Jonsson, Finnur, ed. *Edda Snorra Sturlusonar.* Udgivnet efter Handskrifterne af Kommissionen for det Arnamagnaeanske Legat. København, Denmark: Gyldendalske Boghandel – Nordisk Forlag, 1931.

Kroonen, Guus. *Etymological Dictionary of Proto-Germanic.* Leiden: Brill, 2013.

Lafayllve, Patricia M. *Freyja, Lady, Vanadis: An Introduction to the Goddess.* Denver: Outskirts Press, 2006.

Larrington, Carolyne, transl. *The Poetic Edda*, revised edition. Oxford: Oxford University Press, Oxford, 2014.

Lecouteux, Claude; transl. Jon E. Graham. *Demons and Spirits of the Land: Ancestral Lore and Practices*. Rochester, VT: Inner Traditions, 2015.

Lecouteux, Claude; transl. Jon E. Graham. *The Hidden History of Elves & Dwarfs: Avatars of Invisible Realms*. Rochester, VT: Inner Traditions, 2018.

Lecouteux, Claude; transl. Jon E. Graham. *The Tradition of Household Spirits: Ancestral Lore and Practices*. Rochester, VT: Inner Traditions, 2013.

Mainer, John T. *They Walk With Us: Stories by John T. Mainer.* New Haven CT: The Troth, 2015.

Mallory, J.P. and D.Q. Adams, editors. *Encyclopedia of Indo-European Culture*. Chicago, IL: Fitzroy Dearborn Publishers, 1997.

Meyer, Elisabeth Marie. *Die Bedeutungsentwicklung von Germanischen *moda-*. Halle, Germany: Buchdruckerei des Waisenhauses, 1926.

Motz, Lotte. "Of Elves and Dwarfs" in *Arv: Tidscrift for Nordisk Folkminnesforskning (Journal of Scandinavian Folklore)* Vol. 29-30, 1973-4. Published by The Royal Gustavus Adolphus Academy, Uppsala; distributed by The Almqvist & Wiksell Periodical Company, Stockholm, Sweden.

Munin, Janet, ed. *Polytheistic Monasticism: Voices from Pagan Cloisters*. Alresford, UK: Moon Books 2022.

Paulus Diaconus, *History of the Lombards*. Transl. William Dudley Foulke. Philadelphis: University of Pennsylvania, 1907.

Paxson, Diana. *The Essential Guide to Possession, Depossession, and Divine Relationships*. San Francisco: Weiser Books, 2015.

Paxson, Diana. *Trance-Portation: Learning to Navigate the Inner World.* San Francisco: Weiser Books, 2008.

Poetic Edda: see Larrington.

Prose Edda: see Sturlason.

Rochholz, E(rnst) L(udwig). *Drei Gaugöttinen: Walburg, Verena und Gertrud, als deutsche Kirchenheilige. Sittenbilder aus germanischen Frauenleben.* Leipzig: Verlag von Friedrich Fischer, 1870.

Rodriguez, Louis J. *Anglo-Saxon Verse Charms, Maxims and Heroic Legends.* Chippenham UK: Anglo-Saxon Books, 1993.

Rose, Winifred Hodge. *Heathen Soul Lore: A Personal Approach.* Urbana IL: Wordfruma Press, 2022.

Rose, Winifred Hodge. *Heathen Soul Lore Foundations: Ancient and Modern Germanic Pagan Concepts of the Souls.* Urbana IL: Wordfruma Press, 2021.

Rydberg, Viktor. *Teutonic Mythology: Gods and Goddesses of the Northland,* translated by Rasmus B. Anderson. Norroena Society, 1907.

Saxo Grammaticus, ed. Hilda Ellis Davidson, transl. Peter Fisher. *The History of the Danes, Books I-IX.* D.S. Brewer reprint, 1999.

Schöll, Hans Cristoph, *Die Drei Ewigen: Eine Untersuchung über Germanischen Bauernglauben.* Jena: Eugen Diederichs Verlag, 1936.

Schreiwer, Robert Lüsch, and Ammerili Eckhart. *A Dictionary of Urglaawe Terminology.* Bristol PA: Deitscherei.com, 2012

Schreiwer, Robert Lüsch. *The First Book of Urglaawe Myths: Old Deitsch Tales for the Current Era.* Bristol PA: Deitscherei.com, 2014.

Sheffield, Ann Gróa. *Frey: God of the World.* Lulu, 2007.

Sheldrake, Merlin. *Entangled Life: How Fungi Make Our Worlds, Change Our Minds & Shape Our Futures.* New York: Random House, *2021.*

Simek, Rudolf. *Dictionary of Northern Mythology.* Cambridge: D.S. Brewer, 1993.

Simpson, Jaqueline. *Icelandic Folktales and Legends.* Berkeley: University of California Press, 1972.

Storms, G(ustav). *Anglo-Saxon Magic.* New York: Gordon Press, 1974 (reprint of 1948 publication)

Strömback, Dag. "The Concept of the Soul in Nordic Tradition," in *ARV: Journal of Scandinavian Folklore*, Vol. 31, 1975. Stockholm: The Almqvist & Wiksell Periodical Company.

Sturlason, Snorre. *Heimskringla or The Lives of the Norse Kings.* Ed. and transl. Erling Monsen, A.H. Smith. Mineola: Dover Publications reprint, 1990.

Sturlason, Snorri. *Edda.* Transl. Anthony Faulkes. Everyman, Charles E. Tuttle, Vermont. 1995.

Tacitus, transl. Herbert Benario. *Agricola, Germany, and Dialogue on Orators.* Norman: University of Oklahoma Press, 1991.

Waggoner, Ben, *et al. Our Troth, 3rd Edition.*
Volume 1: *Heathen History*, 2020.
Volume 2: *Heathen Gods*, 2021.
Volume 3: *Heathen Living*, 2022.
Philadelphia: The Troth.

Watkins, Calvert. *The American Heritage Dictionary of Indo-European Roots.* Boston: Houghton Mifflin Harcourt, 2011.

(Note: the title of the journal 'Arv' changed slightly over time; in each reference above I give the title as it appeared in that issue of the journal.)

Photo Credits

Photo Credits
Listed if legally required.

Cover image: Winding path
Perengstrom, CC BY-SA 4.0 <https://creativecommons.org/licenses/by-sa/4.0>, via Wikimedia Commons
https://upload.wikimedia.org/wikipedia/commons/0/02/Winding_path_over_Kullaberg.jpg

Page 1: Mountain hiking
Paxson Woelber, CC BY-SA 4.0 <https://creativecommons.org/licenses/by-sa/4.0>, via Wikimedia Commons
https://upload.wikimedia.org/wikipedia/commons/5/55/Hiking_in_the_Talkeetna_Mountains_of_Alaska.JPG

Page 4: Mountain view in Robson
Jakub Fryš (talk · contribs), CC BY-SA 4.0 <https://creativecommons.org/licenses/by-sa/4.0>, via Wikimedia Commons
https://upload.wikimedia.org/wikipedia/commons/f/fd/Mountain_view_in_Robson_valley.jpg

Page 5: Odin sculpture Epcot Center.
Eden, Janine and Jim from New York City, CC BY 2.0 <https://creativecommons.org/licenses/by/2.0>, via Wikimedia Commons
https://upload.wikimedia.org/wikipedia/commons/b/bb/Odin_%2849564069552%29.jpg

Page 6: Freya sculpture Epcot Center.
Eden, Janine and Jim from New York City, CC BY 2.0 <https://creativecommons.org/licenses/by/2.0>, via Wikimedia Commons
https://upload.wikimedia.org/wikipedia/commons/f/fe/Freyja_%2849560740206%29.jpg

Photo Credits

<u>Page 23:</u> Three Norns, Ribe Vikinge Center
Västgöten, CC BY-SA 3.0 <https://creativecommons.org/licenses/by-sa/3.0>, via Wikimedia Commons
https://upload.wikimedia.org/wikipedia/commons/7/7c/Ribe_VikingeCenter_-_the_3_norns.jpg

<u>Page 52:</u> Odin at the Fountain of Wisdom
Derbeth, CC BY 4.0 <https://creativecommons.org/licenses/by/4.0>, via Wikimedia Commons
https://upload.wikimedia.org/wikipedia/commons/d/d6/Brunnen_der_Weisheit_Thale_Wotan.jpg

<u>Page 67:</u> Sculpture, Woman Thinking
ÁWá, CC BY-SA 3.0 <http://creativecommons.org/licenses/by-sa/3.0/>, via Wikimedia Commons
https://upload.wikimedia.org/wikipedia/commons/8/81/A_woman_thinking.jpg

<u>Page 70:</u> Cleft in the limestone cliff known as the Fairy Steps by Martin Dawes, CC BY-SA 2.0
<https://creativecommons.org/licenses/by-sa/2.0>, via Wikimedia Commons
https://upload.wikimedia.org/wikipedia/commons/4/43/Cleft_in_the_limestone_cliff_known_as_the_Fairy_Steps_-_geograph.org.uk_-_3935087.jpg

<u>Page 73:</u> Hedgehog
Hrald, CC BY-SA 3.0 <https://creativecommons.org/licenses/by-sa/3.0>, via Wikimedia Commons
https://upload.wikimedia.org/wikipedia/commons/a/aa/West_European_Hedgehog_%28Erinaceus_europaeus%291.jpg

<u>Page 76:</u> Flying raptor bird
Peter Gronemann from Switzerland, CC BY 2.0
<https://creativecommons.org/licenses/by/2.0>, via Wikimedia Commons
https://upload.wikimedia.org/wikipedia/commons/d/dc/Milvus_milvus_-_near_Brienzersee%2C_Canton_of_Berne%2C_Switzerland_-flying-8_%281%29.jpg

Photo Credits

Page 82: Fractal image
Optoskept, CC BY 4.0 <https://creativecommons.org/licenses/by/4.0>, via Wikimedia Commons
https://upload.wikimedia.org/wikipedia/commons/5/5c/Fractal_Detail_No_1_by_Optoskept.jpg

Page 96: Two wolves
Caninest, CC BY 2.0 <https://creativecommons.org/licenses/by/2.0>, via Wikimedia Commons
https://upload.wikimedia.org/wikipedia/commons/3/36/Two_Grey_Wolves_%284394641125%29.jpg

Page 98: Thor sitting
Hermann Ernst Freund, CC BY 3.0 <https://creativecommons.org/licenses/by/3.0>, via Wikimedia Commons
https://upload.wikimedia.org/wikipedia/commons/9/9a/Thor%2C_siddende%2C_st%C3%B8ttet_til_sin_hammer.jpg

Page 101: Small silver-mounted drinking horn, grave find.
The Swedish History Museum, Stockholm from Sweden, CC BY 2.0 <https://creativecommons.org/licenses/by/2.0>, via Wikimedia Commons
https://upload.wikimedia.org/wikipedia/commons/0/06/Drinking_horn%2C_mouth_mounting_%286881053943%29.jpg

Page 103: Reconstructed Viking hall, Borre, Norway
Wolfmann, CC BY-SA 4.0 <https://creativecommons.org/licenses/by-sa/4.0>, via Wikimedia Commons
https://upload.wikimedia.org/wikipedia/commons/4/4d/Midgard_vikings_enter_Viking_Age_centre_Borre_Horten_Norway_GILDEHALLEN_Rekonstruert_festhall_trebygning_2013_vikingstil_Reconstructed_Viking_inspired_banquet_hall_Utskj%C3%A6ringer_Ornamental_wood_carvings_Takspon_Wooden_roof.jpg

Page 105: Gallehus horn
Nationalmuseet, CC0, via Wikimedia Commons
https://upload.wikimedia.org/wikipedia/commons/3/38/Tegning-af-guldhorn_DO-1501_original.jpg

Photo Credits

Page 114: Field of grain
Susanne Nilsson, CC BY-SA 2.0
<https://creativecommons.org/licenses/by-sa/2.0>, via Wikimedia Commons
https://upload.wikimedia.org/wikipedia/commons/9/9f/Grain_%2828590523792%29.jpg

Page 115: Witches' dance, Austria
Iryna Pustynnikova, CC BY-SA 4.0
<https://creativecommons.org/licenses/by-sa/4.0>, via Wikimedia Commons
https://upload.wikimedia.org/wikipedia/commons/e/eb/Witches%27_dance.jpg

Page 116: Witches in masks
Iryna Pustynnikova, CC BY-SA 4.0
<https://creativecommons.org/licenses/by-sa/4.0>, via Wikimedia Commons
https://upload.wikimedia.org/wikipedia/commons/7/7f/Witches_in_Masks.jpg

Page 120: Collection of Nehalennia altars
Ben Pirard, CC BY-SA 3.0 <https://creativecommons.org/licenses/by-sa/3.0>, via Wikimedia Commons
https://upload.wikimedia.org/wikipedia/commons/9/93/Leiden-Nehalennia-votiefaltaren.JPG

Page 125: Straw doll
Siegbert Brey, CC BY-SA 4.0 <https://creativecommons.org/licenses/by-sa/4.0>, via Wikimedia Commons
https://upload.wikimedia.org/wikipedia/commons/c/c5/Strohfigur_Fahren_2023_%282%29.jpg

Page 126: Maibaum
Triplec85, CC BY-SA 4.0 <https://creativecommons.org/licenses/by-sa/4.0>, via Wikimedia Commons
https://upload.wikimedia.org/wikipedia/commons/c/c2/2022-05-01_Maibaum_Tauberbischofsheim_W%C3%B6rtplatz_3.jpg

Photo Credits

Page 127: Maypole and Ratshaus
Jacquesverlaeken, CC BY-SA 4.0
<https://creativecommons.org/licenses/by-sa/4.0>, via Wikimedia Commons
https://upload.wikimedia.org/wikipedia/commons/d/d9/20040913_Sontra_Rathaus_Maypole_82.jpg

Page 131: Swedish Valborg
Bengt Nyman from Vaxholm, Sweden, CC BY 2.0
<https://creativecommons.org/licenses/by/2.0>, via Wikimedia Commons
https://upload.wikimedia.org/wikipedia/commons/4/46/Valborg_2304_%286989901896%29.jpg

Page 163: Valkyrie bronze statue
Mik Hartwell from Copenhagen, Denmark, CC BY 2.0
<https://creativecommons.org/licenses/by/2.0>, via Wikimedia Commons
https://upload.wikimedia.org/wikipedia/commons/e/ec/Valkyrie%2C_Copenhagen.jpg

Page 173: Doorway
Derek Harper / Door, No 10 Cathedral Close, Exeter
https://upload.wikimedia.org/wikipedia/commons/0/03/Door%2C_No_10_Cathedral_Close%2C_Exeter_-_geograph.org.uk_-_1082850.jpg

Page 176: Heimdall listening
"Heimdallr. An illustration from Fredrik Sander's 1893 Swedish edition of the Poetic Edda. Reprinted with Erik Brate's 1913 translation which in turn is published by Project Runeberg at http://runeberg.org/eddan/ from where the image is taken. All works republished by Project Runeberg are in the public domain."

Page 194: Earth goddess garden sculpture:
Eric Yarnell, CC BY-SA 4.0 <https://creativecommons.org/licenses/by-sa/4.0>, via Wikimedia Commons
https://upload.wikimedia.org/wikipedia/commons/0/03/Earth_Goddess_sculpture%2C_Atlanta_Botanical_Gardens.jpg

Photo Credits

Page 199: Matrons Aufanie
Matronis Avianiae J. Vogel (LVR-LandesMuseum Bonn), CC BY-SA 4.0 <https://creativecommons.org/licenses/by-sa/4.0>, via Wikimedia Commons
https://upload.wikimedia.org/wikipedia/commons/d/d3/Matronenaltar.jpg

Page 200: Matron with fruit in lap
Ji-Elle, CC BY-SA 3.0 <https://creativecommons.org/licenses/by-sa/3.0>, via Wikimedia Commons
https://upload.wikimedia.org/wikipedia/commons/c/cc/Statue_de_d%C3%A9esse-m%C3%A8re-Mus%C3%A9e_barrois.jpg

Page 220: Tapestry tree
SEN Heritage Looms - Sophia Tsourinaki, CC BY-SA 4.0 <https://creativecommons.org/licenses/by-sa/4.0>, via Wikimedia Commons
https://upload.wikimedia.org/wikipedia/commons/7/71/TAPESTRY_WEAVE_ON_A_FRAME_LOOM.jpg

Page 231: Tree-trunk carving of Frau Holle
"Schnitzerei 'Weinende Frau Holle' am Ostufer des Oderteich. Kassandro, CC BY-SA 4.0 <https://creativecommons.org/licenses/by-sa/4.0>, via Wikimedia Commons

Page 235: Exposed tree roots
Peter Trimming / Roots! CC BY-SA 2.0
https://upload.wikimedia.org/wikipedia/commons/c/c9/Roots%5E_-_geograph.org.uk_-_1403768.jpg

Page 240: Foggy woods
Waldimnebel: Reinhard Hurt, CC BY-SA 3.0 <https://creativecommons.org/licenses/by-sa/3.0>, via Wikimedia Commons
https://upload.wikimedia.org/wikipedia/commons/4/4d/Waldimnebel_%28189870391%29.jpeg

Photo Credits

Page 241: Troll becoming a hill, illustrator : JNL, FAL, via Wikimedia Commons
https://upload.wikimedia.org/wikipedia/commons/a/a1/Troll_becoming_a_mountain_ill_jnl.png

Page 243: Tall tree-trunk
Eyþór Björnsson from West Side Kópavogur City, Iceland, CC BY 2.0 <https://creativecommons.org/licenses/by/2.0>, via Wikimedia Commons
https://upload.wikimedia.org/wikipedia/commons/5/5b/Ein_er_me%C3%B0_%C3%A1sum..._-_Flickr_-_Ey%C3%BE%C3%B3r.jpg

Page 244: Red face in rock
Aleph79, CC BY-SA 3.0 <https://creativecommons.org/licenses/by-sa/3.0>, via Wikimedia Commons
https://upload.wikimedia.org/wikipedia/commons/7/7f/Rock_Face.jpg

Page 245: Sun through tree branches
Noah Wulf, CC BY SA 4.0 <https://creativecommons.org/licenses/by-sa/4.0>, via Wikimedia Commons
https://upload.wikimedia.org/wikipedia/commons/8/83/Sun_Through_Tree_Branches.jpg

Page 247: Old graveyard
Rosser1954, CC BY-SA 4.0 <https://creativecommons.org/licenses/by-sa/4.0>, via Wikimedia Commons
https://upload.wikimedia.org/wikipedia/commons/0/05/Old_Kirk_site_and_graveyard%2C_Ochiltree%2C_East_Ayrshire._View_south-west.jpg

Page 254: Dewy flower
Brocken Inaglory, CC BY-SA 3.0 <https://creativecommons.org/licenses/by-sa/3.0>, via Wikimedia Commons
https://upload.wikimedia.org/wikipedia/commons/6/6f/A_small_flower_refracted_in_rain_droplets.jpg

Photo Credits

Page 255: Small Waterfall by Mick Garratt, CC BY-SA 2.0 <https://creativecommons.org/licenses/by-sa/2.0>, via Wikimedia Commons
https://upload.wikimedia.org/wikipedia/commons/6/68/Small_Waterfall_-_geograph.org.uk_-_2586064.jpg

Page 261: 'Zauberlehrling' Kreuzschnabel, CC BY-SA 3.0 <https://creativecommons.org/licenses/by-sa/3.0>, via Wikimedia Commons
https://upload.wikimedia.org/wikipedia/commons/8/8b/Zauberlehrling_Erneuerung_2018.jpg

Page 269: Geothermal and glacier Iceland Virtual-Pano, CC BY-SA 4.0 <https://creativecommons.org/licenses/by-sa/4.0>, via Wikimedia Commons
https://upload.wikimedia.org/wikipedia/commons/3/3a/Hveravellir_thermal_energy.jpg

Page 271: Rainbow over the wind farm turbines by Jacky Barrett, CC BY-SA 2.0 <https://creativecommons.org/licenses/by-sa/2.0>, via Wikimedia Commons
https://upload.wikimedia.org/wikipedia/commons/3/33/Rainbow_over_the_wind_farm_turbines_-_geograph.org.uk_-_1821529.jpg

Page 278: Rock-Giantess formation Devil's rock face P. James Franks, CC BY-SA 3.0 <https://creativecommons.org/licenses/by-sa/3.0>, via Wikimedia Commons
https://upload.wikimedia.org/wikipedia/commons/0/05/Devil%27s_Rock_face.JPG

Page 279: Dreaming woman Noahbuchanan, CC BY-SA 4.0 <https://creativecommons.org/licenses/by-sa/4.0>, via Wikimedia Commons
https://upload.wikimedia.org/wikipedia/commons/2/2b/Dreaming_Woman.jpg

Photo Credits

Page 289: 'Dwarf' face
York Museums Trust, CC BY-SA 4.0
<https://creativecommons.org/licenses/by-sa/4.0>, via Wikimedia Commons
https://upload.wikimedia.org/wikipedia/commons/1/1d/Early-medieval_%2C_Mount_%28FindID_652588%29.jpg

Page 311: Bronze Dwarf on street corner
MOs810, CC BY-SA 4.0 <https://creativecommons.org/licenses/by-sa/4.0>, via Wikimedia Commons
https://upload.wikimedia.org/wikipedia/commons/7/75/Dwarf_from_Pabianice_%284%29.jpg

Page 319: Dwarf street-guardian
Babewyn, CC BY-SA 4.0 <https://creativecommons.org/licenses/by-sa/4.0>, via Wikimedia Commons
https://upload.wikimedia.org/wikipedia/commons/7/7c/Radabweiser_schwedenstr-13_2023_09_17_nah.png

Page 343: Nordendorf fibula
Found in 1843 in an Alemannic grave field of mid 6th to late 6th century A.D. near Nordendorf, Bavaria, Germany. The fibula bears a runic inscription on the back side of its head plate: (first line) logaþore wodan wigiþonar (second line) awa (l)eubwini.
Bullenwächter, CC BY-SA 3.0 <https://creativecommons.org/licenses/by-sa/3.0>, via Wikimedia Commons
https://upload.wikimedia.org/wikipedia/commons/b/bb/Fibula_Nordendorf_I.jpg

Page 349: Thor sculpture Epcot Center
Eden, Janine and Jim from New York City, CC BY 2.0
<https://creativecommons.org/licenses/by/2.0>, via Wikimedia Commons
https://upload.wikimedia.org/wikipedia/commons/9/98/Thor_%2849563402798%29.jpg

Photo Credits

Page 375: Phantom galaxy
NASA's James Webb Space Telescope, CC BY 2.0
<https://creativecommons.org/licenses/by/2.0>, via Wikimedia Commons
https://upload.wikimedia.org/wikipedia/commons/d/d8/The_Phantom_Galaxy_Across_the_Spectrum.jpg

Page 377: Plowed field
Johann Jaritz / CC BY-SA 4.0, CC BY-SA 4.0
<https://creativecommons.org/licenses/by-sa/4.0>, via Wikimedia
https://upload.wikimedia.org/wikipedia/commons/f/fa/Poggersdorf_Linsenberg_Landschaft_mit_Birnb%C3%A4umen_11012019_5938.jpg

Page 381: Goðafoss
AwOiSoAk KaOsIoWa, CC BY-SA 3.0
<https://creativecommons.org/licenses/by-sa/3.0>, via Wikimedia Commons
https://upload.wikimedia.org/wikipedia/commons/9/93/Godafoss_-_panoramio_%283%29.jpg

Page 388: Still pond
Margret Ottner, CC BY-SA 4.0
<https://creativecommons.org/licenses/by-sa/4.0>, via Wikimedia Commons
https://upload.wikimedia.org/wikipedia/commons/7/7d/Stockenweiler_Weiher%2C_Gemeinde_Hergensweiler%2C_Kreis_Lindau%2C_Bayern_01.jpg

Page 392: Sky over Munich
Kritzolina, CC BY-SA 4.0 <https://creativecommons.org/licenses/by-sa/4.0>, via Wikimedia Commons
https://upload.wikimedia.org/wikipedia/commons/e/eb/Sky_over_Munich_02.jpg

Page 399: Sparky camp fire
Mark limb, CC BY-SA 4.0 <https://creativecommons.org/licenses/by-sa/4.0>, via Wikimedia Commons
https://upload.wikimedia.org/wikipedia/commons/9/9f/Sparky_camp_fire.jpg

Photo Credits

Page 411: Völva
By Vangland, CC BY-SA 4.0
<https://creativecommons.org/licenses/by-sa/4.0>, via Wikimedia Commons
https://upload.wikimedia.org/wikipedia/commons/7/78/V%C3%B6lva.jpg

Page 416: Midsummer bonfire in Finland
Tumi-1983, CC BY-SA 3.0 <https://creativecommons.org/licenses/by-sa/3.0>, via Wikimedia Commons
https://upload.wikimedia.org/wikipedia/commons/9/96/Midsummer_bonfire_in_Pielavasi%2C_Finland.JPG

Page 422: Yggdrasil by Jeroen
Jeroen van Valkenburg, CC BY 2.0
<https://creativecommons.org/licenses/by/2.0>, via Wikimedia Commons
https://upload.wikimedia.org/wikipedia/commons/1/13/Yggdrasil_-_by_Jeroen_van_Valkenburg.PNG

Page 423: Moonrise over bare trees
Sardaka, CC BY-SA 4.0 <https://creativecommons.org/licenses/by-sa/4.0>, via Wikimedia Commons
https://upload.wikimedia.org/wikipedia/commons/6/6f/UNSW_moonrise_001.jpg

Page 434: Mist mountain reflection
Arnaud Jaegers ajaegers, CC0, via Wikimedia Commons
https://upload.wikimedia.org/wikipedia/commons/c/cf/China%27s_mist_mountain_%28Unsplash%29.jpg

Page 459: Roots of yew
BabelStone, CC BY-SA 4.0 <https://creativecommons.org/licenses/by-sa/4.0>, via Wikimedia Commons
https://upload.wikimedia.org/wikipedia/commons/e/e9/Roots_of_yew_tree_at_Waverley_Abbey.jpg

Photo Credits

<u>Page 458:</u> Fractal spiral
PantheraLeo1359531, CC BY-SA 4.0
<https://creativecommons.org/licenses/by-sa/4.0>, via Wikimedia Commons
https://upload.wikimedia.org/wikipedia/commons/2/25/Spirals_in_self-similarity.jpg

Index

Note: The indexing software counts words in different formats, such as italics or capitalized words, as different words. You might find the word you're looking for listed more than once, such as 'elves' and 'Elves.' Also check listings for singular and plural words, such as 'Dwarf' and 'Dwarves.'

Æcerbot, 191, 193
Æsir, 33, 56, 58, 59, 60, 61, 62, 68, 77, 78, 90, 157, 159, 185, 199, 212, 283, 284, 285, 287, 463, 464, 468, 471, 476
Alfar, 185, 463, 476
alveig, 183
Ansuz, 61
Asgard, 25, 38, 40, 42, 59, 67, 143, 147, 149, 151, 153, 154, 155, 163, 165, 176, 178, 233, 284, 454, 456, 457, 463, 465, 476
Ask and Embla, 59, 156, 233, 234, 475
Asmoði, 109, 366
astral, 292, 428, 429, 433, 435, 436
Auðhumla, 44, 58, 76, 218
Aurgelmir, 57, 280
ausinn Óðreri, 55
ausinn vatni, 55, 56
Balder, 7, 16, 17, 18, 25, 27, 28, 29, 150, 151, 152, 153, 154, 155, 157, 158, 159, 161, 163, 164, 165, 167, 168, 169
Bede, 208
Berchta, 122, 125, 133, 136, 196, 217
Berchte, 121
Bestla, 54, 55, 56, 57, 58, 464, 476
Bifröst, 10, 19, 175
blessing-water, 256

Index

Bolthorn, 57
Borr, 58, 464, 471
Brisingamen, 25, 325, 366
Buri, 58, 464, 466
Dagaz rune, 87, 88, 89
Dain, 155
darshan, 362
daughters of Ægir, 181
Disablot, 132, 208, 209, 217
Disarsalr, 209, 210
Disir, 7, 8, 11, 22, 124, 135, 199, 208, 209, 210, 211, 212, 213, 214, 215, 216, 464
Disting, 208
Donar-Oak, 236
Dream of the Rood, 232
Durinn, 318, 319
Dvalin, 155
Dwarf, 291, 292, 293, 295, 299, 300, 301, 302, 303, 304, 307, 316
Dwarf-fathers, 155, 158
Dwarves, 14, 144, 185, 291, 302, 311, 313, 318, 319, 320, 321, 464, 476
Eikthyrnir, 456, 457
Eir, 36, 40, 68
Elf, 20, 117, 119, 122, 133, 135, 139, 140, 291, 296, 297, 299
Elf-shot, 20, 291
elves, 129, 134, 180, 246, 293, 295, 297, 476
Elves, 297, 480
entropy, 250, 403
Eostre, 133, 135, 137, 138, 140, 141, 385
Erce, 192, 194, 196, 197
etheric, 147, 149, 292, 296, 428, 433, 435, 436

Index

Fenja and Menja, 275, 277
Fenris, 84, 89, 393
feorhcynn, 234
Ferah, 230, 232, 233, 465
fermentation, 61, 63, 65
fettering, 299
Fire and Ice, 466
firibarn, 234
fjarghus, 226, 228
Fjörgyn, 41, 226, 227, 228, 229
Fjörgynn, 41, 226, 227, 228, 229
flower essences, 253
Forseti, 155
fractal, 432
fractals, 432, 433
Frau Holle, 133, 136, 371, 389, 467
Frey, 59, 72, 73, 259, 372, 383, 384, 385, 435, 453
Freya, 7, 8, 21, 24, 25, 48, 68, 72, 189, 294, 366, 369, 385
Frigg, 8, 9, 11, 15, 16, 17, 18, 19, 20, 22, 29, 30, 31, 32, 33, 34, 36, 37, 38, 40, 41, 42, 43, 44, 45, 46, 47, 48, 49, 68, 69, 70, 73, 75, 77, 78, 79, 81, 120, 121, 154, 155, 162, 165, 168, 196, 226, 228, 229, 367, 368, 369, 387, 397, 400, 447, 448, 463, 465, 467, 471, 473
Friia, 28, 29, 38, 168
frith, 3, 42, 158, 227, 357, 364, 372, 373, 465, 473
frith-king, 372
Fulla, 29, 37, 38, 39, 40, 154, 165, 168
fylgja, 21, 22, 159, 418, 466
galdor, 154, 291, 302, 303, 304, 305, 307, 310, 320
Gallehus horn, 104, 105, 485
gand, 20
gandr, 462

Index

Gebo, 355, 356
gemynd, 61, 62
Gerda, 453
Giantesses, 181
Giants, 262, 264, 268, 275, 468, 470, 472, 476
Ginnungagap, 43, 464, 466, 468, 470, 476
Gjallarhorn, 62, 179, 189
Gna, 36, 40, 68
Grani, 452
Griðr, 74, 75, 76, 77, 78, 79, 80, 81, 89
hag-ridden, 297, 299
Hallows-Tide, 217
hama, 21, 291, 292, 293, 294, 295, 297, 299
hamingja, 151, 154, 247
hamrammr, 294
Harke, 121, 196
Hati, 25, 147, 149, 152, 169
Hausos, 138, 141
healh, 70, 71
Heimdall, 62, 79, 175, 176, 177, 178, 179, 183, 185, 186, 187, 189, 406, 407, 408, 470
Heiptr, 144
Hel, 38, 167, 365, 387, 464, 467, 468, 476
Helgi, 168, 169
Hermod, 38, 165
Hertha, 226
Hervör, 452
Hidden Fire, 451, 457, 458, 461
Hlidskjalf, 50, 62, 368
Hlin, 35, 40, 360, 467
Hoðr, 149, 154, 157, 158, 159, 161, 163, 166, 167, 169
Hœnir, 59, 463, 475

Holda, 109, 116, 117, 119, 125, 133, 134, 136, 258
Holle, 109, 119, 133, 134, 136, 196, 217, 371, 372, 379, 380, 385, 387, 389, 396, 467, 478
housewight, 242
housewights, 247
Hringhorn, 152, 163
Huginn, 62, 305, 368, 369, 370, 397
Hugr, 13, 187, 369, 468
Hvergelmir, 48, 145, 456, 457, 465, 468, 476
idises, 124, 213
Iðun, 384
Irminsul, 236, 239
Jarnsaxa, 104, 181, 182, 183, 185, 469, 470
Jera, 71, 417
Jötnar, 176, 177, 178, 185, 261, 262, 263, 264, 265, 267, 269, 272, 273, 274, 275, 277, 457, 468, 469, 472, 476
Jotunheim, 19, 155, 167, 185, 277, 476
Kvasir, 56, 59, 61, 62, 63
Landdisasteinar, 211
Landvidi, 88, 89, 393
Landwights, 244, 246, 250, 252, 253, 255, 258, 259, 318, 320, 321, 468
Lebensbaum, 231
Lif and Lifthrasir, 156, 157, 234
Ljöfn, 35
Loki, 17, 156, 161, 189, 294, 370, 467
lybbestre, 307
lybesn, 307
Maane, 10
mægen, 104, 105, 106, 108, 109, 247, 318, 320, 366, 384, 470
Magni, 104, 105, 106, 108, 384, 385, 468, 469, 474
Mani, 25, 143, 145, 147, 149, 153

Index

Mannus, 266
Martin of Tours, 236
material plane, 427, 435
Matron, 124, 199, 205, 209, 210
Matron Cult, 199
Matron Goddesses, 124
matronae, 200, 204
Matronae, 124, 135, 217, 469
Menglöd, 453
mental plane, 428, 436
Metod, 144
Mimameiðr, 453
Mimir, 48, 57, 59, 61, 62, 90, 91, 156, 387, 389, 390, 464, 470, 476
Mimir's Well, 54, 56, 59, 61, 62, 63, 66, 389, 390, 470, 476
Mimisbrunnr, 53
Moði, 104, 105, 108, 470, 474
modraniht, 208
Moon, 10, 24, 25, 73, 143, 144, 145, 146, 147, 149, 150, 152, 153, 167, 218, 243, 244, 250, 256, 259
Moon-Bane, 25
Moon-Dis, 25, 150, 153
Mothernight, 208, 215
Mothers' Night, 208
Mothers-Night, 217
Mundilfari, 145, 167
Muninn, 62, 305, 368, 369, 370, 397
Nanna, 25, 38, 143, 146, 147, 149, 150, 151, 152, 153, 154, 155, 158, 161, 162, 163, 165, 166, 167, 168, 169
Nauthiz, 123, 355, 411, 413, 417
Nauthiz rune, 123
Nehalennia, 120, 121, 124, 133, 136, 203

Nerthus, 41, 133, 191, 197, 204, 226, 227, 263
Nibelungenlied, 309
Njorð, 59, 226, 227
Noösphere, 61, 470
Nordendorf fibulae, 106
Norn, 7, 21, 26, 223, 476
norns, 210, 471
Norns, 21, 22, 23, 24, 33, 36, 47, 121, 124, 202, 221, 472
Oak of Dodona, 239
Odainsakr, 156, 157, 164, 165, 166, 167
Odin, 4, 7, 8, 9, 10, 11, 12, 13, 14, 15, 16, 17, 18, 19, 20, 22, 28, 29, 30, 31, 41, 42, 44, 45, 46, 47, 48, 49, 50, 51, 58, 62, 75, 77, 79, 80, 81, 84, 86, 89, 90, 91, 92, 93, 94, 95, 96, 97, 154, 155, 162, 165, 168, 229, 234, 305, 368, 369, 370, 390, 396, 401, 452, 453, 454, 456, 463, 464, 465, 468, 469, 470, 471, 475, 476
Odin, Vili and Ve, 58, 464, 469, 476
Óðrœrir, 49, 55, 56, 62, 471
önd, 181
ordeals, 378, 379, 380, 403, 413, 471
orlay, 24
orlays, 215
ørlög, 24, 33, 62, 68, 213, 470, 471, 472
Ostara, 72, 134, 135, 137, 138, 139, 140, 141, 191, 385
patronage, 32, 54
Perkwunos, 226, 228, 229, 465
Perthro, 417
planes of being, 427, 433, 436
Ragnarök, 62, 84, 86, 88, 106, 157, 166, 178, 234, 393, 469, 470, 472, 474
Ravens, 50, 51, 306
resonance, 433, 435, 447

Rig, 179, 187, 188, 189
Rigsthula, 179, 188
Roskva, 110
Rydberg, 25, 57, 167, 168, 454, 457, 481
Saga, 37, 68, 211, 214, 297, 387, 478
Schicksalsbaum, 231
Second Merseberger Charm, 7, 18, 25, 28, 167
Seven Sleepers, 298, 306
shrine, 210, 268, 269, 270, 272, 273
Sif, 104, 110, 111, 112, 113, 114, 473, 474
Sigrdrifa, 452, 453
Sigurd, 452
Sigyn, 370
Simon the Magus, 294
Sinhtgunt, 25, 28, 29, 145, 146, 147, 149, 167, 168
Sjöfn, 35, 473
Skaði, 272, 276
Skirnir, 453
Skoll, 147
Sky-Wolves, 147
Sleipnir, 452
Snotra, 35
Sol, 10, 145, 147, 148, 151, 153
Sons of Borr, 234
spiritual plane, 429, 432, 433
stag, 372, 456
strange attractor, 388, 389
straw doll, 125
sumble, 157, 158
Sun, 10, 24, 25, 50, 72, 88, 113, 114, 145, 146, 147, 150, 151, 153, 243, 244, 245, 250, 256, 259
Sunna, 25, 28, 29, 145, 147, 154, 168

Index

Svipdag, 453
Swan-Maidens, 146
Swinburne, 141, 142, 226
Syn, 68, 172, 360, 474
Thidrandi's death, 214
Thjalfi, 110
Thjazi, 276, 454
Thor, 8, 10, 11, 14, 15, 20, 29, 30, 100, 104, 105, 106, 108, 109, 110, 111, 112, 113, 114, 226, 228, 229, 233, 264, 294, 365, 384, 385, 417, 455, 456, 457, 463, 465, 468, 469, 470, 471, 473, 474
Thorgerd and Irpa, 211
Thorlings, 104, 106, 108, 474
three Marys, 207
Thrudgelmir, 58
Thrudheim, 366
Thruðr, 104, 106, 108, 110, 473, 474
Tiw, 267
Tree of Life, 225, 238, 457
Tuisto / Tuisco, 266
tuntre, 231
Tyr, 46, 47, 267, 366, 367, 463
Tyrfing, 452
Utgard Ranger, 375, 409
Valkyrie, 7, 21, 163, 169, 452
Vanaheim, 59, 155, 167, 476
Vanir, 53, 54, 56, 59, 60, 62, 90, 185, 199, 212, 390, 470, 476
Var, 34, 68
vårdträd, 231
Varin's Bay, 147
venom, 370
Verðandi, 221, 470

Index

Viðar, 2, 74, 80, 83, 84, 86, 87, 88, 89, 91, 92, 93, 94, 95, 96, 97, 393, 394, 468
Volla, 28, 29, 38, 168
Vør, 35, 67, 68, 69, 70, 71, 73, 74, 75, 79, 80, 81, 172, 447, 448
Wælburga, 135, 136
Walburga, 115, 118, 119, 120, 121, 122, 123, 124, 125, 128, 129, 133, 134, 135, 136, 385
Walpurgis night, 115
Walpurgisnacht, 115, 118, 119, 128, 129, 130, 131, 132, 133, 135
Walpurgistide, 125, 127, 129, 132, 134
wave-mother, 181
Well of Memory, 61, 90
Well of Wyrd, 33, 124, 221, 470
Wild Hunt, 9, 117, 121, 123, 134, 257, 258, 385
Windhound, 121, 128
Winter Solstice, 215
Winternights, 209
witch, 23, 116, 130, 135, 296, 297, 307
Witch Ride, 295
Witch-Bridle, 295
witches, 14, 115, 116, 117, 118, 119, 120, 130, 132, 134, 135, 193, 295, 297
Wodan, 28, 167, 168
Wode, 398, 405, 406, 408, 475
Woden, 396, 397, 400, 401, 402, 404, 471
woodwives, 123
World Mill, 181
World-Mind, 60, 61, 390, 394, 397, 470
Wynn, 458, 459
Wyrd, 36, 44, 48, 114, 150, 155, 162, 221, 387, 476
Yew, 232, 458, 459, 461

Index

Yggdrasil, 53, 55, 62, 239, 281, 285, 420, 422, 458, 475, 476, 493

Ymir, 57, 58, 59, 60, 267, 280, 281, 313, 319, 390, 464, 466, 468, 469, 476

Yuletide, 125, 157, 208, 210, 215, 217, 385

Here is my portrait of our housewight Elmindreda, busily at work in her spirit-garden where she grows soul-nourishing spirit-food for us and all the wights of our homestead.

About the Author

Winifred Hodge Rose is an Elder of the Troth, an inclusive, international Heathen organization. She has followed a Heathen path for more than thirty years, serving as a scholar, writer, leader, teacher, priestess, and oracular spaewife in many Heathen venues.

Winifred grew up as the daughter of a US diplomat stationed in various countries during the 1950s and 1960s, and later lived for years in Greece and Germany. She learned foreign languages through immersion, and learned to observe and adapt to different cultures and world-views. These experiences have supported her efforts to understand, as well as possible, ancient Heathen world-views and adapt them for modern Heathen use, and led to her self-study of ancient Germanic languages, literature, and etymology.

She has Bachelor's and Master's degrees in the natural sciences, and a Master's degree in political science. Winifred is now retired from her career as a senior research scientist working on methods for watershed and natural resources management on military installations in the US and Germany. She's blessed with two grown children, three growing grandsons, and a good life in the Illinois countryside with her blacksmith husband Dean Rose (and various critters).

Nowadays she considers herself an independent scholar of Heathen theology and philosophy, and spends most of her time involved with thinking, studying, spiritual practice, writing and publishing on these topics.

A Word about Wordfruma Press

Fruma means 'origin, beginning' in Anglo-Saxon, and *ordfruma* means the fount or the source. The Anglo-Saxon word *Os* refers to a God of the Esa or Æsir tribe, and the Rune Poem for the rune Os / Ansuz goes as follows:

> *Os is 'ordfruma' of every speech,*
> *The support of wisdom and the benefit of the wise,*
> *And for every earl, prosperity and hope.*
> (my translation)

The Esa-God referred to here is Woden or Odin, the fount and origin of speech, eloquence and wisdom. Since my work relies in large part on understanding the roots and sources of words, I have made a play on words here, changing *ordfruma* to *wordfruma:* "the origin of words". The origin or wellspring of meaningful words flows from godly inspiration: a divine gift that underlies the formation and emergence of our entire species, *homo sapiens*. Wordfruma Press thus honors the gift of speech, and the origins of the gift: all of the Holy Ones.

The trademark logo pictured here, conceptualized by myself and created by Forest Hawkins, shows the rune Ansuz, an analog of Os, rising up from a wellspring. Ansuz takes shape as a fountain that represents the power of speech and wisdom. The shape of the logo also represents the Well of Wyrd and the World-Tree, with dew from the Tree dropping into the Well. Wordfruma Press publishes scholarly and inspirational Heathen works.

Other Publications from Wordfruma Press

Heathen Soul Lore Foundations: Ancient and Modern Germanic Pagan Concepts of the Souls, 2021 (575 pages)

Heathen Soul Lore: A Personal Approach, 2022 (423 pages)

Oaths, Shild, Frith, Luck & Wyrd: Five Essays Exploring Heathen Ethical Concepts and their Use Today, 2022. (164 pages)

Idunn's Trees: A New Tale of the Norse Goddess Idunn, 2022 (children's illustrated story and activity book, 52 pages)

Celebrating Heathen Yule, 2023 (booklet, 45 pages)

Mothers-Night Blot and Yule Celebration, with Heathen Words for Yule Songs, 2022 (booklet, 28 pages)

TM

Notes

www.ingramcontent.com/pod-product-compliance
Lightning Source LLC
Chambersburg PA
CBHW070836020526
44114CB00041B/1391